A LANTERN ON THE STERN

LIVERPOOL'S SEAFARING HERITAGE

THE LIVERPOOL MASTER MARINERS' CLUB

Volume Two
The Later Years

Edited by

Bob Evans

This book is dedicated to my comrades in the
Liverpool Master Mariners' Club
For friendship over half a century.

Previous books by Bob Evans:

A Dog Collar in the Docks
Mersey Mariners
The Way to Liverpool
The Training Ships of Liverpool
H.M.S. Eaglet
The Indefatigable
The Mersey Mission to Seamen

First Published 2007 by Countyvise Limited,
14 Appin Road, Birkenhead, Wirral CH41 9HH.

Copyright © 2007 Bob Evans

The right of Bob Evans to be identified as the author of this work has been asserted by him in accordance with the Copyright, Design and Patents Act 1988.

British Library Cataloguing in Publication Data.
A catalogue record for this book is available from the British Library.

ISBN 978 1 901231 97 7

The first thought about a title for this book was 'The Seadogs of Liverpool', but sense prevailed as these anthologies stretch across the world and a wider title was required. As ever, Captain Graeme Cubbin produced what was necessary. If seafarers can produce a 'wake', the 'light on the stern' will uncover their stories ... convoluted, but apt!

If men could learn from history, what
lessons it might teach us!
But passion and party blind our eyes,
and the light, which experience gives
Is a Lantern on the Stern
Which shines only on the waves behind us.

Samuel Taylor Coleridge

INTERNATIONAL REGULATIONS
FOR PREVENTING COLLISION AT SEA
(1938 Edition)

Article 10.
STERN LIGHTS
The white light required to be shown by this Article may be fixed and carried in a lantern, but in such case the lantern should be so constructed, fitted and screened that it shall throw an unbroken light over an arc of the horizon of 12 points of the compass, viz., for 6 points from right aft on each side of the vessel so as to be visible at distance of at least a mile. Such light to be carried as nearly practicable on the same level as the side lights.

3

Barrie Youde was a serving Liverpool Pilot from 1966 to 1988 and retired on health grounds. He at once changed careers and read law. Barrie was called to the (legal) Bar in 1990. He remains in legal practice with R. A. Wilkinson & Co., from which firm his services are retained by the United Kingdom Maritime Pilots' Association. He has published a number of books … 'Beyond the Bar', 'Sitting on a Bollard' and 'Sitting on Another Bollard'. We happily print his poem … 'The Light at the Stern'… with his warmest good wishes, in the hope of conveying the spirit in which it was written

THE LIGHT AT THE STERN

Attend at the stern, Mr Lamptrimmer,
Replenish and polish the light,
The followers-on, Mr Lamptrimmer,
Will all wish to have us in sight.
Attend to the light, Mr Lamptrimmer,
The weather is closing-in thick,
Attend to the light, Mr Lamptrimmer,
Be sure that you turn-up the wick.
We're a Liverpool ship, Mr Lamptrimmer,
We're one of a privileged breed.
Our fathers before, Mr Lamptrimmer,
Were looked-to by others in need.
So let us be right, Mr Lamptrimmer,
Our ancestors all taught us how;
And let it be bright, Mr Lamptrimmer,
As others may look to us now.
We'll weather the storm, Mr Lamptrimmer,
As long as we're willing to learn.
We're on watch tonight, Mr Lamptrimmer,
Please look to the Light at the Stern.
God has us in sight, Mr Lamptrimmer,
Expecting no more than our best:
And Such, in due course, Mr Lamptrimmer,
Determines our ultimate rest.

Barrie Youde

Foreword

Colin Jones
President of the Merseyside Master Mariners' Club

The membership of the Club, now approaching its Diamond Jubilee, represents a broad spectrum of maritime experience. Ship Masters and Pilots, Marine Engineers and Shipping Company executives, not to mention many like myself, who left the sea to pursue careers ashore ... a diverse crew with a common bond which stems from shared experience within an industry which was not just a job, but a complete way of life.

The relentless decline of the British Merchant Fleet, which started in the sixties, means that most of the companies which formed the backbone of Liverpool shipping such as Blue Funnel, T & J Harrison, Elder Dempster, etc., are now distant memories, but the flag loyalties and memories of the men who served in these fleets and others, are still strong. Certainly there has been no shortage of material submitted by members for inclusion in this book ... incidents and accidents in war and peace, some humorous, some dramatic, but all written by men who made their business in great waters.

Who better to act as compiler and editor, than Bob Evans, an Honorary Life Member of the Club, whose name has been synonymous with the welfare of seafarers in the Mersey ports for almost half a Century.

Captain Roland Owens
Master of the Merseyside Master Mariners' Club

It is my honour to be the Master of the Merseyside Master Mariners' Club in this its 59th year and my pleasure to be able to write the Foreword to this book. Our members enjoy meeting to keep in touch with old shipmates and acquaintances and to make new friends and, of course, to 'swing the lamp'. It was felt that the experiences of the members represented a way of life that is fast disappearing with the decline of the Merchant Navy as we knew it and that it would be a great pity if this was allowed to go unrecorded. Canon Bob Evans, an Honorary Member, volunteered his expertise to compile, type and organise these yarns into a book of two volumes and the subsequent publication is a tribute to his experience and heroic endeavours. Here are the stories of the seafarers, some of whom have had remarkable careers and others who have had extraordinary experiences. They make a very good read.

The Master, the Chaplain and the President

Preface

For almost half a century I have been in contact with the Master Mariners' Club as Chaplain. My first connection in 1960 was with the Club-ship LANDFALL, which sat in Canning Dock opposite Kingston House, the headquarters of the Mersey Mission to Seamen. In those long past years, there were Masters who had survived the bitter experiences of the Battle of the Atlantic, the Russian Convoys and all the dangers of war at sea. They had always been in peril and their daily courage kept our nation alive. Without them we would not have survived.

My happy task was to be the Chaplain-Superintendent of the Mersey Mission to Seamen and for some years I was also the Chaplain to H.M.S. EAGLET, the Royal Navy Reserves. Even in retirement I have never lost contact. The real work of the Padre is to listen ... if only I had taken notes at the time! Seafarers are great talkers ... they call it 'swinging the lamp'.

Casually over yet another lunch I suggested to the Master Mariners that their tales ought to be recorded and that I was happy to undertake the task. The response was slow so I wrote an urgent plea ... it really worked! The intention was to produce a book of some three hundred pages. In the end there were over five hundred pages and the end-product was two volumes. I suspect that there could be another two volumes!

This is an anthology of seafaring memories. Very little editing was needed as the stories speak for themselves. In many cases I had to condense and even omit sections and for that I apologise to the contributors.

Many good folk have helped in the formation of the anthology and nothing would have been achieved without them. I did start on a list, but the books themselves must be their thanks. You are many and I thank you all. Perhaps, there could have been many more photographs ... but space was at a premium. Captain Colin Lee has 'doodled' to good effect and we had much fun uncovering designs of stern lights. The painting of the tug, BROCKLEBANK, on the back cover is one of my efforts! My sternest critics are my family ... the proof readers, coffee providers, computer buffs and tolerant listeners to my enthusiastic burblings. John and Jean Emmerson of Countyvise are understanding with their printing expertise and are good friends over many years. However, I am aware that there will ever be blemishes, mistakes, misjudgements and omissions and they can only be attributed to me with apologies.

People are unbelieving when I tell them that 95% of our trade goes by sea. We chance to live on an island! We need the seafarer.

My greatest joy is that I have shared my life with seafarers and through them I find my vision and understanding of mankind.

To them I dedicate these books.

Bob Evans,
November 2007.

THE TITLE THAT MIGHT HAVE BEEN
THE SEA-DOGS OF LIVERPOOL

The Sea-Dogs of Liverpool: Tell me about them.
Just look at a ship and let nobody doubt them,
Whose ships drew the world rather closer in thought,
Who traded in every approachable port,
Archangel to Adelaide, East unto West,
Built Liverpool into the biggest and best
In the world, for a while, not so far long ago,
Through trade, (nothing more, no great glamorous show,)
Who looked to the world and the world would look back,
And a deal would be done, trading barrel and sack:
Who smiled in the face of the poor xenophobe
And profited Liverpool, London & Globe.

The Sea-Dogs of Liverpool: Tell me about them.
Their merits are many. None ever did shout them.
Each learned as a boy in a cockleshell boat,
From his father, the paramount, "Keep it afloat."
Each grew with the basics of, "Hand, reef and steer"
As he rose to maturity, year after year,
Until he showed fitness, by trust and by laws,
And a ship would commission him: "Sir, this is yours,
To navigate, ministrate, keep it, protect it,
And run it for profit, that's why we have decked it.
Now sail it, and honour each promissory note;
And come back to Liverpool. Keep it afloat."

The Sea-Dogs of Liverpool: Tell me about them.
I've grown with them, own with them, so much about them.
Honour is mine to have sailed in their fleet:
For a pilot, a Liverpool ship 'neath his feet
Is the tallest of feelings, the top of the range,
Inheritance drawn from the Flags of Exchange.
Each Sea-Dog is human: some better, some worse;
Some heroes, some zeroes, some need a wet nurse:
But history shows that the record is sound:
Success is not gained when a ship runs aground.
The commonhold thread of each maritime note
Is, "Liverpool, Liverpool, keep it afloat."

Barrie Youde

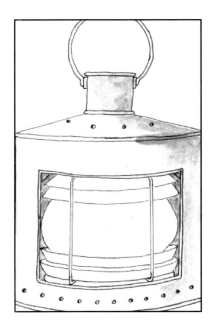

Merseyside Master Mariner's Club

Commodore Sir Bertram Hayes Hayes, K.C.M.G., D.S.O. in 1938 was the first President and the first Chairman was Captain E.A. Wood. The Club did not meet during the war and was re-established in 1946. The new President was Commander the Honourable F.H. Cripps, D.S.O., RN. The Club in its present form was founded in 1949.

President:		*Master:*
1949	Sir Burton Chadwick, Bart.	Commander The Hon. F.H. Cripps, DSO, DL
1950	Sir John R. Hobhouse, MC, JP	Capt. H.G. Dickins
1951	Capt. W.H. Coombs, CBE, RNR	Capt. H.G. Dickins
1952	Capt. W.H. Coombs, CBE. RNR	Capt. G.G. Astbury, DSC
1953	Sir Rex Hodges, JP	Capt. G.G. Astbury, DSC
1954	Sir Rex Hodges, JP	Capt. G.G. Astbury, DSC
1955	Sir Rex Hodges, JP	Capt. L.H. Des Landes
1956	Capt. G.G. Astbury, DSC	Capt. H.F. Pettit
1957	Capt. G.G. Astbury, DSC	Capt. G. Ayre, FRGS
1958	Capt. G.G. Astbury, DSC	Capt. V.E. Thomas
1959	Capt. L.H. Des Landes	W.R. Brotherton
1960	Capt. H.F. Pettit	Capt. D. Rankin, OBE
1961	Capt. G. Ayre, FRGS	D. Archibald, OBE
1962	D.Archibald, OBE	Capt. J.H. Wright, RD, RNR
1963	Capt J.H. Wright, RD, RNR	Capt. F.W. Skutil, CBE, RNN (R'td)
1964	Capt. F.W. Skutil, CBE, RNN (R'td)	Capt. J. Whitehouse, OBE
1965	Capt. J. Whitehouse, OBE	Capt. H.F. Pettit
1966	Capt. H.F. Pettit	Capt F.W. Skutil, OBE, RNN (R'td)
1967	Capt. F.W. Skutil, CBE, RNN (R'td)	
1968	Capt. F.W. Skutil, CBE, RNN (R'td)	J.D. Home, TD
1969	J.D. Home, TD	J. McKendrick
1970	J. McKendrick	N.P. Brooke
1971	N.P. Brooke	E.A. Jenkins, OBE
1972	N.P. Brooke	E.A. Jenkins, OBE
1973	E.A. Jenkins, OBE	E.P. Moss
1974	E.A. Jenkins, OBE	E.P. Moss
1975	E.P. Moss	J. Morton
1976	E.P. Moss	J. Morton

11

	President:	**Master:**
1977	J. Morton	Capt. A.J. Braund
1978	J. Morton	Capt. A.J. Braund
1979	Capt. A.J. Braund	W.H. Bell
1980	Capt. A.J. Braund	W.H. Bell
1981	W.H. Bell	J. McKendrick
1982	J. McKendrick	W.H. Higgins
1983	W.H. Higgins	Capt. L.W. Roberts
1984	Capt. L.W. Roberts	Capt. R.H. Baldwin
1985	Capt. R.H. Baldwin	Capt. S.M. Threlkeld
1986	Capt. S.M. Threlkeld	Capt. J.P. Brand
1987	Capt. J.P. Brand	F. Whitehurst
1988	F. Whitehurst	Capt. M.H.D. Embleton
1989	Capt. M.H.D. Embleton	Capt. D.M. Belk
1990	Capt. D.M. Belk	Capt. W. Taylor
1991	Capt. W. Taylor	Capt. T.C. Mullings
1992	Capt. T.C. Mullings	Capt. G.F. Kay
1993	Capt. G.F. Kay	Capt. M.A. McClory
1994	J. Blaasse	Capt. M.A. McClory
1995	A.E. Proffit	Capt. A.G. Cruickshank
1996	T.H. Smith	Capt. G.M. Bryson
1997	E.G. John, MBE	Capt. D.A. Watt
1998	J. McKendrick	Capt. J.F. Scrivens
1999	P. Gannicliffe	Capt. M.D.R. Jones
2000	P.J.H. Tebay	Capt. P.H. Daniel
2001	G.R. Davies	Capt. B. Luke
2002	L. Ensor	Capt. G.M. Taylor
2003	E. Dickinson	Capt. G.M. Taylor
2004	W.F.B. Wood	Capt. D.N.B. Nutman
2005	D.L. Large	Capt. D.H. Allen
2006	Capt. D.l. Drummond	Capt. M.P. Bestwick
2007	C.E. Jones Esq.	Capt. R. Owens

Volume Two Contents

Captain John Hanney
Master Mariner

Captain John Hanney makes an interesting and historical contribution.

STORM AND TIDAL SURGE

In September 1952, I joined the Glen Line liberty ship, S.S. GLENBEG in London, together with three other young Midshipmen, who were usually Apprentices with the Company for four years. Going down river, the ship anchored at Holehaven, in sight of Southend Pier. There we loaded a full cargo of ammunition for the Korean War, plus small quantities for British forces en route. Loading from barges by army  personnel was slow, and our Chinese deck crew spent time coaching the army men in winch driving. There was a mixture of British and American steam winches which were temperamental. Barge arrivals and departures meant that loading began daily after l000 hours and finished before 1600 hours. Outward to Korea, our ports of call were Suez, Aden, Singapore, Bangkok, Labuan (Borneo) and Hong Kong.

In Hong Kong, we delivered small consignments to British bases, and wherever we went, we were treated as lepers ... tail-end Charlie in the Canal, and explosives anchorages miles from human habitation. On passage from Bangkok to Labuan, we were beam on to the north east monsoon and all the 'tween deck ammunition broke loose in heavy rolling. The Chinese crew and we four Midshipmen spent long hours doing our best to secure the cargo in all five hatches, and with steel upon steel, there was a very unnerving jerk at the end of each roll when the cargo shifted to the low side. Re-lashing with wires and timber seemed to be endless. Homeward cargo was mainly sawn timber, and on deck, heavily damaged tanks from the war required 'tween deck shoreing. The timber cargo was loaded in the Rajang River, Sarawak.

Copenhagen and Rotterdam were our European ports for unloading and. as standard procedure by company standing orders, bridge watches were doubled in all waters north of Ushant. The ship had no radar or gyro compass, and the echo-sounder appeared to be unreliable. Due to bad weather and poor visibility, we four Midshipmen were instructed to take soundings every half hour throughout the night when we were en route from Copenhagen to Rotterdam, using the deep sea sounding machine. We took turns with the sounding machine, two at a time.

Years ago, the long length of piano wire had two brass tubes attached, each made to contain a glass tube closed at the upper end and coated internally with silver dichromate. A 28 lb. lead was attached at the very end, and water pressure, appropriate to the depth of water measured, discoloured the internal coating. The sounding could be obtained by comparing the undisturbed coloured coating against a boxwood scale.

The Navigating Officers were critical of our readings, asserting that the depth of the sea should be considerably greater than our readings showed and that we must have been doing something wrong. Perhaps the echo sounder was correct after all?

On arrival at Rotterdam, the mooring posts at our berth were under water and the mooring men in the boat had great difficulty in getting our lines attached. Wires had to be used, because our mooring lines would not sink.

Most of the labour force did not turn up for work and we heard later that exceptional flooding had occurred and that the missing men were probably engaged in rescue work or were even drowned themselves. Later we discovered that due to the tidal surge that we had been through, three hundred and seven people lost their lives on the East Coast of England. Loss of life in Holland and Belgium was over two thousand.

I presume that the shallow soundings we obtained across the North Sea were due to an enormous shift of sea water which flooded the Thames Estuary, Canvey Island, the east coast and worst of all, huge areas of Holland and Belgium.

We Midshipmen were unaware of the scale of the disaster until we had been at home for some time and the press had got to work. Food and work were the priorities in our lives. The disaster occurred on the night of January 31st- February 1st, 1953, the storm surge being due to a combination of a prolonged northerly gale and a high tide.

We know that this tidal surge disaster was the prime mover in getting the Thames barrier built. Recent research indicates that the height of the Thames barrier may have to be increased, plus many other anti-flood safety measures

I was to leave GLENBEG on February 16th, 1953 in London. Incidentally, Midshipmen were indentured for four years and did not actually sign on or off.

Thank you, Captain John Hanney. That really was a piece of history. And here we go again! Seafarers in their years of sea-going will have observed many volcanoes ... active, dormant and extinct. They are mainly concentrated in the ring of fire encompassing Indonesia, the Philippine islands and Japan. John chanced to be in the vicinity of Mount St. Helens a few days after its eruption and in common with many seafarers he saw Mount Fuji, Krakatoa, Mount Etna, Vesuvius and Stromboli, among others. Read on.

THE LAST VOYAGES OF M.V. VOLCANO OBSERVER

VOLCANO OBSERVER was a British built, small bulk carrier, registered in Greenock, and designed specifically to carry iron ore from Narvik and other Norwegian ports to Bidston Dock, Birkenhead, to supply the Shotton steel works. Ore was delivered by rail to the steel works near Connah's Quay and Chester.

The ship had completed a fifteen-year 'Time Charter' with the British Steel Corporation and her final cargo had been unloaded at Dagenham. I joined her there on January 4th, 1975, having been appointed second-in-command. The British crew were not the best and they had probably spent all their money over Christmas and New Year.

Our orders were to take bunker fuel at Vlissingen and then proceed to Durban for a cargo of coal for Japan. At the time, unknown to all on board, negotiations were in progress with a view to selling the ship. It appeared that negotiations had broken down and we received new orders to proceed to Melilla … a Spanish enclave on the North African coast of Morocco, for a cargo of iron pellets which were destined for Lubeck. We arrived at Melilla on the 11th of January.

On the following day, a Sunday, the opportunity of putting our lifeboats in the water was not to be missed. Loading continued around the clock until we sailed on Monday, January 13th for Lubeck

Most noticeable as we proceeded under pilotage to Lubeck,

was the difference between the dark east bank on our port side, with the brightly lit west bank on our starboard side ... East and West Germany, at night.

The cargo was unloaded on January 22nd to 24th and we departed 'in ballast' for another cargo of pellets from Melilla. We were there from February 2nd to the 6th including a two-day wait at anchor. Dagenham again was our destination for the delivery of the second cargo of iron pellets. Melilla is a remarkable place. A walled city, all the pavements were made of marble and most of them had elaborate coloured designs. Architecture was a mixture of Moorish and Spanish, and palm trees lined the main streets. Time did not allow for much exploration.

On February 13th at Dagenham, some of the crew signed off and on the 14th replacements signed on and joined the ship. Sailing on the 15th 'in ballast' from the Thames, fuel oil 'bunkers' and fresh water were taken over night at Flusching and the next day, we passed Dungeness, Beachy Head, and St. Catherine's Point. On February 17th, Portland Bill was passed in the early hours. As we had a sick Third Engineer on board, we had to divert to Falmouth to land him into hospital for treatment. There was no one available to replace him at such short notice, and so in the late afternoon of the 17th we set sail for Durban via somewhere, short-handed.

The ship's single Doxford diesel engine used a lot of fresh water for cooling and it was quickly apparent that fresh water capacity would be the controlling factor in the range of the ship. Her previous life had been on short sea passages and so it had never been a big issue.

The Canary Islands were passed on February 23rd and plans were already in hand to call at Dakar for fresh water, fuel and fresh stores ... vegetables, salads, fruit and milk. Dakar in Senegal is about 14½° north, 17½° west, and is the most westerly point on the African continent. Our water supplies would not have lasted to Cape Town. Happily, a new Third Engineer Officer joined us, and when we sailed on the 27th / 28th midnight, the ship was fully manned. The owners were still hoping to book coal cargo from Durban to Japan.

Ever since we left the English Channel, there was very little useful work for the crew. Our stores of paints, ropes and wires were at a rock-bottom minimum, presumably because the owners had anticipated the sale of the ship. The normal and routine maintenance work would have been pointless, as the whole deck area was to be re-built and the existing structures above main deck level would be removed. This entailed hatches, hatch coamings, hatch covers, and all the machinery for the opening and closing of the 'pontoon'- type mechanical steel hatch covers. After exhausting all the necessary maintenance work on our fire-fighting equipment, and every detail of safety equipment, it was difficult to find things meaningful to keep the crew occupied. A small amount of paint was found and so, in good weather, the largest hatch on the ship was opened, and 'goal posts' were painted on the forward and after bulkheads, simulating a football pitch. It was not long before the only football we had was kicked from the bottom of the hold over the side. The A.B. responsible was not popular. Our E.T.A. message to Dakar included the usual details of the ship and in the short list of requirements of water, fresh food and the odd item of stores, were two footballs, which we hoped would be available while we spent a short stay in Dakar. The crew were more interested in the delivery of the footballs than in the delivery of fresh fruit and vegetables.

Somewhere north of Ascension Island, a radio message was received with new orders to proceed to the Panama Canal to await further orders. So with the right hand down a bit, or more correctly 'Starboard easy the wheel', we turned around and headed for the Caribbean. The course alteration was very popular with all on board because we were now ventilating the accommodation after a long spell of sultry conditions due to a following wind. The ship was designed for northern European waters.

Barbados was sighted on March 11th and after passing St. Lucia, having lost the Atlantic swell, the engines were stopped for two hours of adjustments. On the 12th, 13th and 14th we slowed down and altered course to get a cool breeze blowing through the ship. The cooling effect was most welcome. On arrival at Cristobal, the northern entrance to the Panama Canal, we went alongside after a day at anchor, and more fuel, fresh stores, and of course fresh water was taken on board. On completion, back we went to the anchorage to await further orders. We read our mail and our return letters were given to the agent for posting. After much 'discussion / negotiation' with port health officials, I obtained permission to go ashore and travel to Panama should the opportunity arise.

While we were at sea, the ship had been sold to an American oil company which intended to convert the ship to an oil drilling vessel. The ship was very suitable for this purpose, as she had been built to withstand hard knocks experienced in the heavy iron-ore trade. The oil company spent a few days in deciding where we were to go for the conversion work and I was able to visit Panama City, which involved a train journey at least the length of the Canal. I spent a whole day away from the ship, with an early start and a late return. While I was in Panama, I visited an English sailor twice, as he had been hospitalised for some injury. He was very appreciative of my visits, more so for the conversation in English than for the shopping that I did for him. It was much later that I was told that it was a dangerous thing to walk about in Panama City, alone and unarmed.

The choice of port for the ship's conversion was between Galveston, Texas and Sasebo, Western Kyushu, Japan. The new owners must have been negotiating with the two shipyards while we awaited their decision. Sasebo won the contract and a week or so must have passed, because we went alongside once again for food stores and fresh water. While we were in one of the Canal lakes, we got permission to fill some of our ballast tanks with fresh water from the lake, and even then we did not have enough water to reach Japan non-stop. So after the Canal passage, our next destination was Honolulu ... for water. When the ballasting was almost finished, I had reason to admonish one of the crew about the dangerous situation into which he had put himself, inside a ballast tank. He replied very politely in broad Scottish Hebridean accent ... "Sir, lions only drink water, but you should hear them roar!" I had a job to keep a straight face.

With the Pacific Ocean ahead of us and no schedule or time-scale to keep, it was decided that a little exploration was in order without going too far out of our way. As it would be in daylight, we headed for Clipperton Island, which is a little over 10° north and about 109° west. Having no detailed chart, we could not go too close, but through binoculars, I could make out a very tattered French flag. The island was very small, with no habitation, and only a few trees were visible. It looked very similar to the cartoonists' drawings of 'desert islands'. It was certainly very remote.

The next landfall was one of the Hawaiian islands, and for some time we were able to see steam rising from the edge of the land where volcanic lava was pouring slowly into the sea.

The passage south into the South Atlantic and then north-west into the Caribbean was all in relatively calm weather. So the daily football sessions took place without any heavy pitching or rolling. Doldrums and the Sargasso Sea were encountered, and our meals became more and more luxurious and even exotic as an inventory of meats, fish and poultry revealed that we would have surplus food, even if we were to be ordered to Japan. In spite of the week or more in Cristobal, our daily fare became an almost unlimited matter of choice and quantity was never a problem ... all the more so when we entered Pacific waters. For the whole of the sea passage, the wind barely reached Force 4 of the Beaufort Scale, when white horses become obvious to the naked eye.

We berthed alongside on arrival at the harbour in Honolulu, and as there was no commercial pressure either for our berth, or for our departure, we spent a night tied up, filling our tanks with fresh water at a leisurely pace. Sailing the next day, we headed west on a latitude of about 22° north, south of the Tropic of Cancer and then on to take a look at Wake Island. Although there may not have been a lot to see, we had to keep out of the prohibited area declared by the U.S. government, and so in the end saw nothing. The ship's speed was a leisurely 10 knots, so at each port of call, there was time for our mail to catch up with us. Letter writing and sun-bathing were the most common off-duty occupations. We had no swimming pool and the design of the upper deck hatch covers did not lend themselves to the game of deck tennis. We had no equipment anyway. Some of the most enjoyable times of the day at sea were to be seen at sunrise and sunset, when colours of the sea and sky change rapidly. Flying fish were seen daily and there were always some seabirds about. They sometimes followed us for days, just waiting for the cook to dump the garbage from the galley.

Somewhere north of the Island of Guam, we altered course to the north in longitude 144° east and, in daylight, we zig-zagged to look at a 'string' of volcanic islands, some of which were in the Mariana group, sometimes known as the Ladrone Islands. Most of them looked very inhospitable, with their volcanic shapes running steeply down to the sea. Not having detailed charts, we could not approach too closely. Only a few of them were active and there was no sign of vegetation of any sort. 'Occasionally visited by fishermen' was the comment in the Pilot book and that probably dated from the 1930's. With the unusual and sometimes weird-shaped islands astern of us, we headed for the islands to the south of Kyushu at the south-western extremity of Japan and for a brief period we crossed the strong Kuro Siwo current. This is a warm sea current, sometimes called the Japan Current, vaguely comparable with the Gulf Stream in the Atlantic. It sets in a north-easterly direction, skirting the Japanese islands and runs into the north Pacific Ocean. Just as fog is common on the Grand Banks, so it is where this warm current meets the cold waters south-east of Japan.

Having crossed the Kuro Siwo, we were then in an area frequented by fishing boats. Fishermen all over the world are well known to be a potential hazard to shipping. At night, bright lights often obscure their navigation lights and it is often impossible to tell whether a fishing boat is stationary or moving, or fishing or not fishing. They are still subject to the International Collision Regulations. The best advice is to KEEP CLEAR.

We had left Panama on March 31st and I have no record of dates after that until I left the ship on May 12th.

We continued to eat well, consuming the best of steaks, salmon, shellfish, ice cream, etc., in addition to the fruit and vegetables which had been purchased during our stays in port. We knew that a quantity of food had to be left behind and so we made the most of it.

The last part of our sea passage was northward off the coast of Kyushu, passing the island of Yaku-Shima which is 6,348 feet high, and the cities of Kagoshima and Nagasaki. We were too far off to get any good views. Our arrival at Sasebo was routine and we tied up alongside a berth in the harbour.

After the formalities and paper work were completed, our agent informed us that we were all to fly together from Fukuoka to Tokyo and then onwards via Anchorage, Alaska, to London. The Officers refused point-blank to fly on the same plane as the crew ... not for snobbish reasons, but because many of the ratings were badly behaved. On board ship they were subject to ship's discipline, but after signing off their contracts, they could become difficult. With head office being informed, bookings were re-arranged and the crew members left before the Officers and we went on separate flights.

After the two Melilla voyages, the ship had sailed in ballast, which means that she carried no cargo ... no pay load. The ballast had to be used to submerge the hull sufficiently for the propeller to be adequately below the water. Ships do carry solid ballast on occasions, but sea water in tanks is by far the most common form. The ship's cargo capacity would be between 8,000 and 10,000 tons.

The VOLCANO OBSERVER was handed over as she was at the Sasebo dockyard, and together with all her sea-going equipment I expect that there were two footballs ... one in each cargo hold!

A NEAR MISS, A CLOSE SHAVE OR JUST GOOD LUCK

In March 1982, my ship, a large bulk carrier, was chartered to carry 130,000 tons of coal from Queensland to Europe, and the charterers specified the Cape Horn route because they said that it was shorter than the Cape of Good Hope route.

South of New Zealand, we encountered a ferocious storm, and for ten hours or so, the ship was unmanageable. A helmsman replaced the autopilot, but still had difficulty keeping within 40° of our intended course. Bad weather and poor visibility continued for 17 days to Cape Horn, and our only sightings were icebergs on the radar. Cape Horn was passed on the morning of March 31st, and our Radio Officer obtained a weather forecast from Port Stanley, and further contacts were arranged to be made by radio-telephone. Heading north-east and between the squalls, glaciers, ice and snow were visible at over 100 miles on Tierra del Fuego, as the sun shone briefly over the land.

On the afternoon of April 1st, Jason Island in the north west of the Falkland Islands group was observed, and on the next morning, our Nigerian Third Mate said that he had seen a large fishing fleet on the radar during his 2000 - 2400 hours watch. Local and international radio programmes made it obvious, that we had crossed just ahead of the blacked-out Argentine invasion force.

The pre-arranged radio-telephone weather forecast from Port Stanley never materialised. Instead, I managed to get the programme frequency in which musical requests were being played locally. At frequent intervals, 'edicts' were announced by the disc jockey in English. The Argentines were allowing the continuation of these requests in Jimmy Young programme style ... "Mrs. X in East Falkland would like you to play a record for Mrs. Y in West Falkland." The English disc jockey apologised at the beginning of the programme, stating that there were certain constraints because there were two Argentine soldiers in the studio with guns pointing at him.

In between records, the following Edicts were announced:

Edict No. 1:- Anyone who goes outside his house must carry a large white object.

Edict No. 2:- As from noon today local time, everyone must drive on the right side of the road.

Edict No. 3:- Will Doctor Alison Blainey proceed to the Hospital immediately together with her children. Each one of you must carry something white.

Edict No. 4:- The following British personnel are still missing ... names and ranks were all given. They must report to the airfield immediately. Any islander found hiding them will be shot.

Edict No. 5:- All shops, schools, offices and public buildings will remain closed until further notice.

There were about 8 – 10 'edicts' altogether.

These are memories of twenty-five years ago. We knew that there were political problems, but we had no idea that an invasion would take place. I think I was the only one on the ship who heard the radio programme and I am fairly certain that we were the only British merchant ship anywhere near the Falklands.

John was educated in Warwick School and at the famous Outward Bound Sea School, Aberdovey, where he was Captain of the Quarterdeck Watch, course No. 88, 1949. He took his 'tickets' in Liverpool and Warsash, Southampton. His sea-going was with Alfred Holt & Co., T. & J. Harrison, J. J. Denholm and a number of other freelance companies. On coming ashore, he was occupied in various management activities, but found the most satisfying task was teaching adults to read and write. He summed everything up in typical nautical fashion ... 'a dogsbody and right or left hand man for anybody'.

Ed Dickinson
Master Mariner

Ed Dickinson, like so many Master Mariners, has started writing his memoirs and, happily for me, they have proved an excellent source of material. In truth, every Master Mariner could and should write a book as in many ways they are a dying breed, not these days being replaced in great numbers. Ed gives us a lively picture of 'life at sea and on the docks'.

Having signed my Indentures with the Elder Dempster Line on December 16th, 1952, I joined the intermediate (just 40 passengers) mailboat, M.V. TARKWA, in Liverpool and was introduced to the soul-destroying job of cargo watching. The dockers were already down the hold when I climbed down the ladder at 8 a.m. and I assumed, when they trooped up the same ladder at 9 a.m. to be replaced by another gang, that they had been the nightshift. I was rather surprised to see them return at 10 a.m. and made the other, obvious assumption that they had been on meal break. Another gang change at 11 a.m. really confused me and I had to ask one of the men what was going on. He

replied that each gang worked one hour about. I knew that cargo was only being worked from 8 a.m. to 5 p.m. and could not resist the comment that only half a day was being worked for a full day's pay. "I've done my bit" was the indignant reply, "three years in the Western Desert!"

I doubt that the same sentiment was ever expressed by one of Rommel's men and neither will I forget the Japanese foreman's reply in Osaka five years later as we were discharging scrap metal from the United States, when I complimented his men for their hard work. So much for the spoils of war! It did not take a genius to read the writing on the wall.

As we sailed into the Irish Sea on my first trip, I had to take all the flags down and, finding the Company House flag jammed by the main aerial, I climbed up to the truck at the very top, cleared it and reported back to the Bridge. Expecting to be complimented on my initiative by the First Mate, who had spotted me just before I started back down, I was treated to a stream of expletives which, broadly translated, meant that I was not allowed aloft for the first six months at sea as the Company insurance did not cover the possible consequences. Pity no-one had told me!

After almost a year at sea, I was on the fo'c'sle of one of the Company's old 'Explorer' class ships, DAVID LIVINGSTON, as we delivered her to the breaker's yard at Greys in Essex. The intention was to tie up alongside an old wooden jetty and we already had a bow line onto a bollard at the end of this jetty when a strong ebb tide, which the Thames River Pilot had obviously underestimated, took full advantage of the broadside we were offering it to carry us downstream. In the seconds it took us to throw the turns off the drum end, our bow line had lifted the end of the jetty clear off the piles. I will never forget the look of horror on the face of the longshoreman as, with his back pressed against a wooden shelter, the floor under his feet rose up and crashed down again. A second attempt put us safely alongside and I still have the Red Ensign the ship flew on her final voyage.

I transferred to another ship in London, only to be transferred again when we arrived in Lagos, Nigeria. This time it was to the M.V. EBOE, one of the Company's newest vessels, trading between West Africa and the United States. Our first port there was Newport News in Virginia, which was a huge American Naval Base. On that and on every occasion that we visited Newport News, we took delight in dipping our ensign, as naval etiquette demanded, on passing each aircraft carrier and warship, to see a white uniformed figure race aft from the Bridge in order to dip their ensign in recognition of the courtesy. Simple pleasures, perhaps!

Just two years into my Apprenticeship, I was on an old liberty ship, the S.S. ZINI, on our way back up to West Africa from the Cape when we called in a place called Walvis Bay. It seemed to consist mainly of a canning factory, on the edge of the Namibian desert, and we were to load about five hundred tons of … yes … tinned fish. We had signed on about six months earlier in London, although our deck crew were mainly from Stornaway. They were all excellent seamen, but perhaps a little too fond of the drink. The Captain had long stopped their tap on board, their shore leave was stopped, and they received no money to go ashore at Walvis Bay. However, they all arrived back at the quay the next morning, far too drunk to man stations. No one had realised that the cannery was run by Scots and sported a Scottish Club … even if they had ready cash, they would not have been allowed to pay!

Almost every trip to West Africa in a cargo ship involved crossing sand bars, such as Bonny and Evscravos in order to enter the Niger delta. This often involved fresh water rationing for the crew, as less water meant that more cargo could be carried as we bumped and scraped our way over. Shortly after, the Captain would spot his favourite native river Pilot, by a particular old code of signals flag, amongst the group of dug-out canoes waiting for business. A derrick would be positioned over the side and the Pilot, his entire family and their canoe would be lifted on to the foredeck and remain with us until we returned to the bar. The long journey up the creeks to Sapele for logs and sawn timber was always the most interesting, starting with 'the bend', which involved a ninety degree turn to port. This usually resulted in the ship's bow being buried in the muddy bank, burying the Chief Mate and Carpenter in the rain forest until astern engine movements and the river current carried us back into midstream. Then, we were able to continue our journey. The soft river bank at that point was filled with deep vee's, showing how often this happened.

Arriving at Sapele, which consisted of a sawmill in the middle of a small settlement, together with huge rafts of logs which appeared periodically from up river, we dropped anchors fore and aft before mooring ropes were carried ashore by small boats. These lines disappeared into the bush and the call "Slack away, slack away" continued until there was barely enough left to turn around the drum end of the winches. Eventually, we would hear the call "Heave away" and the lines would tighten to the throbbing of a couple of trees, hundreds of yards away. The ship would be positioned between anchors and ropes so that log rafts could be brought alongside for loading. There were few places in the world where ships of 7 - 8,000 gross tons would be tied up to trees!!

I finished my Apprenticeship as Uncertificated Fourth Mate on the Company flagship, M.V. AUREOL, left Elder Dempster Lines and never went back to Africa.

With a brand new Second Mates Ticket, I joined a Panamanian-registered tramp ship in Immingham, to find that I would be the only Englishman on board. The Owner was a Yugoslav named Ante Topic, who had a Liechtenstein passport and was living in Monte Carlo. The Captain, another Yugoslav, named Zarko Grgic had settled in New York. My intention was to complete an eighteen-month voyage so that I would have enough sea time in to return to college for my First Mates Ticket. I nearly turned around and went home again, but was persuaded to stay and I have to say I never regretted it.

All ship's business, including log books and letters to the Owner were in English, but the language used on board was Italian, as most of the Ratings on board were from the Trieste region, although we also had many Yugoslavs. Some, with passports, had never returned to their country after Tito took power. Others, like the Captain, had become naturalised Americans, or had escaped and were sailing on Italian work permits. The ship was run efficiently, if sometimes illegally, to make money for the Owner, with safety being given scant regard. My first trip on PANAMANTE was to Port Sulphur up the Mississippi and, due to the ship's position required for loading, a temporary gangway had to be rigged using a davit of the port lifeboat. It took the Bosun two hours to free it, using a chipping hammer, grease and brute force. We never had a lifeboat or fire drill, but I made sure that at least one lifeboat could be lowered before we sailed.

Apart from the sulphur, which turned all the silver coinage in the pockets of your clothes black, even though hanging up in a wardrobe, we carried bulk cargoes of coal, iron ore and scrap metal. In the case of the metal, loaded by chute and electro-magnet crane in the US, it was only after discharging in Japan six weeks later, having crossed the Pacific, that we found the perforated water-tight bulkheads between the holds!

It may be of interest to note that, on arriving at the port of Osaka in Japan, we had on the Bridge a Japanese pilot, a Yugoslav Captain, an Italian helmsman and a very Anglo Saxon, yours truly, manning the engine room telegraph. The Pilot issued all engine and helm orders in English and the Captain translated these into Italian, more necessary for the helmsman than for me! Who in this world needs Esperanto?

The Panama Canal was, I believe, the only place in the world where the Captain had to relinquish his responsibility for the ship to the local Pilot who, although American, was able to issue all helm and engine orders etc. in the language of the crew.

It used to be the practice, on British Merchant Ships at least, that on long ocean voyages especially, sighting another vessel was an excuse to practice on the aldis lamp by calling and asking 'What ship and where bound?" One long night watch, en route from Panama to Honolulu, I tried calling a ship which, just on our port bow and travelling in the opposite direction, appeared not see my call sign. Thinking that the Officer-on-Watch may be in the chartroom, I called again and again until he had passed our beam and, realizing that he had chosen to ignore my approaches, I sent one final signal, consisting of two words, the first of which began with an F and the second with an O. Almost immediately he responded with a single long flash meaning "message received" and his lack of social grace was immediately forgiven.

Being an old Liberty ship, propelled by a steam reciprocating engine and with no facilities such as a washing machine, one of the ship's Engineers must have studied under Heath Robinson for, down on the engine room plate, a ringbolt had been welded to the base of one of the main pistons. By leaning over the safety rail, it was possible to hook a line with a small piston hanging from it, which was led over a convenient block so that it would pound the weekly wash in a steel drum, which could be filled with hot cooling water and flakes shaved off a long bar of Sunlight soap. I learned, after the first wash, that more than two minutes of this treatment would shred a shirt. I also learned that shirts, tied by the tail to a washing line on deck would, in a stiff breeze, require no ironing at all and separate collars flattened to a mirror could be peeled of later perfectly smooth.

Before returning to the Atlantic Ocean, we loaded a full cargo of sawn timber in British Columbia. It was consigned to a port on the United States east coast. Prior to departure, the Captain insisted on entering the ship's draught into the log book himself. This seemed strange, but the heavy list we developed on our way south only righted itself as we filled our depleted, double-bottom fuel tanks at San Pedro in California. I was to learn that profit from any extra cargo, over and above the Owner's contract, would be to the Master's account!!

The Americans then, as now, operated a very strict immigration policy. All visitors, including seamen, had to have a limited period visa. For this, you needed a passport or some other proper identification from your country of origin. Sadly, the Yugoslavs without this were unable to get visas. Apart from the odd successful ship jumper, it was amazing how efficient the immigration authorities were in picking up and returning offenders who were just stretching their legs and after a bit of shore recreation.

With National Service after me at home, I managed to transfer on to another Company ship, the S.S. BIMINI, registered in Bahamas and still flying the Red Ensign, in order that I would be able to register at College without being called up, when I eventually got home. This involved calling in the Immigration Office in Philadelphia, on my way by train to Baltimore from New York, in order to extend my visa. There was an absolute refusal until an ex-GI turned up who had 'fond wartime memories of Blighty' and thought I might know some of his old English acquaintances. The answer was 'No', but it got me my visa extension.

Having a 14-month trip as a ship's Officer under my belt, I was able to register at College for my First Mate's course. For my final three years at sea, I was to serve in the Shaw Savill and Albion Line, starting as Fourth Mate and working my way back up to Second Mate.

The Captain on my first ship in Shaw Savill, the M.V. DELPHIC, had been decorated for heroic exploits during the war. His experiences may have had something to do with a certain eccentricity when in port, if always of a sober character when at sea. It was well known that he had a catapult, with which he would diligently chip the paint off the funnel to pass the time. As Officer of the Watch carrying out cargo duties, one evening I was summoned to his cabin. He suggested that I might like a drink. Just to be sociable, I felt it wise to accept and asked for a beer. He then produced his famous 'catapult' along with a bag of nuts as ammunition and suggested I tried it out. When I asked what the target might be, he pointed to a calendar on the small corner wall of his cabin. I could not resist asking him to choose a day. 'Today', he almost shouted, but sadly I missed hitting even the wall. This was not to be the end of the story. He disappeared into his night cabin to reappear with a service revolver, which he handed to me after spinning the chambers. "Got some ammo somewhere" he said, and went to look. Fortunately, he couldn't find any, and I quickly finished my beer, mumbled something about being needed on deck and left.

I later sailed to New Zealand on a ship called KARAMEA, where another Captain had the habit of finding a bar ashore that had a piano, which he would play with obvious skill, and start a singsong. As the pubs all officially closed at 6 p.m. in those days, he would invite all and sundry back to his ship for a drink, borrowing as necessary to supplement his stock. He also had a tape of himself telling jokes, which he would play on his recorder and lead the laughter until it was finished! At that point, he would decide that it was his bedtime and tell all his guests to 'bugger off'. Eventually the last customer, having found no one else to provide drink, would disappear down the gangway.

One of the remotest places a ship could visit in Australia

would be Wyndham, up in the northwest corner. The only thing there was a meat works, a general store, a pub, and a few houses for key personnel. The place closed down for the summer, when it was too hot to work and seasonal workers, living in wooden barracks, came up from the south. The scenery was like Arizona, dry and dusty with a few stumpy trees. Just behind the cattle pens, where up to about 1000 head would await their fate, was a large, red-layered mountain. Every few days, the permanent stockmen would ride around this mountain to a collection point. There incoming herds from central Australia could be fed and watered, until their turn came to be cut out, counted and driven back round the mountain to the pens. The head stockman, being an agreeable fellow, was happy to lend me a horse and saddle. I spent two happy afternoons herding cattle with one grizzled old stockman telling me that, when I got home, I could say that I had herded cattle in the Kimberleys. The foreman was to complain in the pub later that at least one of the crew who had followed me couldn't ride to save his life and if he had injured himself he, the foreman, would have been in trouble. Thankfully, no one realized that I had never ridden a horse before in my life, but I had watched a lot of John Wayne films!!

I left Shaw Savill Line in 1962, with enough sea time to sit my Masters Ticket, which I passed successfully. Then, I had a short, celebratory holiday before starting to look for shore employment in the shipping business. I was to work with ships and ship owners from then until I retired in 1996.

Thank you, Ed Dickinson, for an interesting and detailed account of your time at sea. Writing for your grandson has given all of us much pleasure.

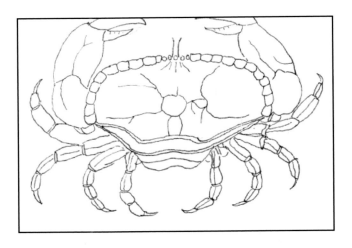

Captain Tony Gatt
Master Mariner

Captain Tony Gatt shares a couple of memories of life at sea and ... even, in it.

SHARKS CAN BITE

Back in 1955, I signed on a ship called the BARON ELGIN for a trip to Jamaica. After a lengthy passage ... she was a coal-burner and did seven knots with a following wind ... we arrived at a place called Savanna-la-Mar, where we anchored in the bay and started loading sugar off barges.

Every day we would watch as sharks circled the ship looking for scraps (no chance off a Hungry Hogarth ship!), but finally a few of us plucked up courage to go ashore in one of the rickety canoes plying for trade.

All went well on the shore-bound trip, but coming back when all had had a few beers, one of the ABs decided to give everyone a song. Unfortunately, he decided to stand up to do so ... and the inevitable happened.

The canoe went bottom up. Luckily we could all swim (I think), but I reckon no Olympic swimmer could have beaten us to the jetty as we thought of those sharks!

Tony continues.

When I was Third Mate on one of the United Baltic Corporation's ships in the 60's, one of the runs we had was from London's Surrey Commercial Docks to Leningrad ... as it was called then.

In Leningrad, we were issued with a pass that had to be shown to the armed guard as soon as we stepped off the gangway. Similarly, all Russian personnel boarding the ship had to show their passes.

One day, we had a small fire in the poop deck and someone (one of the dockers, presumably) raised the alarm. The fire brigade duly arrived, but they had a heated argument with the guard, who was not going to let them up the gangway without a pass. Finally, they got on board and extinguished the blaze.

Power and pomposity are a sad mixture

Angela Gatt tells us a salutary tale of life at sea.

MEDICAL EXPERTISE

On voyage to West Africa, whilst sailing with my husband, who was Chief Officer on board, I was set the task of looking after the Medicine Chest, as I was a trained nurse. On my way to do this one day, I came across an Engineer limping badly and struggling to get up to his cabin. I helped him up to his cabin where he told me he had fallen down the Engine Room stairs and had hurt his ankle.

He got on to his bunk and I went to get equipment to treat him. As I bandaged his ankle, I noticed his speech was slurred and he kept drowsing off to sleep. I also noticed to my horror his pupils were noticeably uneven, classic signs of a head injury. He said he was not aware of hitting his head when he fell.

I thought I had better be sure of my facts before asking the Captain to head for port so I checked on my patient every half hour,.by waking him up and checking on his speech and eyes.

After a couple of hours, I arrived to wake him up only to find him dressed and preparing to go on watch. Still convinced we had an ill man on board, I asked my husband and the Captain for their opinion.

Can you imagine how I felt when it was revealed that the slurred speech and drowsiness were probably due to drink and that he also had a glass eye!

Thank you, Angela Gatt for that little pearl.

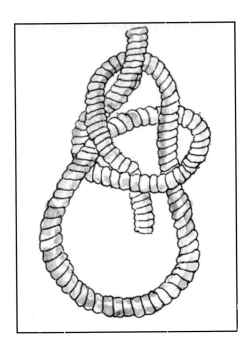

Captain David Campbell
Master Mariner

Captain David Campbell even looks 'nautical' with a 'full set', and our friendship, as with so many characters in this anthology, goes back a long time ... especially in the Royal Naval Reserve, based in H.M.S. EAGLET. He tells a good tale and, in spite of our differing accents we communicate remarkably well!

REPELLING BOARDERS

After the War, Prince Line resumed the 'Round the World Service' with five ships permanently based in New York. Each round voyage took five months. The ships did not call in the U.K. and we were expected to do fifteen months to two years on board.

Ellermans and Silver Line did a similar service, with for example, the CITY OF CHIGAGO and the SILVERBRIAR and SILVERPLANE.

We used to 'pay off' in New York

every five months. We never had much money, but when needed there was always the British Apprentices Club in the Hotel Chelsea on 23rd Street ... run by Mrs. Spalding. I recall plenty of sandwiches and chocolate cake and a dance with some rather nice American girls on Saturday evenings. I was very friendly with one girl, she even came to stay at my home when she visited U.K. ... but that is another story and definitely not for publication! However, some stories can be told.

In 1951, I was the Senior Cadet on the JAVANESE PRINCE and the following incident occurred when we were at anchor off the village of Wawa on Luzon in the Philippine Islands.

I was on cargo watch with the Third Mate, and about midnight I went for'd to check that No. 1 hatch was still secure (we were loading bagged sugar in other hatches) and found the hatch opened and a gang of men, some armed, already on board. One of them took a swing at me with an iron bar. I departed rapidly down the deck and raised the alarm. The Chief Officer called the Master and obtained the firearms, while I called the other Cadets. We had two Winchester rifles and six Colt revolvers. Shots were fired over their heads and some of them jumped over the side whilst others tried to mingle with the stevedores, who were living on the after deck. We did manage to capture seven of them and eventually I was left in charge of our prisoners who were manacled to the rails on the port side of the boat deck. I was armed with a revolver and a pocket full of ammunition. One of them slipped the hand cuffs ... his wrists were so small ... and he jumped over the side. I have no idea what happened to him as I remained on the boat deck. Some hours later, the others were handed over to the local police who came on board.

The following morning, I went with the Chief Officer through the jungle to the town of Nasugbu, where they were being held in the police station. The Police Chief confirmed that they were insurgents, but said that he could only hold them for twenty-four hours unless we were prepared to delay sailing to give evidence. Signed statements were not acceptable. This was not possible, as we had completed loading, so twenty-four hours later they were all set free.

It had been an interesting and exciting night for our passengers and crew and to have the firearms on board probably prevented a more serious incident. They were certainly more effective than fire hoses, which are currently suggested as a means of repelling pirates.

Thank you, Captain David Campbell. But there is more!

WHO AM I?

Part of David's claim to fame (not his words!) was his time as Master of the HEBRIDEAN PRINCESS. Hebridean Island Cruises organizes voyages around the Western Isles.

The vessel carries 48 passengers and 34 crew members and probably is best described as a small Country House Hotel which floats. In fact the main number of the crew aboard are hotel staff and not seafarers and not really used to ship's discipline. They were prone to use Christian names for everyone irrespective of rank! David dealt with that little problem ... "Not wishing to appear unduly aloof, I explained to them that I too had Christian names ... Captain or Sir!"

Life in the Western Isles is certainly different. Once David found himself in the pub at Craignure on Mull in March and asked what time was closing time. He was informed that it would be about October. As David added, it was a wonderful area to potter around and he was lucky that someone thought it worthwhile to pay him for the pleasure. Rather wistfully, he concluded that anchoring every night was a sailor's dream.

Thank you, David.

Captain David Peters
Master Mariner

All seafarers start somewhere in their career. It is normally at the bottom of the ladder and invariably involves livestock. The surprising result is that most animals did survive together with their minders. So here we go again. The story teller is Captain David Peters.

MUCKING OUT!

I was a WORCESTER cadet and joined my first ship in Tilbury Docks in September 1953. It was a twin-Doxford shelter-decker SOCOTRA, one of P & O's black-funnelled bastards, as we were wont to call them as they plodded up the Thames past the WORCESTER moored at Greenhithe. She managed twelve knots flat out, but was in fact a comfortable vessel with excellent accommodation even though she was built in 1943.

We had a cynical Second Mate called Kit Morris, a splendid chap who sent me down aft to check the mooring lines. Imagine my horror to find the Lascar crew killing a sheep, for it was the end of Ramadan. My discomfort caused some comments.

Later that evening, the other first-trip Apprentice, Norman Maclean, and I were called up to the Chief Officer's cabin to be told that we were on daywork for the outward voyage to Japan. And, above all, we would be looking after thirteen thoroughbred racehorses going to new owners in Penang, Singapore, and Hong Kong.

My only experience of horses was that of the milkman's horse with two vicious hooves at the rear end, and a set of teeth at the front, and a large body keeping the front and back apart. Needless to say, we had no choice and next day settled down to get bitten regularly as we entered the boxes over the front edge, but we persevered, and upon arrival at Port Said we had the customary vet aboard. He had us taking temperatures by tickling the base of tails and inserting the thermometer. We kept the tail up by twiddling the said instrument. So far so good, but three days later in the Red Sea, I lost a thermometer and the Mate shouted at me to get it back. That entailed inserting one arm and fishing! Fortunately I found it.

By the time Singapore came, I had fungus on both feet, badly. A gully-gully man came up to me and said he would cure it, if I gave him some hairs from the horses' tails. This I did ... he used them apparently to tie around warts and moles and pull tight, cutting the offending objects off neatly. He covered my feet with an evil-smelling liquid, which dried into a crust. He left me on No 4 hatch and returned later with his cut-throat razor scraping the encrusted feet. Pink and cured!

The upshot of the horse episode was that we were each given about 750 Straits dollars for our efforts, which was approximately £50 each ... equivalent to six months wages. It was only when I became Chief Officer that I found out how much the Mate and Old Man received. Apprentices and Cadets were cheap labour or better still canon fodder, but we learned. All part of life at sea!

The Mate was called Cook and he was known as Choo

Choo Cook, because on the 4 - 8 watch he would come up for stars and whilst the Char Sahib, Fourth Mate with a Second's ticket, worked out the position, he would be a steam train with the Apprentice, the signal man. He then 'choo-choo'd all around the bridge, obeying the signals and when he went through the wheelhouse it was a tunnel!!

Moving on, after I left P & O as Master, I came ashore and one January went to the Boat Show at Earls Court. It was the time when Ted Heath had his first MORNING CLOUD and we were all gathered at the 'Guinness Stand' after the show had closed. That was when the stories started.

When my turn came, I said that I had been Second Mate on the SURAT, another P & O cargo ship on the far East mail run.

We were anchored at Deep Water Point at Port Swettenham, now Port Klang, along with a Blue Funnel ship, possibly the AUTOLOCUS, but I could not be sure.

During my midnight to four watch, I took the motor lifeboat over to the Blue Flue and painted a large white patch under each quarter, returning later when it had dried and painted a large red L for learner. Feeling pleased with myself, I went to bed and was awakened by the phone ringing at 0730 and it was 'Father' who required my presence on the Bridge. He asked me if I was responsible for painting the other ship with L plates and I said 'Yes, Sir'. He then pointed to our black funnel to find that loadlines had been painted on it. This evoked much merriment and Ted Heath then said it was a farfetched tale and he did not believe it.

A voice from the back of the crowd came loud and clear. "I was the chap who painted the loadlines on his ship." It turned out that we had both had a bollocking from our respective Captains. C'est la vie.

And here is another memory from David Peters.

49

FIRE AT SEA

It was on my second voyage as an Apprentice in P & O SOCOTRA. This time on the Calcutta run, under charter to B & I, one of the P & O subsidiaries. I was on the 4 to 8 watch with the Char Sahib, Peter Hayward, a nice chap like most of those who went to sea.

Choo Choo Cook, the First Mate, came up to take stars and while the Fourth worked them out, we played trains. By this time, we were off the North African coast parallel with Algiers. It was the 28th March, 1954 ... a very significant date. I was Bridge lookout and about 0630 spotted a large mushroom of smoke ahead of us. We called Captain Leonard Henry Howard and a little later we could confirm that it was a large passenger-type vessel stopped and well alight mainly from the engine room.

It turned out to be the EMPIRE WINDRUSH. She was built as the German MONTE ROSA in 1931 by Blohm and Voss for the Hamburg America Line and was of some 14,000 tons. During the Second World War, she was commandeered by the Third Reich and served as a troopship, but this was curtailed as she struck a mine in the Baltic and was out of action until repaired. She became part of the war reparations and was taken over by the New Zealand Shipping Company in 1947 under the auspices of the Ministry of Transport. She was en-route from Japan to UK.

SOCOTRA rescued about six hundred souls, none of whom were injured. The sea was flat calm and, along with other rescue vessels attending, we landed the survivors at Algiers. WINDRUSH sank a few days later when under tow to Gibraltar.

Being a keen photographer, some of the pictures in the press came from my camera and for this I received the princely sum of £40 which I shared with the other three hard-up Apprentices.

One anecdote was that a boat came alongside and asked where we were bound. We said Calcutta via Aden. They said that they had only just come from that beastly place and would not go again. With that they pulled over to another ship.

One day we came through the Straits of Messina between Italy and Sicily, northbound for Genoa. We came up to the Isle of Stromboli to find that the volcano was extremely active. I was Second Mate at the time and as we approached, I persuaded the Captain to pass between Stromboli and Stromboleccio. The ship was SURAT and he agreed. The time was about 0030 and the scene was very spectacular. The twelve passengers begged the Captain to go around again, which he did, and the result was that we had to deploy the fire hoses as we risked setting the ship on fire. The mess on deck next morning was another matter and took a long time to clear.

The Gulf of Lyons at the northern end of the Mediterranean is another place where weather phenomena are apparent. Leaving Genoa one trip southbound, I went on the Bridge at midnight to find that a major thunderstorm was in progress with the lightning turning night into day. The two masts had St Elmo's Fire on the mastheads and the magnetic compasses were revolving at high speed. The rain was so intense that the sea-state was flat; the noise from the lightning was quite incredible. The whole thing lasted for roughly two hours and at the end we found that we were tired, probably from the incessant noise.

I had a very interesting career at sea, and upon coming ashore worked as a rep for Escombe McGraths, the loading broker for P & O, booking cargo on the ships that I had sailed on. Money for old rope, but good things came to an end and I joined a small firm Lockett Wilson Line, the forerunner of the Cross Channel Ferries. Slater Walker took them over and asset stripped, so I started my own trailer and forwarding business to the Continent and Scandinavia with a large fleet of vehicles. I had a merger, then came a management buy-out before I retired to North Wales, where I now reside.

You cannot keep a good man down and happily another offering appeared from David Peters.

IT CAN BE COLD

I found myself posted to the KARMALA which was a 'Victory Ship' built by the Bethlehem Shipyard Company in the U.S. during 1944 and, as we all know, was supposed to do one or two trips across the pond before heading for the scrapyard.

However, the mighty P. & O. decided that along with the KHYBER, they would do very nicely on the Calcutta run. To this end, I joined in the Royal Albert Dock as Senior Apprentice for the coastal voyage to Hamburg, Bremen, Rotterdam for dry-dock, then on to Antwerp and R.A. Dock to complete loading … then out to Red Sea ports, Colombo, Madras, Calcutta, Visakapatnam, Madras and Colombo for crew change and home.

The Hamburg/Bremen stops were uneventful, but when we arrived in Rotterdam we dry-docked at Heijplaats near the Waalhaven in the floating Dockdroog and, as it was the depths of winter, we froze into the dock for nearly three weeks. Unfortunately, we lost three of our Indian crew who froze to death on the drydock loos in the middle of one night, which did not make anyone very happy, but eventually we left and headed on into the voyage.

When we finally arrived in Calcutta, we first went into King George Dock to discharge opposite the coal berths, then out into the river on the bore tackles before moving into Kidderpore Dock to load the usual tea, flax, etc, for U.K. and continental ports. By this time, it was extremely hot, and as the Cadets' cabin was directly above the boiler room I had taken to sleeping on the Bridge Deck. So far, so good.

The call at Visakapatnam was uneventful and at Madras about 0200 hours, I was awakened by a cracking sound which came from various parts of the ship. I could not see anything wrong so went back to sleep. Imagine my surprise at sunup, when I noticed all the bulkheads were crazed and the paint was falling off in large sheets. The deck paint was also lifting revealing various holes, as also appeared in the bulkheads. When the crew turned to, they were immediately put on to stripping the bulkheads of paint, and when we weighed it all on the wharf we found that we had put ashore 35 tons of paint. I counted 44 coats on several pieces and they went back to the battleship grey from the war. The upshot of this was that the welders had to repair all the holes before we could apply a coat of varnish to seal the bare steel but it had saved the Company a modicum of money, time and crew effort.

The explanation given by the pundits was that it was so cold in the Rotterdam drydock that the ship had contracted and in the heat of the tropics, i.e. Calcutta, it had expanded, so cracking the paint. Interesting.

LONELINESS

You ask what it is like to be in the middle of the Indian Ocean and not seeing any ships for days.

Well, I was Second Mate on the ADEN, one of the Federal Steamship vessels, chartered to P & O for the Aussie run. We left Aden, having bunkered and filled up with Aden water, which was so disgusting that we all cheerfully drank an equally disgusting brew, Allsops lager.

From memory, it was twenty-one days from Aden to Melbourne and we saw nothing at all for ten days except many albatross and flying fish. It was at the time of the S.W. monsoon. So we bowled along at sixteen knots, rolling 10/20 degrees at times, until at about 0700 we espied another ship dead ahead steaming towards us. It turned out to be the PINJARRA, another P & O ship, homeward bound having loaded iron ore somewhere on the east coast of Oz, and as she obviously had a large GM she was rolling heavily, maybe 30 degrees or so. It caused great excitement and the ensigns were run up and both dipped in salute, normal practice in the Company when two vessels met. Boy, how the guys there must have been feeling, rolling as she was doing!

Eventually after Melbourne we completed discharge in Sydney at Piermont and lay there for three weeks, fitting out the freezer holds to load meat from Brisbane, Townsville and Cairns, finishing at Wyndham, 50 odd miles up the River Durack in the northwest of Oz. Wyndham was a meat-packing station and freezer plant which took in cattle trains of up to six wagons at one end. The cattle would be slaughtered and every part of the animal was utilised. Hinds-quarters, fillets, ribs, etc. The bones were barrelled, which were made in the plant, and I think we loaded about 10,000 tons. The loading bay at the warehouse was about three miles from the wharf, which had a 47-foot rise and fall of tide. The three wagons were hauled by a diesel loco, called Kate, alluded to as the hardest worked woman in Wyndham! It took nearly three weeks to complete loading and the locals, what there were of them, made us very welcome in the only pub on a dusty main street. It was full of Cornishmen, so I was in my element being a Cousin Jack. Total population of Wyndham was 125 white Aussies and a handful of Aborigines.

Life at sea was good, particularly when on the 12 to 4 watch, as it meant that I could get all my paperwork completed without any interruptions. Not only was I Navigator, but also Cargo Officer with the Mate, and I also looked after the Ralston indicator. This machine, when loaded with various blocks representing cargo in the decks, plus oil and water, gave us the meta-centric height of the ship. This meant that the stability of the vessel could be worked out on paper, as was Company policy.

I used to enjoy calm nights on the Bridge watching the stars and seeing the early sputniks with their intermittent flashes distinguishing them from the shooting stars.

One particular incident that comes to mind was when I was Second Mate on the SINGAPORE, a steamship on the Far East run. On the outward trip, I saw the Chief Engineer and put to him that we should save up about 200 tons of fuel oil for the return from Yokohama to Hong Kong, the idea being that we could arrive in H.K. early and start loading cargo with the ship's crew instead of waiting for the coolies to come aboard, which was scheduled for four days after our arrival. What happened was that a sampan wallah would come out to the ship on the typhoon buoys and he would hand over a brown envelope with some H.K. dollars in and he would be directed to the necessary hatch for loading. After discharge of his cargo, he would be given the Mate's receipt which then went into the Agents' office, who issued the Bill of lading to the shipper. He then put this into the bank and was credited with his deposited money. The sampan wallah then took another load to the ship and the whole process was repeated for many sampans. The net result was that the crew loaded approximately 1,000 tons of cargo, leaving 1,500 tons to be loaded by the coolies. The ship's personnel profited; the cargo owners profited; and all were happy until an ogre from Head Office came out on the ship and stopped this corrupt practice for all six ships on the Far East run. The next voyage, H.Q. wanted to know why their stevedoring fees had doubled in H. K.

The moral of this story was that everyone gained, including the shipping line but once the practice was stopped, no-one gained. And they say that the Chinese are not resourceful!

Well done, Captain David Peters.

Captain Gerald Kay
Master Mariner

Captain Gerald Kay tells a charming tale ... more wild life!

MONKEY BUSINESS

In the 1950s our ship sometimes carried Rhesus Monkeys from Calcutta to U.S. East Coast ports. We understood these monkeys were for Medical Research and were used by Dr. Salk to develop the polio vaccine.

On sailing day from Calcutta, the last item of cargo to be loaded on deck would be 5 or 6 large cages, each holding about 25 of these little monkeys. They were very cute creatures and were spoilt by the crew giving them tit-bits every day. Needless to say, the job of cleaning out and feeding them with the food provided by the Shippers fell to the Apprentices. We only carried these monkeys when generally good weather could be expected, but even so, sadly, we had one or two mortalities during the voyage.

The cages were not particularly robust and the monkeys were quite adept at trying to get out, so various extra security precautions had to be taken, which kept Chippy busy. However, despite this, the inevitable happened one particular voyage, and we had twenty-five monkeys loose all over the ship.

Unfortunately, one of them got into the Old Man's cabin and attempts to catch the little devil caused the inevitable bowel reaction ... oh dear, what a mess the Old Man's cabin was in by the time it was caught! Needless to say, we all knew who was going to get blamed and required to clean up ... the Apprentices, poor lads.

It took at least a week to catch the rest of them. A monkey hunt and chase took place every day as and when one was spotted ... they were everywhere from stem to stern. Gloves were an essential item of wear, together with a large piece of sacking to throw over them if you were lucky enough to corner one! Despite all this effort, by the time we arrived in Savannah 3 or 4 were still roaming around the ship. Strangely enough, the U.S. Department of Agriculture and Customs were not at all concerned that we had monkeys loose on board. Whilst in Savannah the Consignee managed to catch one monkey, whilst one of the Longshoremen caught another and took it home with him, just before we sailed!

So there we were with 'over-carried cargo' (two monkeys) sailing south down the Eastern Seaboard, en route to the Florida Straits and on into the Gulf of Mexico. Next port Galveston, then on to Houston.

Just before we arrived in Galveston, one of the seamen caught one of our 'passengers', and when we berthed, he offered the monkey to a Longshoreman who would only offer him $5. Our seaman wanted a lot more and decided to wait and see if he would get a better price in Houston. Unfortunately for him, half-way up the Houston Ship Channel, the poor monkey died. That was one very upset sailor! As the Houston Ship Channel was a very polluted area at that time, the atmosphere probably put paid to the poor monkey. So now we only had one monkey left on board.

We continued with the voyage, loading at various Gulf

Ports, and the remaining monkey, having the run of the ship, became quite a lot tamer and everyone treated him as a pet. Early in the loading programme, we berthed at Port Sulphur on the west bank of the Mississippi to load a part cargo of sulphur in bulk. The sulphur is loaded by conveyor belt which leads to a chute over and down into the Hold. Loading had been in progress for some hours, and I was on duty when the Gangway Watchman reported that he had just seen Charlie, the monkey, going ashore. He had leapt off the bulwark rail and on to the framework of the cargo elevator. Some while later, as I was watching the loading at No. 5 Hold, I glanced over the side at the conveyor belt and ... who should I see riding on the belt, spluttering with the dust but our friend Charlie. He went straight into the chute, straight down, and popped out at the bottom! I have never seen anyone get out of a hold so fast as that yellow monkey, not even a Docker when the whistle goes! The next day Charlie did not seem any the worse for wear, despite his adventure!

And so the voyage progressed, eventually we sailed from the Gulf Coast with a lovely full cargo of cotton, timber, canned citrus, etc. Charlie had decided going ashore was not a good idea, and so he was still with us as we proceeded homeward across the Atlantic.

As the weather got colder, Charlie decided the Engine Room was a nice warm place to take up residence for the rest of the trip, and he adopted the Fifth Engineer, Dave, as his best friend. Dave was on the 8-12 watch and he used to sew canvas save-alls for the Engine Room ladders in between checking round the machinery. Charlie was fascinated by this activity and sat on the bench next to Dave as he used his palm and needle, watching the needle come up through the canvas. Eventually, he cottoned on to what was happening and used to grab hold of the needle and the twine and pull it up through the canvas! Who says you can't teach a monkey new tricks!!

Eventually, we arrived in London and officialdom required a declaration of any animals on board. "Oh dear" said Jobsworth, "We can't have this state of affairs ... a monkey loose on board". The R.S.P.C.A. were called to take Charlie in to quarantine, but Charlie wasn't having any, and after two or three days the R.S.P.C.A. gave up trying, and Jobsworth must have decided life was too short to pursue the matter further, and so Charlie stayed with us. We went on leave ...leaving instructions to our reliefs to look after Charlie.

A few weeks later we all returned and were glad to find Charlie still alive and kicking. He obviously had decided, after his escapade with the sulphur, that it was much better staying on board ... going ashore was a mug's game.

So, off we sailed again, fully loaded with general cargo for the Red Sea ports, Ceylon (as it then was) and India, calling at numerous ports, but Charlie was not for going ashore.

Eventually, we arrived back in India, our next-to-last discharge port Madras (as it then was) and this is where Charlie's and our troubles were to begin. Because we had called at ports on the African side of the Red Sea, the Indian authorities would not allow us to berth as the monkey might be carrying Yellow Fever. So we had to lie anchored off until the monkey was caught and very sadly destroyed. The ships' crew made a half-hearted attempt to catch poor Charlie, without success that day. The following day, Police and quarantine personnel boarded and after a lot of chasing around, Charlie disappeared under the canvas cover of No. 4 Boat. Everyone gathered round holding the cover tight while the Police Sergeant threw a tear gas canister into the boat. We waited twenty minutes or so before carefully lifting one very small section of the canvas ... a brown streak shot out though the gap, shot across the Boat deck and straight through the open skylight of the Engine Room, before anyone realised what was happening!! Charlie could not be found in the Engine Room, despite searching for what was left of the day. So, the Police, etc., trooped off ashore to return the next day.

During the Middle Watch, the white band on the funnel was seen to be smeared with filthy black marks all round. On closer inspection, lo and behold there was one very-oil covered, miserable-looking monkey sitting on the funnel rail. Poor Charlie must have fallen into the oily bilge during the search the previous day.

In the morning Charlie was still sitting on the funnel rail, looking very sad ... the oil had done him no good, poor thing. When the Police arrived, a marksman shot him, a sitting target. It was probably a mercy in some ways as he was in a bad state. Needless to say we were all very sad to see his demise.

And that was the end of Charlie and the end of the Monkey Business.

And that was a poignant story ... thank you, Gerald. Now, he moves on some thirty years and paints a real picture.

A TRIP UP THE HUDSON RIVER IN THE FALL

It was autumn, October 1980, and we were carrying a cargo of bananas from Honduras to Albany, the capital of New York State, some 150 miles up the Hudson River. I recall one of our other ships had gone up to Albany years before, a most unusual destination at the time and it had always been at the back of my mind how I would love to make that journey. So I was delighted to suddenly find myself going there.

We arrived off the Ambrose Light just before dawn on a beautiful clear morning, and picked up the New York Pilot. We passed under the Verrazano Bridge just as the sun was coming up over the horizon, with Staten Island on our port hand, and then shortly, the Statue of Liberty. By the time we were passing the sky-scrapers of Manhattan, the low sun was up, and as the streets of Manhattan run approximately East-West, as we passed the end of each Street, the early morning sun shone along each one, quite an unusual sight as we alternated between brilliant sunshine and then shadow of the high buildings of 'The Big Apple'.

After passing under the George Washington Bridge and the North end of Manhattan, we changed Pilots off Yonkers. From here onwards, we entered a different world away from the cities of New York on the East bank and New Jersey to the West, a land of hills and trees, cliffs and mountains.

There were many points of interest on the way up-river, the first after leaving New York City behind, was, of all things, 'Sing-Sing', the State Penitentiary!! A grim-looking cluster of barrack-like buildings, enclosed by high concrete walls, topped with menacing watchtowers ... an obscene blot on an area of beautiful countryside. A few miles further up was a very neat-looking nuclear power station. The River at this part ran between open countryside and on our port bow we could see in the distance the Catskill Mountains

Next, we passed round a bend and into a ten-mile stretch of river which was almost like a gorge. Ahead was a graceful suspension bridge over the river, called 'Bear Mountain Bridge', with Bear Mountain looming 1,500 feet above us on the port side. On the starboard side the railroad track ran right alongside the river, disappearing through tunnels blasted through the rock at various points where the rock stuck out into the river.

Through this gorge we eventually came to a very sharp bend at West Point, which is the Military Academy of the U.S.A., situated up on the top of cliffs to port, looking haughtily down at the river, at least 150 feet below. It was here during the War of Independence that the Colonists drew a heavy chain across the river to stop the British coming up. On the starboard side was Foundry Creek, which was where an iron foundry was established to make the chain. Incidentally, coming down the river at night was a hair raising experience. Approaching this bend at West Point, we seemed to be heading straight for black nothingness, knowing it was solid rock ahead, waiting until only two thirds of a ship's length away before turning to go round the bend ... quite horrific! The Pilot, in typical laconic American style said after we were round, "You know Cap, that's quite an interesting little turn to make in dense fog". I thought, "My God, I hope I'm not there!"

However I digress. On we went upriver past Tarrytown, then Poughkeepsie ... a name that has always intrigued me for some reason. By now there were a great many trees each side, so many varieties, birch, beech and maples all in different stages of autumn colours, ranging from still bright green, through every colour and shade you can imagine of green, yellow, brown and brilliant red. As the maples turned bright red, at places where the steep hillside came right down to the river bank, by half closing your eyes, they looked like tongues of fire sweeping up the hillsides. A really wonderful sight!

By this time, about 50 or 60 miles to go, the river got so narrow that a ship of our size would not be able to turn. The channel was blasted out of rock, where necessary, and it was only 400 feet wide, while we were 575 feet long. We passed Hyde Park, which was President Roosevelt's home, and their neighbour's home, the Vanderbilt's ... very grand houses in beautiful grounds! We also passed beautiful modern homes of the wealthy each side of the River, and some very affluent farm homesteads.

On we went upriver, passing boat marinas, villages, through the middle of industrial towns, past wharves where cement was shipped out in barges ... due to lots of limestone in the area ... back through farmlands, steep hills, large wooded areas, another industrial town, under bridges, under power lines, clearing them by 10 feet. On and on went the day, the sun shining all the time, passing yachts, pleasure cruisers, tugs pulling barge trains downriver, being buzzed by curious weekend fliers in tiny planes flying level with our Bridge ... the pilots giving us a friendly wave! Families on the banks picnicking, gave us a friendly wave too, until they suddenly realised they were too close to the waters' edge, our wash was bringing a three-foot tidal wave after us and they were scrambling for dry land! Even our Pilot's family was out to give us a wave as we went by where they live, but they had enough sense to keep back from the waters' edge!

Finally we made it to Albany, before it got dark. It was a long and tiring run up the river, but very interesting. The river just seemed to go on for ever, and it ran generally north, in the morning the Catskill Mountains were in the distance on our port bow. By Noon the Mountains were abeam of us, and now, having reached Albany at 4.30 on a beautiful, quiet, sunny evening, they were just a shadow on the southern horizon at sunset. The colours of the 'Fall' were magnificent, and with so much else to see as well, I felt lucky to have had this experience

That was well written. Gerald started his career as an Apprentice with T. & J. Brocklebank in 1946, up to Second Mate in 1957 when he was promoted to Chief Officer. Brocklebank traded from U.K. with general cargo to the Red Sea, India and sailed back sometimes via the U.S.A. In 1973, he was promoted Master with what had become Cunard-Brocklebank and served in Bulk Carriers in worldwide trade. From 1979 to 1985 Gerald served in refrigerated vessels carrying bananas. His final job ... 1986-87 ... he was employed by J. Marr & Son of Hull as Master of the Ocean Weather Ship.

Captain Roland Owens
Master Mariner

Captain Roland Owens, the present Master of Master Mariners' Club started his career in H.M.S. CONWAY and in 1956 became an Apprentice in Ellerman Hall Line, remaining with that Company for some seventeen years. Next he joined Kuwait Shipping, Co., which became United Arabs, Co., and soon assumed Command. The big slump of 1986 found him in various jobs, ending before his retirement at the turn of the Century engaged in seismic surveys in the North Sea and as liaison Master on supply and anchor handling vessels. Here is the first of his tales ... with an excellent punch line!

AN UNEXPECTED ENCOUNTER

It was my first voyage as Third Mate. I flew out to Gibraltar in August, 1960, with five other Officers, stayed overnight and then joined the CITY OF SINGAPORE. She had called in Gibraltar for a crew change whilst on passage from India to the East Coast of U.S.A.

Whilst discharging cargo at Boston, the vessel was boarded by officials from the Department of Agriculture who conducted a search of the hatches with magnifying glasses! They were looking for grain weevils. After two days of intensive scrutiny, two dead, minute khapra beetles were found behind flakes of rust on the bulkheads of No. 1 hatch 'tween deck, where a cargo of Mirabolam nuts was stowed.

This was sufficient for the Department of Agriculture officials to call for the four hatches to be fumigated. Work was stopped and the vessel shifted to a lay-by berth off Park Street, a derelict area. The contractors prepared to fumigate. As the entire process would take twenty-four hours with methyl bromide in the hatches, the vessel was shut down and everyone was evacuated to stay ashore. The Officers went to the Emmerson Hotel, while the Indian crew was dispersed to various Seamen's Hostels.

Being Third Mate, it fell to me to be on duty through the night of the fumigation process to assist the fumigation operatives. So during the afternoon, the Radio Officer and I went ashore to see the hotel I would not be staying in. The Emmerson was a fine, old hotel at the top of Main Street. After lunch, Sparky and I found a bar on the mezzanine floor which had the appearance of a gentlemen's club ... dark green wallpaper, leather chairs and a fine bar. At that time of day it was quiet and cool, outside the temperature and humidity was high.

We had just ordered a beer from the bar-tender and decided that at the price charged, we could just manage two when we were joined by a small, wiry, elderly gentleman. He was dressed in country style, Stetson, string-tie, check shirt with his suit. He introduced himself to us and urged us to join him at his table. As he invited and offered to buy us another beer, we were persuaded. He told us that he was from West Virginia and came to town regularly. He seemed lonely.

During our conversation, another party of five gentlemen came in and sat round a table near the bar. The four young men were in smart dark suits, horn-rimmed spectacles and crew cuts and were in earnest conversation, whilst their older companion sat to one side and said nothing all afternoon.

Our West Virginian companion now suggested that we join his friends at the other table and we were duly dragged across. They politely made space for us and continued with their discussion which soon proved to be totally incomprehensible to me as it was about political campaigning, I think.

Sparks and I talked, the politicos discussed, the West Virginian dozed and the quiet gentleman in the rimless glasses regularly ordered fresh beers and drinks.

About 5 p.m., I had to leave as I had to walk back to the ship to take over from the Second Mate. I left the hotel in bright sunlight and heat which brought on a distinctively groggy feeling for which I blamed Senator Lyndon B. Johnson, soon to be the Vice-President.

SINK OR SWIM

The Gulf of Aqaba is a deep rift valley with high mountains of bare, brown rock on either side. The entrance, the Tiran Straits, in contrast is shallow and reef-strewn with the narrow, but safely navigable, channel close to the Sinai shore.

Approaching after dark at 1930 hours, on the 16th October, 1980, and just as the vessel was in the narrower stretch of the channel, an Israeli patrol boat ahead blinded us with its search-light. Having read our name … IBN QUTAIBAH … they proceeded to interrogate us as to our business and destination, etc. over the VHF radio. This was not unexpected as the vessel was registered in Kuwait and at this time the Israelis occupied the Sinai Peninsula, having a military base in Sharm El Sheik which we were just passing.

Having been allowed to continue, we steamed up the Gulf of Aqaba, arriving early the next morning off the port and town of Aqaba, which is located at the head of the Gulf in the eastern corner, whilst the Israeli port and town of Eilat is in the western corner. Halfway between them is the border, a wire netting fence neatly dividing both the shore at the head of the Gulf and the anchorage.

Anchoring is only possible on a shelving bank of sand, extending about a mile from the beach whereupon it becomes too deep to safely anchor. In this restricted area were fifteen vessels at anchor with a further twelve drifting about awaiting their turn.

Our call came that morning and we anchored without the aid of a Pilot in the designated anchorage ... five shackles on the port anchor in 35 metres of water, with the starboard anchor just on the bottom, to reduce swinging in what was a very congested anchorage.

On quiet days, holiday-makers on pedaloes came out sightseeing around us, we were that close to the shore. Discharging the cargo with barges was fairly complicated, but in the early hours of the 28th and by 0530 hours we were ready to weigh anchor and depart. On getting underway the engine did not run properly, with a tendency to stall, then speeding up. We could not now re-anchor, nor safely turn in such a restricted space so we had to go ahead towards the shore and try to turn to port when clear of the anchored vessels.

Due to the problem with the engine controls, we went faster than desired. As we rounded the innermost vessels, we came to a gentle stop. We were aground on the sand. Looking over the starboard side, I could just make out the shape of the wire net swimming enclosure belonging either to a hotel or spa or the King of Jordan. "Good heavens!" I thought ... or something like that ... "Now I will have to report that not only are we aground, but that this 26,000 dead-weight ton ship is in a swimming pool!"

The carpenter reported that he had sounded the double bottom tanks and all appeared sound. Attempts to free the vessel with the engines was unsuccessful, but by discharging water ballast from the starboard side tanks and with the aid of the freshening morning off-shore breeze at 0710 hours the vessel slid clear. As it was now light enough, I could see that we were not in fact in the swimming enclosure, but close.

Having got underway again, the Chief Engineer worked on the main engine controls whilst we proceeded out of the anchorage. This unfortunately took us into Israeli territorial waters where another patrol boat waited. After explaining ourselves and apologising for our incursion, we were able to make our departure without further incident.

Thank you, Captain Roland Owens.

Captain Maurice Bestwick
Master Mariner

Captain Maurice Bestwick, the Master of the Club, 2006, affords us a smile … although I must confess that the technical detail was a little confusing for me.

OOPS!

In the 1960s, serving as Second Officer on board a small tanker in the Far East, the Chief Officer, who had recently joined, asked me to help as he was having trouble stripping the last of the ballast out of No. 3 centre tank, which was immediately under the centre castle.

After checking that all was O.K. with the pump room and valves, we used a mirror to reflect the sun into the tank and sure enough we could see the water draining, but strangely the level was not reducing. As the tank was clean of vapours, I climbed in to get a better view and 'lo and behold' there was a beautiful fountain of water coming into the tank through a hole in the hull.

After due discussion with the Master and Chief Engineer, it was decided to stop the ship and fit a fish bolt. Whilst the Engineers prepared the fish bolt, three heaving lines were joined in the shape of a letter Y. The Chinese crew passed the heaving lines over the bow, and worked two ends down the starboard side and the third end down the port side until they were opposite the area of the hole.

They spread the two ends apart and pulled in the third, until they came to the knot. A sounding rod and line was passed through the hole in the tank and the two ends of the Y pulled up catching the sounding rod and line. The Chief Engineer was busy checking everything was O.K. with the fish bolt and washers. Eventually being satisfied he asked for the end of the sounding line to attach the fish bolt to it. Nobody seemed to have it when it was noticed that the Master was holding the sounding rod. He had separated the rod from the line and thrown the line over the side.

Oops!

Turning the colour of the funnel, red, he muttered something about he really ought to be on the Bridge and departed. The Chief Engineer was not best pleased. Needless to say, the process had to be repeated and eventually the fish bolt was successfully fitted, and the tank drained of water.

Conversations with the Master for the next few days didn't refer to the incident, but out of his hearing we did have a laugh at his expense.

A mite later in his career Maurice Bestwick has another tale … and this one has a cryptic title. Read on.

SHELL ON THE ROCKS

As Chief Mate of the Shell Tanker VALVATA, 36,000 tonner, we had loaded a cargo of Boscan Crude at Bajo Grande in the Maracaibo Lakes of Venezuela. Boscan crude is carried as a heated cargo, being the next best thing to tar or asphalt and it solidifies at about 100° F. The cargo was bound for

Gothenburg and Malmo, and after clearing the Islands (West Indies) I was informed that the Pumpman had been hurt.

It turned out that the Pumpman had been taking the noon bunker dips on the main deck and hearing a wave break over the deck had broken the Golden Rule (grab something and hold on) and ran for a ladder only to be caught and thrown against something resulting in a compound fracture of the ankle.

Loaded with a full cargo, we probably had about 6 to 7 feet of freeboard. 'Pumps' weighed in at about 18 stone. With about 14 days steaming to Gothenburg, we obviously had to decide where to divert to land 'Pumps'. The Old Man decided that 'Pumps' needed medical treatment as soon as possible, so we turned about and headed for San Juan in Puerto Rico. The Old Man cabled in to the local Agents advising that we needed to rendezvous with a tug to take the Pumpman off and get him to hospital.

At about 2200 hours the next night, we arrived at our rendezvous point and eventually an American Coastguard vessel joined us. This craft was a fibre-glass motor cruiser with a two man crew. Apparently, no tugs were available. Bearing in mind the size of 'Pumps' who was secured in the Neil Robertson stretcher, and that we were in the North Atlantic with quite a swell running, we attempted to transfer him to this craft, which one minute was level with the deck and the next was ten or more feet below us.

'Pumps' was gradually growing paler and paler, realising that if we dropped him in the 'ogin' he hadn't a hope in hell of surviving. Commonsense prevailed and I reported to the Master that it was too dangerous to attempt the transfer. 'Pumps' was quite relieved.

After discussion with the Port Authority it was agreed that we would take a Pilot, enter San Juan Harbour, turn in a turning basin, offload 'Pumps' to a now-available tug, depart from the harbour and resume our voyage to Gothenburg.

It did not quite work out as planned.

We ran aground about midnight, on sand, immediately under Puerto Del Morro Castle, a local tourist attraction. The next hours were spent trying, by various means, to pull her off the sand ... engines were put to full astern, all to no avail. To lighten the forward draught, cargo was transferred from a forward centre tank to a centre tank aft.

The local radio referred to the incident as a new drink 'Shell on the Rocks'. Eventually, the following afternoon with the assistance of a powerful salvage tug we were re-floated, towed out to sea and resumed our passage. The Pumpman was landed to a tug at some time in the night and made a full recovery.

We proceeded into the Atlantic with a trim of about three feet by the stern, not a good trim on a loaded tanker in the Atlantic. However, having been up for about thirty-six hours, I decided to leave transferring the cargo to bring the vessel back to an even keel until the next day.

That following day with the assistance of two Apprentices we started transferring the cargo from aft to forward, and as lunch was approaching, I instructed the Apprentices to stop the transfer at an appropriate ullage.

Whilst in the middle of my lunch, a Steward lent over my shoulder with a message from the Third Mate to the effect that there was 'black stuff all over the foredeck'. Departing hastily from the saloon, I dashed forward stopping the pump on my way, and continuing to the foredeck where I closed the valves on the tank that had been overfilled. Apparently, the Apprentices were hungry too and were enjoying their lunch!

My nicely-painted green foredeck was now covered with Boscan crude, which was rapidly cooling and solidifying.

I climbed a ladder to the next deck up and leant on a bulwark to contemplate what I was going to do to clean up the mess. The Chief and Second Engineers arrived full of suggestions and an offer of 300 gallons of diesel to help. I suggested that shovels may be a better offer. Shortly after, the 'Old Man' arrived and enquired "What was I going to do about the mess?" My reply was "I am giving it some thought". Bearing in mind what had happened the last few days, he was not impressed with my answer and suggested that I remove a digit and get on with the job.

At this stage my Liverpool sense of humour took over and he was even less impressed when I suggested that on arrival at Gothenberg "I will order a load of gravel, a steam roller and tarmac the b******d".

The Chief and Second Engineer fell about laughing.

The rest of that story must remain in your imagination. Captain Maurice Bestwick was born in Bootle but brought up in Wallasey. He was educated at the Wallasey Grammar School and went straight to sea after 'O' levels at the age of sixteen. He did not have the benefit of a pre-sea school or Outward Bund course. Like so many he went in at the deep end!

1957 to 1970. Seagoing with Shell Tankers Ltd starting as an Apprentice and leaving as Chief Officer to join Land and Marine Engineering Ltd as a Berthing Master. L & M installed offshore pipelines to enable tankers to load or discharge to tankage ashore. They operated in the Persian Gulf, Nigeria and on the River Mersey.

1975 to 1979. Employed as a Marine Officer with the Port of London Authority working at all London Dock systems including Tilbury Docks and at the Thames Navigation Service.

1979. Maurice joined the Manchester Ship Canal Company as an Assistant Harbour Master, managing the Towage fleet of

10 tugs and progressing to Senior Assistant Harbour Master, Deputy Harbour Master and finally becoming Harbour Master in 1996 until retirement in 2003.

Thank you, Captain Maurice Bestwick.

Captain John Felice, R.N.R.

Over the years we all acquire friends ... far too many have 'gone over the side' ... but happily many of us are 'still at it'. Captain John Felice seems to stretch back into the middle ages of time, not only in H.M.S. EAGLET and the Sea Urchins, but with Blue Funnel and India Buildings, the 'Kremlin'. John was Manager of Marine Personnel, a well known character ... but these days we share food together and swing the old lamp with undiminishing fervour. Here are some of John's more up-lifting thoughts.

WHAT'S IN A NAME

Most of the Captains had nicknames. It may be wiser not to attach names. One had his hair cut so short that they called him .... BELSEN. And who will recall the character who only allowed 'one egg per man for breakfast' and there are no prizes for his appendage ... ONE EGG. Yet another was called ... ALE HOUSE ... because when on leave he was accustomed to push the baby's pram to the pub, tended to indulge rather well and would arrive home minus one child. RADAR ... always had his head in the Radar. There are or two more, but as this might be read before the 2100 hour cut-off, they have been censored. However one tale is outstanding and one wonders if he was ever called by an ecclesiastical title.

THE BISHOP

Many years ago, in a Blue Funnel Cargo Liner, on passage to Singapore with some sixteen passengers, including the Bishop of Borneo elect, en route to take up his appointment. Unfortunately, an elderly passenger died on board the ship whilst crossing the Indian Ocean. His wife requested that as there was a Bishop on board and as they had no family anywhere in the world, perhaps he could be buried at sea.

The Captain, of the old school, however, insisted that as Master under God, it was his duty to carry out the service. The Bishop reluctantly accepted this and preparations were made for the committal, with the body enshrouded in canvas, boiler irons inserted at the feet and the last stitch through the nose, as per custom.

The body was placed on the hatch cover and the Captain began the service accompanied by the Bishop and the ship's crew. In the midst of the prayers, there was a call from the Bridge as a close quarter situation had arisen. The Captain hastily ran to deal with the problem.

The Bishop seized the opportunity, carried on with the service and got to "For I am the light and resurrection". Meanwhile, the Captain, having dealt with the problem and descending from the Bridge, heard this. He shouted "No, you're bloody well not! I am." And then he continued his God given rights!!!

John, that leaves me speechless with delight. No wonder we enjoy your company at table!

78

Captain David Thompson
Master Mariner, B.Sc., M.B.A, F.N.I

Dave Thompson is a figure in my past history in the early '60s... yet another Blue Funnel man! He claims to have led Captain Len Holder and Dick Hutson a merry dance at Holm Lea, before it became AULIS. Dave spent fifteen years with Alfred Holt and took command with a number of U.K. registered vessels, trading world-wide. He came ashore in 1979 as a Nautical Surveyor in the Liverpool Marine Office of the Department of Trade ... his boss was Captain Cyril Roberts who also figures in this book. He retired in 2001 as Chief Surveyor with the Maritime and Coastguard Agency Headquarters in Southampton.

Going to sea in the 1960s was not a lot different from what it must have been like over the previous sixty years or so ... at least, it was in Holts. Strong, over-built cargo ships, carrying up to twelve passengers, all had a large funnel in the middle, three hatches at each end and lots of crew ... 50 or 60 at least. They plied on regular voyages out of Liverpool (Blue Flue) and out of London (Glen Line), mainly to the Far East, some to Australia. The ships had rudimentary radar fitted, but otherwise nothing much had changed on the navigation side of things since the turn of the 20th Century. The container revolution, reduced manning, flagging out, etc. were all still beneath the horizon.

ANIMALS

If animals were carried as cargo, it was usually the Midshipmen's responsibility to look after them and we got paid a bonus ... about three pounds as I recall. Some animals had more luck than others. Before even getting off the quay in Birkenhead to start a voyage to the Far East, a poor dog met its death at the bottom of the lower hold, after jumping up on to an open hatch. The Middies had decided to take it ashore for some last minute exercise in a local hostelry. At the resulting enquiry in India Buildings, they had to admit taking the poor hound to a pub prior to its unleashed rush back on board and its death leap. The Marine Superintendent also got them to admit to having a pint of beer. As indentured Apprentices are forbidden to frequent Taverns or Alehouses, he was outraged. "A pint of beer!" he screamed. "Oh Sir, that's nothing ... we can drink much more that that," piped up the Senior Middie. Not the best line of defence!

In the early days of air-conditioning, the engineers like kids with a new toy would crank the temperature down to such an extent that it felt like entering an ice field when coming in off the deck. As Senior Midshipman on FLINTSHIRE in 1963, I looked after a young Boxer dog, going out to a military family in Singapore. Possibly due to the temperature differential inside and outside the accommodation, the dog frothed at the mouth, collapsed and died halfway across the Indian Ocean and was duly despatched over the side. In Singapore, the Major took my explanation philosophically and I was therefore surprised when a month later, I was called up to see the Captain to answer a telegram from the Major's wife. She wanted to know what hymns were sung at the dog's funeral. As her husband was busy fighting communists in the Indonesian jungle, it was an early lesson in prioritising.

Homeward bound in the Bay of Biscay on DOLIUS, we had two Burmese cats living in the Half-deck with us. It was normal practice at that time to double up the watches at about that stage of the voyage. Thus we were working 4 on 4 off, rather than 4 on 8 off as in the normal watch system. So with less sleep and a full gale blowing, the last thing we needed was a howling cat ... they sound very much like a baby crying. At about three in the morning, I could take no more and slung the noisiest cat out of the door on to the boat deck. Unfortunately, the wind caught the cat and whisked it away. I thought now was not the best time to explain to the Master and Mate that I had apparently just thrown 50% of our cat cargo into the Bay of Biscay, so said nothing, though we did search the ship. A day and a half later as we were entering the lock system in Gladstone Dock, one of the mooring party yelled up that we had a cat on the lifeboat. Sure enough, there was the lost moggie with its claws firmly embedded into the canvas cover. Eight lives to go!

LOOKOUTS

Up to the late 1960s when the accommodation block moved aft and ships got bigger, except in bad weather the lookout was posted on the fo'c'sle between dusk and dawn. Communication with the Bridge was by bell. In Holts if a light was seen to port ... one strike, to starboard ... two strikes, and right ahead ... three strikes. The relief lookout, to avoid giving his mate a heart attack as he stood alone on the fo'c'sle, would whistle as he climbed the fo'c'sle ladder. That is what most of them did. One joker, however, took the element of surprise to another level. He went over the ship's side and hand by hand, dangling over the sea, heaved himself round the outside of the fo'c'sle bulwark until he was right forward, over the bow. He then raised himself over the gunwale, seemingly directly out of the sea, right up into his mate's face. Change of trouser time!

Another problem of keeping the lookout isolated on the fo'c'sle was that they may occasionally be the worse for wear, if too many beers are taken prior to going on watch. In the still of the night, all alone, it is easy to doze off. Such was the fate of one A.B. who sat on a mushroom vent and closed his eyes. With the aid of engine vibration, the top of the vent slowly turned on its spindle until our man was facing directly aft. He woke with a start to apparently see what looked like a huge ship bearing down on him. He yelled out, rang 3 strikes on the bell and dived for cover under the windlass!

By the late '60s, the lookout moved aft to the monkey island, above the wheel house. This was not without its problems. One night the magnetic compass went haywire. The problem was tracked down to a Tennant lager can which the lookout had stashed under the binnacle cover of the standard compass. Nowadays, aluminium cans would go undetected.

COMMAND

By the mid '70s, I was in command myself and hopefully had learned the valuable lessons from my various mentors in Ocean Fleets. I had left for pastures new, too young for promotion. As it happened, the promotion prospects were becoming non-existent for all in Ocean Fleets as the fleet was in decline.

In 1978 with three years in command under my belt, I was in charge of a big off-shore project in Santos, Brazil. Having spent months laying a complex set of anchors way out to sea, my vessel was now manoeuvred within a few hundred feet of the beach in preparation to pull a huge sewage pipe out into

Santos bay. As we were going to be working flat out for the next couple of weeks, I decided that a quick spot of R & R was called for.

Leaving a skeleton crew on board ODIN, I led a happy band ashore on one of our tugs. The following morning, we delicately gathered ourselves together and set off back to the ship in the tug. Although the weather remained fine and clear with little wind, the sea had changed overnight and a swell was running into the bay, caused no doubt by some violent storm 1000s of miles out in the Atlantic.

The tug lay off and we studied the state of affairs. There was no chance of getting alongside and therefore no chance to get back on board. The situation went steadily downhill as the morning drew on and local surfers played the waves around ODIN.

Retaining chains started to break from the pulling wires and I could see the project and my job rapidly going down the pan. That was when I had the great Mr. Motivator moment. After all, this was what the past seventeen years' sea experience had prepared me for. As we lay off in the tug, gazing across at the heaving side of the ship, I called everyone together ... about fifteen in all. "What we'll do is swim across, grab one of the huge fenders and the lads on board can pull us onto the deck." To a man, they looked blankly at me and refused to budge.

Thinking they would follow by example, I stripped off and called to them to follow me. Still no takers. In desperation, I dived over the side and struck out for ODIN. On getting across, with the ship going up and down like the side of a house, I well understood their reluctance.

All ended well. I did get safely on board, the chain was re-secured, the swell abated, the crew rejoined in a more conventional fashion and the job was eventually completed on time. I did learn a lesson that day ... always have a Plan B.

A MERCHANT SEAMAN'S WAR

Many years after coming ashore as Chief Surveyor in the Maritime and Coastguard Agency, part of my responsibilities was the Register of Shipping and Seamen in Cardiff. At the end of an official visit, shortly before I retired in 2001, I was asked if I wanted to test the system by calling up my seaman's record.

I had already seen my own on previous visits, so called for my Uncle Jimmy's file. He had been with Shell from the outbreak of the War and had sailed with them as Bosun for years until his retirement in 1968. He died many years ago, but was my catalyst for joining the Merchant Navy

As his file was being put away amongst thousands of others, the Officer in charge of the records remarked that Jimmy's file cover showed that he had never claimed his WW 11 medals. Apparently, unless you filled in an application form after the War, nothing was handed out ... a typical bureaucratic, negative reporting scheme drawn up by a Civil Servant to minimise uptake. My colleague went to explain that it was still possible for Jimmy's next of kin, my father, to claim the medals. I duly got the paper work completed. Dad did get Jimmy's medals and he has since passed them on to me. A good result, but how much better it would have been if Jimmy, somehow having survived the entire War sailing in tankers, could have enjoyed them himself.

And finally, if there is anything that I have learned from 45 years in the Shipping Industry, it is this:

'Keep the water on the outside.'

'When all else fails, look out the bl...y window'.

Many thanks, David Thompson.

Anon

The Suez Canal affair at the tail end of 1956 developed a saga of its own. One of our members has written a 'prologue' to that event and he wishes to remain anonymous.

ALL IN A NIGHT'S WORK

The Suez Canal is the man-made link in the steamship route to the Orient. It is seen by most seamen as a necessary evil. Outward bound, it was an interruption to the peaceful-at sea routine, homeward bound it stood like the last fence of the Grand National. It had to be taken, but it might cause problems. Problems at this stage of a trip meant late arrival home, because just missing a convoy through the canal entailed a twenty-four hour delay

In late September 1956, as we plodded up the Red Sea there was more than usual to speculate upon. Whilst we had been out East, the Canal had been nationalised, rumours about the effect of this on the Canal passage were rife. No doubt the Old Man had some information about this from on high. The situation was however deteriorating. Throughout our passage across the Indian Ocean, Sparks had kept us informed on the ships that were being rerouted around the Cape, presumably in anticipation of action, possibly warlike. Whatever information was available to our owners in Liverpool, no such instruction came to us. There was a strong feeling that every day we steamed north would be an extra ongoing south again.

Twenty-four hours from Suez, we received acknowledgement of our ETA message, with instructions for our transit. These came from the Agents, no longer the friendly in-house firm who had been there since the early days of the Canal, but from their nationalised successors. The instructions were much as expected except for one, in our case, very significant point. 'No vessel was permitted to stop at Port Said ... any cargo must be on-carried ... once clear of the Canal all ships had to proceed directly out to sea.'

Our ship was thirty-five years old and on her penultimate voyage. She had twin screw diesel engines of moderate reliability and electric steering gear with appallingly slow response connected to a disproportionately small rudder, a combination which barely made her manageable even at full speed. Herein lay our problem.

The ship was one of four sisters. In their early days all had been equipped with a rudder extension, which had been rigged for the Canal transit in an attempt to improve their steering. Even so, these ships were almost always Tail-End-Charlies in any Canal convoy, just in case! The crescent-shaped extension mirrored the trailing edge of the single plate rudder to which it had been fitted, held in position by pairs of angle bars on each side. These had to be slotted around the main rudder and bolted into place through the upper pair. At loaded draft, this took place just under the surface. Support was provided by a series of tackles, one of which, attached to a small davit on the poop deck above, was used to lower the extension in a position after it had been manoeuvred around the stern from its stowage place on the after deck. On a good day, rigging would take an hour or so, unrigging it slightly less, assistance from the Agents' launch for the overside-party was essential, otherwise there was the additional chore of using a lifeboat.

We duly arrived at Suez and received the usual cooperation to rig the extension, however, there was no compromise on the Port Said situation. We were not allowed to moor. Agreement was reached on the provision of a launch and it was stressed that the ship would have to be virtually stopped in the middle of Port Said harbour, at night, unable to use helm or engines for as long as it took! What the harbour Pilot's reaction to this was I never knew. It was also apparent that the departure of the southbound convoy would be delayed until we were clear!

As expected, we arrived at Port Said in the wee small hours, considerably behind the rest of the convoy. As a result of nationalisation, the Pilots were new to the job and devoid of experience of this kind. Eventually, the launch appeared and the Mate accompanied by the Second Bosun and a couple of sailors boarded and proceeded aft. The Number One Bosun and the rest of the crew were assembled on the poop. Having been on the ship for years, they were well used to this operation. For my sins, I was posted on the poop to maintain contact with the Bridge.

When all was ready, way was taken off the ship and the job started. From my position, I could not see what was happening under the counter stern, nor could I construe from the constant stream of Chinese being exchanged what progress was being made. The Bridge telephone rang almost constantly, at first requesting progress reports, as time passed becoming more demanding as to how much longer? I stalled on the replies, deciding that trying to be heard over the crew was impossible and anyway the Mate would not appreciate the interrogation at this time. There was a fair breeze blowing which no doubt was affecting the ship, but also made it difficult to reach the bolts under water with the launch rising to the waves.

At last the shouts rose to a crescendo, the crew on deck burst into activity, the extension came into my view being hauled out of the water and eventually the launch appeared with the Mate shouting that "All was clear". Almost before I could relay this to the Bridge, I heard the noise of the engines and the water being churned as the ship gathered way. Activity around me was intense as the extension was worked around the stern to abreast of number six hatch prior to being lifted aboard. Then above the noise, I caught the faint sound of the Mate's Lancashire accent "Tell the Old Man the launch has broken down", or something to that effect! Having got part of the way back to the gangway, the boat was now stopped fifty yards off and being rapidly left astern!

There was no stopping at this stage, the ship had to keep going until she had cleared the buoyed channel before we could anchor. Those were the days before VHF radio. There was no easy way of contacting the shore ... so we sat and waited. At last as dawn was coming up, a different launch hove into view and the Mate and the crew were restored to us. At once he went forward to heave up and we were away. There was plenty to talk about during the rest of the four to eight that morning.

Some five weeks later I was on day one of the Second Mates Course at Liverpool Nautical College when the attack on the Canal took place.

Captain Roddy Tarbuck
Master Mariner

SWORN TO SECRECY

Ship PINE HILL, Canadian Fort - 1956. I was First Mate on this ship, British Crew, and we had completed discharge in London's King George Docks. The Captain and I were told that transport would pick us up next day early, but we didn't have a clue what it was about. As told there was a dark limousine chauffeured by a very smart (good-looking) young Naval Wren. We were whisked up to the Admiralty House in London and ushered in to a magnificent room with a long table, occupied by so much BRASS, believe it or not about twenty in all ... Army, Navy, Air Force, Admirals and Generals. After introductions (thankfully we had our best bibs and tuckers on) we were sworn to secrecy and told whatever passed in that room was not to be passed to anyone ... crew, family, pals ... everyone. The meeting was amazing and came under the heading 'Operation Grapple'.

It transpired our ship was to be taken over by the Navy to take all the equipment (bulldozers, cranes, lorries, diggers) out to Christmas Island, mid-Pacific, for testing of the British nuclear bomb. To unload the cargo ourselves, we would first have pontoons to unload, to be chained together to make rafts with two massive outboards each (this part of the story could go on for ever, the trip out, the unloading ... hunting land crabs with sten guns etc.). The whole loading in London and Portsmouth took about a month, the ship was shrouded with canvas screens on the jetty and could only be boarded through the shed via Naval security.

After about a week of this, the Old Man and I were leaning on the rail looking out on the dock and a tourist boat ... fully loaded with gaping tourists and a cockney avec loud hailer on the stern shouting 'This is a British ship loading all sorts of goodies to take out to Christmas Island in the Pacific for the nuclear bomb testing!!!'

So much for Secrecy.

AN EXAMPLE OF HOW NICKNAMES EVOLVE

A couple of decades ago (names and times desert me) on an SD 14 General Cargo vessel, we had two Cadets on board and as often as possible the First and Third Officers would have them on the Bridge for 'noon sights' (a thing of the past). They were very keen and soaking up knowledge like sponges (we thought). After a few months of this we would have quizzes to test the youngsters. Question:-'What happens every day at noon?' Answer from one of the Cadets ... 'lunch'. He had his priorities right. Needless to say this young lad was called 'LUNCH' for as long as I can remember.

TANKER PRACTICE

I was on a tanker doing relatively short runs up and down the west coast, U.S.A., and as usual with tankers they are about even keel loaded and about 15 feet by the stern in ballast (tank cleaning, stripping etc.). Hence my fore and after bunk in ballast, my head was a couple of feet lower than the rest of me, blood rushing to my head, headaches etc. I had a wonderful Tiger from Goa, getting on in years, but limited English (I'd forgotten my reading of Mhalim Shaib's Hindustani). I explained to him this ballast/loaded situation and would he make my bed with the pillow forward during ballast passage. He never got it right. I went through the explaining process again and I'd try not to upset him. We had just sailed from San Francisco early morning and when I went down to my cabin later, Angelo was standing by my bedroom door with a big grin on his face, pointing to my bed. 'Tik Hay, Sahib'. My bed was made up with two pillows EACH END! He was taking no chances.

TRYING TO GIVE A HELPING HAND TO THE MISSION

We were loading grain up the River Parana Argentina at Rosario. As is usual one loads at several silos ... all a few ship lengths apart. During one of the shifts (warping up by ships ropes) our own anchor picked up another bower anchor, plus about 1 shackle of cable, all in good condition. We hung it off our offside shoulder with several turns of stout rope (all done by Chief Officer Brian Rogers, a most affable giant of a man). Next morning with the help of a local retired Captain Gittins, who ran the Seamen's Mission, we negotiated a good price for the anchor and chain with the local scrap merchant ... proceeds to be split with the Mission and ship.

Unbeknown to us, a nosey Argentine Pilot on a passing ship had seen the anchor hung off and reported it to the Harbour Master, who 'REQUESTED' my presence ashore. I was grilled for quite a while and I, of course, denied all knowledge of selling it, stating that it had carried away whilst we hung it off. I legged it back to the ship as the Harbour Master promised he would visit the ship with a troop of marineros. I briefed the Chief Officer on the situation (still hoping we would get away with it) and said if it looked like going wrong to get up to the Forecastle and cut the lashings with an axe.

Some time later, my office was filled with a very belligerent bunch of Argentine harbour staff, saying at one stage that I could face incarceration, because they were convinced I still had the anchor and that it was in No.1 hatch under the grain. The Chief Officer was standing in my office doorway and without a word spoken, I gave him the nod. He slipped away and in a few minutes I felt and heard the anchor being cut away. My visitors never noticed.

We all marched forward to inspect the area and they threatened to discharge No. 1 to find the anchor. Of course I was on good ground by now and replied 'get on with it', but the port authority would face all costs and delays. I'd called their bluff, but my rear end was making little buttons. They settled to put divers down to look for the anchor ... we gave them a VERY APPROXIMATE position. We had moved upstream in the meantime to another silo. They found the anchor two days later and the harbour master paid another visit to tell me, but with quite good humour, that he thought he had been hoodwinked. TRUE ... it was the talk of the British community in Rosario, how the Mission had lost a good donation.

NO WONDER OIL AND WATER DON'T MIX

During my early days at sea, Engineers and Navigating Officers dined separately (a recipe for bad feeling). The Captain would on occasions invite the Chief Engineer to dine with him on a Sunday. The food was supposed to be the same, but Engineers maintained the Deck Officers received better (it was true). Looking back it was a stupid situation, when each department depends on each other for the safe running of the ship. The ship in question was the LONDON BANKER,

Doxford economy engine, fuel consumption 8/9 tons per day, 10 knots, 1949 – 50.

HOW EATING HABITS ON SHIPS CROSS CULTURES

Apart from Brits liking Indian food with Indian crews and Chinese food with Chinese crews, here is a slightly funny tale. In the late 90s my company London & Overseas Freighters ... 'London Greeks' so called, asked me to take command of a ship called LONDON ENTERPRISE in Japan. It was a Panmax Tanker, one year old on a clean oil run and the Britside of the Company were taking it over from the Greekside. Change of flag, change of Officers, but keeping Philippine crew, who had only served under Greek Officers. The ship was running without a Catering Officer, which the Britside was used to. They asked me would I try to run the ship the same. This was a time of big cost cutting. The British Officers in my Company had always enjoyed a high standard of catering ... silver service etc., uniformed Stewards and Officers, bar and barmen ... very good food. I was justifiably apprehensive. The Philippine catering staff and galley staff never wore hygienically-recommended white coats, hats and aprons and had only done Greek food occasionally as it turned out, because the Greek Officers each had large fridges in their cabins and it seemed each man cooked and ate by himself. Anyway, I had the foresight to take 'THE DAIRY BOOK OF COOKERY' with me... a very good cookery book with coloured pics.

We arrived in Kobe ... myself and sixteen Officers ... sailing in two days, one week before Christmas. I hurriedly got the ship's chandler on board and managed to get 3 months of British-style stores. All the Greeks had left was what looked like 2 tons of Feta cheese and olives in tins. I also had a talk to the Philippine cook, an excellent person who spoke perfect English. All that they seemed to be happy with was pork and chicken. For the British menu, I just photocopied the recipes together with the coloured pictures and the Cook had a go ... not bad at first, but EXCELLENT in a week or two. I'd talked to the Cook about the English style breakfast ... every day the main course was the typical heart attack on a plate ... bacon, eggs, sausage, black pud etc. with another course different every day. He wrote the menus and showed them to me each evening. All went well, the standard of catering was excellent, the catering staff soaking up the new experience of cooking British-style food. As mentioned, I'd stocked up for the 3 months.

After about six weeks, the Cook came up with the next day's menu ... we usually had a beer whilst we discussed it. I pointed out to the Cook that he'd forgotten the 'ENGLISH BREAKFAST'. He told me we had run out of bacon, sausage, black pud etc. "Not possible" I said. We had ordered enough for three months. "Sorry Sir" he said. "We Philippines just love this English style breakfast." I had a good laugh and ordered double next time. An offshoot of this ... we started to enjoy some Philippine dishes for breakfast!

ODD NAMES OF FOOD AT SEA

Porridge - Burgoo or Bergon.
Sardines on Toast - Sharks on a raft.
Cheese - Bungole??

Evaporated milk was called 'Captains milk' because usually he was the only one allowed it. During coal-burning days on the ships I sailed on, the 3 firemen, 1 trimmer and 1 donkey man came off their watch in the evening at one bell (quarter to eight) and their evening meal was cooked especially for them by the Second Cook (one hour's overtime). It was the best cooked meal of the day because it could include a few left-over's from the Officers' table and was appropriately called 'BLACK PAN'

Thank you Captain Roddy Tarbuck … I enjoyed that!

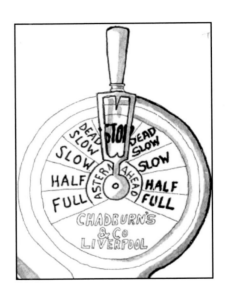

Edmund Drew
Liverpool Pilot

Edmund Drew tells a tale which reminds us that there are hazards in every calling. However, our Liverpool Pilots are not always being faced with life-threatening crises and this little saga proves them to be human ... not that proof is really required!

EMERGENCY

Looking through my diary for 1957, I found a job that has stayed vividly in my memory down the years. I was aged 31 and had my First Class Licence for just over two years. I rang the Shoremaster at ten past five on Monday, 11th February, 1957, and the entry in my diary reads, 'MARTABAN, Duke Street, East Float to sea 0500 tomorrow. Sleep on board.'

The MARTABAN was one of the Paddy Henderson Line of Glasgow cargo/passenger liners trading to the Far East. I knew that there would be a Pilot's room on board, so I decided, in view of the 0500 start, to travel to the ship late on Monday evening. I left my car in Irwell Street and walked up to James Street Station at about 11 p.m. and caught a train to Park Station. From there I walked to the ship in the N.E. corner of the East Float and contacted the Officer on Watch who showed me to the Pilot's cabin. It was arranged that I be called at 0445.

In the morning, I went onto the Bridge and in the darkness introduced myself to the Master. He seemed to me to be quite an elderly gentleman and I noticed, which was not uncommon in those days, that he had First War medal ribbons preceding his row of Second War ones. He was a dour Scotsman and, although he was civil as we shook hands, I had the distinct impression that he was not terribly thrilled to see me, as the ship was usually piloted by Mr. Reg Youde, the company Appropriated Pilot.

As we singled in and made the tugs fast fore and aft, a dock gateman hailed the Bridge and told me that the Dockmaster wanted us to leave the berth at once. He requested that we make our way down to Alfred North lock and make fast there... Highwater that morning was at 0905, 26.1 feet. In those days, there was no VHF communication at all ... not to the tugs, the Dockmaster or with Mersey Radio. The weather, whilst not foggy, was certainly very misty as we backed our way slowly down the East Float, through the North Bridge and into Alfred basin. All the time the Master walked up and down in a fore and aft line, on the starboard side of the Bridge, where I was watching intently but not saying a word. It was breaking daylight when we made fast starboard side in North Alfred lock.

I had an early breakfast in the chartroom as we waited for the tide to make and for the lock become level with the river. All the time the weather was looking murkier and murkier and some ships in the river were blowing their whistles. At 0730, the lock gates opened and we backed out. It was just possible to make out the Liverpool side as we let the tugs go, and with the engine on half speed, we headed over for the other side, hoping of course that no inward ship was going to appear out of the gloom with us on the wrong side of the river! I soon found out that the ship's radar was pretty useless, although it was much better than nothing. We passed a ship waiting to dock in Sandon and, soon after, another with tugs fast-moving towards Gladstone Lock. The visibility was just under half a mile.

By this time, the boat deck was filling up with passengers, who had had their breakfasts and were out to see the leaving of Liverpool. The Master was still walking up and down, with a friendly comment here and there. As we made our way down Crosby Channel, the visibility was decreasing. It was now about three cables and I was bitterly regretting having had that nice big cup of coffee with my breakfast! I was absolutely dying for a pee!

No chance of doing one over the side, as was not unusual in coasters, because of the passengers on the boat deck! I knew that there was no toilet on the bridge, and that the only one would be in the Masters Cabin. As we approached Crosby Buoy, by now on slow ahead, with ships ahead and astern blowing their whistles, I could hear the deep tone of the fog bell on Crosby Buoy. It was now or never before we got on the Crosby bend! I told the Master of my problem, and asked where the toilet was. He looked at me for a moment and then said, "But I don't want you to leave the Bridge Pilot". Then he called out in a loud voice, "Cadet, bring a bucket for the Pilot".

The Cadet was soon back with a smirk on his face and a large, galvanised bucket in his hand. There were no little plastic ones in those days!! I took it into the starboard wing of the bridge and did what was necessary as swiftly as possible … what blessed relief, and handed the bucket back to the waiting Cadet.

We went round Crosby Buoy with visibility two cables or less, but now it was highwater and no tide to worry about. My courses worked out well, and soon we were on the straight for Formby Buoy when the weather began to clear. By the time we were at the end of the channel, we could see the Bar Lightship and the Bar Pilot Boat.

I used the Aldis lamp myself to flash two long and two short to the Pilot boat. As he signed my cards on the chart table, the Captain was a changed man. He shook me warmly by the hand as the boat came alongside and said "Thank you, Mr. Drew, that was an excellent job". He must have looked up my name in the Bridge Log.

As I got into the boat and waved Bon Voyage to the Master, and to the passengers lining the rails, I was indeed a happy man.

Thank you, Edmund. We all have problems. Try preaching the Three Hour Service on Good Fridays, as we used to do in the 'good old days'. Incidentally, this article appeared in the 'Woodside Whispers' ... the Liverpool Pilots' magazine.

Captain John Bakewell
Master Mariner

Captain John Bakewell has recorded memories under the heading of 'Holyhead Yarns'. I worry about Anglesey! Read on.

WHY WE DON'T SWING IN A S.E. GALE!

I had not been at Holyhead long and was Mate of the SLIEVE BAWN. It was blowing a S.E. gale as we approached Dublin and I remarked that "We won't be swinging this morning Captain". "Why not?" said Alex. "I believe she won't come round in a S.E. gale" said I. As we arrived at the swinging basin, Alec said to the Quartermaster, "Hard a port" and to me, "Now I'll show you why we don't swing in a S.E. gale". Of course, the ship would not come round and we crabbed up the Liffey until we reached some shelter near the Dodder buoy when we let go an anchor and eventually got her stern up river to back on to the berth. Safely tied up, he said to me "Did you see the trouble I had? That is why we never ever swing in a S.E. gale".

Captain Glynne Pritchard.

I SHOULD BE SO LUCKY!

Captain Alex Robertson had a great sense of humour. Every time you'd see him, he'd remind you that if it wasn't for him, there's be no Kylie Minogue ... during WW2 he'd saved Kylie's grandfather's life!
John Griffiths.

CAPTAIN ON THE BRIDGE!

One story from the 60s was concerning when John Griffiths was taking one of the mail boats out from the station and the ship was going astern. In those days, the Marine Superintendent (Captain Lord) had his Office overlooking the harbour from close to the sheerlegs. When the ship passed by his window, Captain Robertson got everyone except the Quartermaster to duck, so Captain Lord only saw one man on the aft bridge. Cue ... wobbler!
John Griffiths

SCOUSE FOR TEA!

A Chief Steward was heard to remark when asked what was for dinner, "Where are you eating? The passengers are having Navarin of Lamb Jardinere, the Officers are having Irish Stew, and the Crew are having Scouse ... but it's all coming from the same pan!!!"
Captain Peter Lockyer.

THE EVENING PAPERS

As a young boy, I crossed over to Dublin Bay several times on the old steamboats when my father was Master. I can remember being on the Bridge at night, and the Quartermaster's face illuminated by the binnacle light, and being allowed to 'steer' the ship. Passing close to the Kish Lightship on the way home, we would throw the evening papers overboard in a waterproof canvas bag for the keepers to pick up in a small boat.

Captain Glynne Pritchard

SCHOOL WORK!

Recalling the times when pupils from Holyhead School were able to work on the Cross Channel boats as Stewards is Ray Rowlands, son of the late Captain John Rowlands.

I was one of the lucky few pupils at Holyhead County School who had important family connections with the two mail boats in the late 50s to early 60s, in that my father was able to get me a job as a Steward looking after the Officers and Engineers during the summer holidays. At that time it was good money, although one had to work 24 hours on and 12 hours off. Helping me at the time as steward was Trefor Jones, whose father was also a Master on the boats.

Unfortunately, I was never a good sailor and I knew, if it was promising Force 6 or more, I would be guaranteed to be really sea-sick. I remember in particular one trip that was extremely rough and part of my job was to take a glass of milk down to the Chief Engineer when we reached the Stack Light. All of this involved going down three flights of stairs into the engine room. All I wanted to do, after carrying out my job, was to go straight back to lie down, but the Chief Engineer (who enjoyed his pipe) asked me to go to the First Class shop to get him a box of matches!! This involved a lot of walking up and down flights of stairs, as well as going from the stern of the ship to the bow. I was really cursing him at the time ... but managed somehow or other to hold back my sickness until I had safely delivered his matches.

Another problem during bad weather was trying to carry

and balance a tray of cups and saucers, milk and sugar along the outside deck to get up to the Bridge, when the wind was blowing the sugar all over the place. Also, even worse at night, climbing up the staircase in complete darkness up to the Bridge, which itself was pitch black and trying to find somewhere to put down the tray.

It's such a big shame now that Holyhead teenagers with strong family links with the Ships are denied the opportunities that I and others were lucky to have had.

Ray Rowlands

MARKING THE CORNER!

Turkeyshore Corner was once marked with two large, white-painted, wooden dolphins. Wouldn't have done much good if you were destined to hit it! But, they did mark the shallow bit. They can be seen on the photos of the old HIBERNIA bow up on the corner in fog. A rather pompous head of personnel, named Mr. Shaw, is reputed to have gone to see the spectacle and was invited by the Master, peering over the bridge wing to: "Push us off with your umbrella, Mr. Shaw!"

THE BWANA SWING!

Captain Richard 'Bwana' Jones explains the remarkable 'Bwana Swing'. Strong, southerly gales always made departure from Holyhead's old Station Berth, stern first, extremely difficult. As the STENA HIBERNIA lacked the power of the STENA CAMBRIA in such conditions, it became apparent to me that if we on the former SAINT COLUMBA failed to sail, then the CAMBRIA might have to wait outside the port until the weather moderated.

After studying the charts for many a long hour and visiting the Container Terminal, I realised that by landing the stern of the ship and pinning it on one set of piles on the container berth, there was just sufficient space to swing the ship there, allowing us to proceed out of the harbour bow first.

At the time, I was sailing as Night Master, with Captain Ian Farrell as the Day Master. I think I had been talking to him for some time about the possibility of this manoeuvre, when one day it was blowing a strong gale from the south. The Refit Berth was occupied, the STENA CAMBRIA was outside the port with nowhere to go, and I was in bed while Ian was preparing for the afternoon sailing. The next thing I was informed that I was wanted on the Bridge where I was told, "This is your bloody idea, so we'll do it together".

After a bit of a conflab, we put the idea into practice and, lo and behold, the birth of the 'Bwana Swing'!

Over time, this method was much improved upon, but it could only be performed if tidal conditions were right and, as the piles on the container berth were somewhat small, landing and keeping the stem on them was quite tricky. Although the container service had finished, the cranes were still in position, which on a few occasions nearly caused the old adrenalin to over-flow!! I am not sure how many Masters used this manoeuvre. Captain Ian Farrell and I did it regularly and Captain Hugh Farrell did it at least a couple of times.

Captain Richard Jones

END OF A BERTH

One evening whilst sitting in the mess room of the BRIAN BORORIME or the RHODRI MAWR, there was a rumble and a roar. We ran out to see the water 'boiling' where the Special Berth should have been. It had collapsed into the dock. Minutes later, an ashen-faced Steward, Eric Hughes I think it was, reported aboard and said he was walking across the berth when he felt the ground tremble and got to firm ground just in time! An ancient stream, the Afon Trip, which ran into the original creek and had been diverted through a culvert which drained into the harbour, beneath the Special Berth, must have worn away the foundations until ... WHOOMPH! ... SPLASH! There had been a problem there for years. Divers had been for ever supporting the foundations with sand bags.

Captain Glynne Pritchard.

And the name 'Bwana'? Before joining the Holyhead ships I was working as a surveyor in West Africa, so I was named 'Dick Bwana' by some wag on the SLIEVE DONARD. Actually, the title 'Bwana' is from East Africa, but what the hell ... Holyhead folk have never allowed a few thousand miles of geographical error to stand in the way of a good nickname!!

Captain Richard Jones

THE POWER OF PRAYER

The late Captain Len Evans recalled a voyage in the turbine steamer DOVER in September 1974. We left Holyhead in flat calm conditions, but it was a good Force 12 Northerly in Dun Laoghaire. I was able to berth, but the sea in the harbour was such that she was pitching and rolling alongside the berth. Clearly she was going to suffer major damage, and so I sailed back out into Dublin Bay where I turned circles for the next twelve hours until conditions improved slightly and I was able to go back alongside, discharge cars and passengers and reload. At about 2300 hrs, I had a message from Valley that the wind was now 83 mph. Coming into Holyhead was not funny. At one stage it seemed inevitable that she would smash into the Refit Berth. However, she came around, and I was delighted to tie up in the Station Berth.

After we got alongside, the Carpenter came up to my room, which he never did usually, and said, "Captain, if I was to die, I prayed for you, and she came around". There were tears rolling down his cheeks. He left me a very chastened man ... to think that one of my crew had thought so much!

Captain John Bakewell makes his own contribution to 'Holyhead Yarns'.

REACTION FROM THE MASTER!

Shortly before he passed away in 2005, Captain Len Evans, first Senior Master of the ST. COLUMBA, (later renamed STENA HIBERNIA), shared his reaction to the 'Bwana Swing'.

Leaving Holyhead in a southerly gale could be quite hairy, and we had a grudging admiration for the B & I ships, which used to do a free swing in the harbour.

Swinging stem on the quay was commonplace with our old cargo ships, which would berth bow-in at the Import Berth and they would then breast over with ropes to the Export Berth. We would then swing bow-out, usually stern-on the quay, but bow-on in northerly winds.

We would also swing the ST. COLUMBA on the quay at the Refit Berth when the needs of the refit required, but it was not done in a southerly gale!

AND WE WERE SINGING HYMNS AND ARIAS, LAND OF MY FATHERS, AR HYD Y NOS!

On 5th December 1981, Glynne Pritchard was at the Cardiff Arms Park watching a Rugby International. We were in Bailey's dry-dock, Barry, on the ST. COLUMBA. Captain Len Evans was the Master, but he had gone home over the period of the game. I was the Commanding Officer. Maelor Jones was the Engineer Superintendent. Alun Roberts was the Chief

Engineer. Other Engineers were Victor Williams, John (Scones) Williams, and a Junior Engineer, David Campbell. Dave Bell was the Radio Officer and Dewi Riley the Electrician.

We were fortunate to be staying at the Angel Hotel where the after-match dinner was held. Being a crowd of jolly seafarers, we were well-in with the waitresses and one of them advised us that after the dinner and speeches, a certain door leading down to the function room would be left unlocked, and if we cared to make our way down individually we could join the party!

We all crept down through the door and joined the party. The rugby crowd were so well-oiled by that time that they didn't notice the gatecrashers! It was one of the best evenings I can ever recall! I gave the programme and autographs to my son.

Later, on the 13th December, the ST. COLUMBA was afloat in Barry dry-dock when the wind picked up to S.S.E. 10. There was a scramble to get more ropes out. Glynne recalled that this was about 6 p.m., after normal working hours. After a while the wind abated and about 8 p.m. the Bosun said some of the lads wanted to go ashore and could they stand down? Len said "Hang on for a bit", but finally conceded when conditions remained stable.

Shortly after the majority of the crew had disappeared down the gangway the wind picked up again, piping up to N.W. 10. Our moorings were now on the wrong side! And, most of the crew were ashore.

Capt Len was operating one winch, I was coiling rope, John 'Scones' and other Engineers doing the same. Assorted Cooks, Stewards, Mates throwing heaving lines and running out ropes. We managed to secure the ship.

Len said, "I b****y knew something like this would happen; as I left the house to walk down to the ship I saw the new moon through the window!"

Captain John Bakewell remembers one of his first trips out as Master.

SMOKIN'!

One of my first trips as Master on SILEVE DONARD was with Glynne Pritchard as Chief Officer. We arrived at night in the Boathouse berth with a heavier landing than I would have liked! So we went down the gangway to see if any damage had been done. We couldn't see any damage to the ship, but there was a strong smell of burning. I thought that we couldn't have slid along the piles that much for them to burn. The smell got stronger when suddenly I found that my coat pocket was on fire from my pipe!

MORE MEMORIES

I joined the Holyhead ships on April 14th, 1958. It was a beautiful evening when I stepped aboard SLIEVE BAWN. The Officer of the Watch was the late Alan Thomas and the first thing he said to me was "This is a soul destroying job!!" Needless to say, I stayed another 33 years!

We were sailing from Holyhead to Dublin on the SLIEVE BAWN and we were due to arrive there at around 0800. Before sailing and after the cargo had been loaded, a list of the cargo was put aboard the ship in the safe keeping of the Captain.

On the passage, all panic was let loose from the Captain's room. Somehow the ship's papers had caught fire. I cannot remember how this happened as Captain Butterworth was a non-smoker. However, we called up Dublin and told them that the cargo papers were on fire. We hoped that Dublin would contact Holyhead for copies. On approaching the berth at North Wall, we could see many people milling around plus fire engines and ambulances. Apparently, they thought we had said "Cargo of paper on fire!"

I was Chief Officer on HIBERNIA and Captain John Rowlands was Master. We were approaching Carlisle Pier and suddenly I noticed a Steward coming up the ladder to the Bridge. He had a gun in his hand which was pointing at us! I said "Captain, a Steward is coming up to the Bridge with a gun in his hand". "Don't bother me now" said Captain Rowlands. "Let me get this thing alongside first!!!"

It turned out that the Steward had found a replica gun in one of the lounges and had quite rightly commandeered it!!

There obviously could have been many more Holyhead Yarns, but Captain John Bakewell has his own story to tell of his life at sea before he joined the Holyhead ships in April 1958.

I joined the training ship H.M.S. WORCESTER in January 1946 where I stayed for two years. The Captain Superintendent was Commander Steele, R.N. ... a fine man who was awarded a V.C. in 1919 in the scrap against the Bolsheviks.

In 1948, I joined Shaw Savill and Albion as a Cadet. After three years, I sat the Second Mates Certificate and was appointed Junior Fourth Officer on DOMINION MONARCH. At that time, this ship was the largest motor vessel in the world. We carried 510 passengers, all First Class. The food was fantastic, especially for a 20 year-old starving young man! We also carried a great amount of refrigerated cargo from New Zealand.

My watch on this ship was with the Second Officer where we kept the 12 to 4 watch, often called the 'graveyard watch' during the middle of the night. One night at around 0200, the Bridge telephone rang. It was the band leader (yes we had a band on board) telling us that he was in trouble. Apparently, he had been entertaining a lady passenger in his cabin and when she returned to her own cabin, her husband refused to let her in and threatened to kill her!

The Second Officer told me to go down and sort things out!! The lady was back In the band leader's cabin and in a panic! I said that I would try and reason with her husband, but got nowhere. The only thing to do was to wake the Staff Chief Steward and ask him to find a spare cabin for the lady. Now, the Staff Chief Steward was one of those gentlemen who never drank and was extremely puritanical. He was against all the vices known to man. So I went along to his cabin, knocked on the door, went in and switched on the light. He swiftly sat up in bed, but so did the topless blonde next to him!! Ever afterwards that gentleman groveled to me for the rest of the voyage!

DOMINION MONARCH had Sir Henry Gordon as Captain. There was a Chief Officer, a First Officer, a Second Officer, a Third Officer, a Fourth Officer, with me bringing up the rear as Junior Fourth Officer. At noon, we were all on the Bridge taking sun sights with our sextants. Sir Henry would then walk down the line asking what our sextant readings were. Usually we were all pretty much the same with the exception of Sir Henry's readings, which were often quite a bit different. Nevertheless, we had to use his reading every time and ignore ours! We still got to our destination safely though!!

I stayed with Shaw Savill for nearly ten years, slowly going through the ranks until I reached Second Officer and obtained my Master's Certificate.

We had some great times. Staying for several weeks at a time in New Zealand, I got to know many people, some of whom are still my dearest friends to this day.

There were so many stories which would take too long to tell. However, I was once standing by a ship, CRETIC, in Wallsend-on-Tyne and I, as Third Officer, was accommodated in Whitley Bay with a great friend, the Second Officer, while the ship was being built.

The day came for sea trials which we were invited to attend. The builders had their own people on board as the ship had not been handed over. The Second Officer and I overslept and arrived to see the gangway was no longer in the ship and that the moorings had been singled up. We quickly looked around and saw one of those gigantic buckets. We jumped in and a crane driver hoisted us on board. Apparently, the Captain, who was watching us this from the bridge, turned to the Chief Officer and said "More rubbish coming aboard"!!!

It was on this ship, the CRETIC, that we had to perform two operations. One outward-bound to Australia and one homeward-bound. In 43 years at sea, these were the only operations we ever did. On the outward-bound run, the Fifth Engineer developed appendicitis. Fortunately, we had on board a Surgeon who was working his passage. He was an F.R.C.S. man. Operating tools to hold the cut open were made from brass in the Engine Room. John Walker, the Electrician, fixed bright lights in the dispensary and the Second Officer, Graham Perry, assisted the Surgeon while I was the anaesthetist. I put a tea towel over his face and nose and dropped drops of anaesthetic from a medicine bottle with a slit cut in the cork. The Surgeon instructed me to watch his ears. A nice red colour was OK, but if they turned purple, I was to ease off!! About a couple of weeks or so afterwards, the Engineer was back in the Engine Room fully recovered. Lo and behold, a Greaser on the trip home also developed appendicitis and this time we only had a doctor who had just qualified. I assisted this time and again the op was successful, but as he was sixty we landed him in Aden. He too survived!

Thank you, John Bakewell, it was great to read of your colourful career.

Captain Ian Poole
Master Mariner

Captain Ian Poole started life in Liverpool and was evacuated to a farm outside Wrexham and then to Anglesey ... an English lad in a Welsh-speaking school ... but he was rescued educationally by Merchant Taylors School in Crosby. In 1952 at seventeen years old, he was apprenticed to T & J Brocklebanks and obtained his Masters 'ticket' in 1963. Ian then transferred to Ellerman Papyanni and was seconded to the London office as Fleet Training Officer before taking up command. He was made redundant in 1983. Next came time in the Liverpool office in Freight Sales and eventually he became Manager of the Festival Hall for the International Garden Festival in 1983/84. Finally, he worked in ANC Express Parcels Head Office in Stoke-on-Trent for eleven years. I quote him ... "retired 1998 ... hooray!"

Here are his tales.

A NICE LITTLE EARNER

Early in the 1950s when I signed on as an Apprentice with T & J Brocklebanks, there was a thriving racing community in Calcutta; there may still be for all I know. A lot of the top

British jockeys used to ride there, Kiddepore race meetings were a highlight of the social calendar, both for the expats and the locals. I can't remember how often they were held, but they needed race horses for these prestigious races and that's where we came in!

We cared for dogs too!

The horses (poor things) were loaded in horse boxes onto the after well-deck and secured in place along with all their fodder, hay, curry combs, pills and potions. These weren't any old horses. These were pedigrees used to the very best, much the same as we Brocklebank Apprentices! We were instructed by the Chief Officer that it would be our responsibility to look after these beasts on the voyage out to Calcutta. There were usually either two or four Apprentices per vessel, and the Chief Officer did advise us that as this was outside our normal duties, we would probably get a small buckshee from him if we performed well and the horses survived. As we were only on £8 a month, even a promise was better than nothing. There was only one snag. None of us had been closer to a horse than Roy Roger's Trigger at the cinema; you would have thought they could have recruited some Apprentices with a farming background. Anyway I digress, the horse owners sent a stable lad to instruct us in the necessary skills in handling them and what to feed them. Then he buzzed off back to Newmarket, but what the Mate forgot to tell us was that we also had to carry out our normal duties as well!!

Anyway, we sailed and we muddled through, mucking out, feeding, grooming, being kicked, bitten and barged. However, by the Red Sea we had got the hang of it and were slapping and kicking back. I never knew horses could drink so many buckets of water.

We finally arrived at Calcutta with the horses in fine fettle, but we were absolutely knackered. The owner's representative came aboard to check on the condition of their beautiful horses. They were well pleased and went up to see the Mate to tell him that he had looked after the horses very well and no doubt crossed his palm with silver. The Mate eventually passed a small number of rupees to us, but unbeknown to him, the owner's rep saw us separately and gave us a huge wad of rupees. It seemed like a fortune to us. We were also advised to bet on certain horses. This we did and made a few rupees more.

Funny thing though!! We never did take any of those horses back to the U.K., but I did have a few very tough steaks in the Grand Hotel. Makes you wonder doesn't it!!

This trip set me up to work with other animals. Later on in my career, we carried Alsatian guard dogs for the R.A.F., elephants to a circus in the States, monkeys for the space programme, pythons and various poisonous snakes ... to mention but a few. And I never got a question in any of my tickets on animals!!

NICKNAMES

During the post war period, possibly in the 50s or 60s, it was the practice to hold extensive naval manoeuvres in the Mediterranean.

A Master in Ellerman & Papayanni set sail from Liverpool, bound for the usual ports in the Med. After a rough passage across the Bay of Biscay, fog down the Portuguese coast and very little rest in Lisbon, our hero sailed on into the Med.

Whether through lack of sleep or some other reason, he failed to read the Notice to Mariners warning that night naval exercises were to be held in a restricted area of the Western Med on certain dates, using as legend has it 'live ammunition'. Not knowing any thing of this, course was set for the next port of call, which just happened to pass through this restricted area. During the night, much to the surprise of all on board, they were suddenly caught up in what appeared to be the start of World War 3 ... shells falling to port, shells falling to starboard, torpedoes passing ahead and astern, star shells and tracers lighting the night sky. The Master took the only course of action open to him. It is alleged that he cabled the Admiralty in Malta with the following message.

To C.in C. Admiralty Malta ... CEASEFIRE
Signed   FLYNN

Since that cable that Master was always known as "Ceasefire Flynn"

We also had another Master who rejoiced in the name Captain Effin Williams ... who hailed from North Wales. I always thought this name to be some rather quaint and obscure Welsh name, but although having been brought up in Anglesey myself, I had never come across it. I made enquires about this from my shipmates and was told that I would soon find out about it. I did. Every other word the Master used was 'effin' this and 'effin' that.

THE STRANGE TALE OF THE SHIP'S CAT

We sailed from Birkenhead on the 29th June, 1961, on a nice summer's day, loaded to the gunwales with general cargo, bound for Calcutta with a full crew consisting of Indian ratings,

British officers and a ginger ship's cat. The MANDASOR was not the fastest or best-looking liner in Brocklebanks' fleet, but she was a happy ship, ploughing her way East at a steady 8 to 10 knots. You had to have a happy outlook on life as, at that speed, the voyage took forever. We sailed out of the Mersey with the poop piled high with masses of second-hand furniture, sewing machines and various bric-a-brac, all bought in Birkenhead market by the Indian crew for their families at home as they were paying off on arrival in India.

The ship's cat considered herself to be of Officer status and did not go any where near the Indian crew's accommodation. With the Officers all being newly signed on, she would prowl the cabins selecting an Officer who looked like a 'soft touch' who would share with her his bunk and his curled-up sardine sandwiches. I think she settled in with the Third Mate and all went well until we reached Calcutta. There she fell in love with this huge black tomcat, more like a puma than a cat. He also made the MANDASOR his home, despite being evicted on numerous occasions. The tom endeared himself to the Deck Officers by hiding under the monkey island's compass housing … at night, pouncing out and sinking his claws into our white socks and ankles as we went up to take bearings. To say it gave you a shock is putting it mildly. Nature had its way and the ship was presented with six kittens that made themselves at home, each finding a 'soft touch' to look after them. On the homeward passage, the ship was sold to Greek owners and the Master decided that eight cats were too many. The best thing to do was to have them put down by a vet on our arrival at Middlesbrough. After the MANDASOR berthed, the cats were rounded up and locked up to await their fate; however only five kittens could be found.

The ship was searched, but no trace of the missing kitten could be found. The vet arrived on board and put the rest of the family to sleep. On completion of discharge, the vessel was handed over to its new owners. The Brocklebank funnel was painted out and we were all paid off on the 28th of October, 1961, and went our separate ways to enjoy our well-earned leave. At no time during the couple of weeks of discharging and handing the ship over to the Greeks was the sixth kitten ever sighted.

After a long leave of ten days after a five month voyage (they don't know they are born these days), I joined the MAGDAPUR for a coastal voyage, prior to taking the rest of my leave. We were surprised to learn that we were to load at Wilhelmshaven on the Weser above Bremerhaven. To the best of my knowledge, this was the first and last time a Brocklebank ship ever called at Wilhelmshaven. We were even more surprised to see the old MANDASOR also berthed there, loading a cargo for its new owners, some three ships lengths ahead of us. During the night the sixth kitten mysteriously came aboard the MAGDAPUR and settled down with a 'soft touch' as if nothing had changed. How did the kitten recognise the Brocklebank ship? Was it the smell of the curry and rice? Was the food so bad on the Greek vessel that it would gladly jump on to any ship? Or was there some deeper reason, divine intervention perhaps!! Maybe the good Canon Bob Evans can throw some light on the matter. (Don't put your money on it!)

I suspect we will never know. Funny things happen at sea!!

Thank you, Ian ... I much enjoyed that. But the last word belongs to Ian's wife ... Annette, who was very reluctant to write her story ... these are Ian's words ... "There was no stopping her once she got the bit between her teeth". Read on.

MEMOIRS OF MEMSAHIB - (Thank You Mum)

Just my luck I thought when my husband came home and announced that Brocklebanks had just introduced a 'wives at sea' policy for all Officers from Second Mate upwards. My husband was at the time serving with them as Second Mate and I would have been eligible to sail with him. There was only one small snag; we had an eighteen-month-old son that I could not leave. I was the daughter of a Master Mariner and had always loved the romance of the sea and had listened to all the tall tales of adventure, disaster, laughter and exotic places. Back in 1962, travel was not as common or as easy as it is today, even a trip to London was a major excursion.

I went to see my mother, as I did most days, and told her of this news and bemoaned my fate. She was a very understanding lady and said that I should never let family come between me and my husband and suggested she would look after our son with the help of my sister for the duration of the voyage. Secretly, I think she just wanted to get her hands on her first grandchild. After a lot of soul searching, I decided to abandon my first born for a life on the ocean wave.

My husband and I signed on the S.S. MARTAND on the 27th March, 1962, in Royal Albert Dock London, amid the hustle and bustle of a ship preparing for a voyage of up to six months. Our cabin was a good size, with a pull-out double bed and the furniture and fittings of an Officer's cabin. There were no 'en suite' facilities in those days, however we did have our own Steward (Boy) ... a lady of luxury at last! After one last tearful telephone call to my mother and son we sailed for India.

There were two other wives on board ... the Purser's and the Spark's. This is not the ideal number and there was a certain amount of falling out among the three of us at times, but we all survived each other and lived to tell the tale. We crossed the Bay of Biscay in pretty bad weather and I surprised myself by not suffering from sea sickness. As we passed Gibraltar, the weather improved and we all managed a good sun tan by the time we reached Port Said. We tied up to the buoys to await the next convoy south. It was fascinating to watch the bum boats trying to sell their wares and the Gully Gully Man who came aboard and produced day-old chicks out of our ears, mouths and clothing. The best bit of Port Said, of course, was the mail from home and news of how my mother was coping with our son. No problem there ... he wasn't even missing me!

We sailed through the Canal into the Red Sea and experienced some really hot weather. We had now settled into an onboard routine. I helped the Mate with his office work during the mornings, then came the lunch drinks session with off-watch Officers. Some washing during the afternoon ... no problem drying it in that heat! We had called at Aqaba and saw the barren lunar landscape of the Gulf, followed by various ports in the Red Sea which I had not really heard of. My husband had read in one of the Sunday papers before we sailed, that one could sell a good European woman in Djibouti for several thousand pounds! He was very disappointed when he couldn't even get a French sou for me. So much for the press!

During the passage down the Red Sea, a swimming pool was erected on the boat deck, not the luxury kind you find on the great liners. Our pool was more like one you would find in a junk yard. It consisted of scaffolding poles, old hatch boards and was lined with an old tarpaulin finally filled with sea water. It mightn't be the loveliest, but it was the coolest place on board. None of the wives could swim and as the water was about five feet deep, we took no chances and wore our life jackets when we were in the water much to the amusement of everyone.

We arrived in Aden and the Agent arrived on board with lots of mail. I was a little disappointed to learn that our son was still not missing me, but pleased that all was well.

Our next port was the highlight of the trip as far as I was concerned ... Gan Island, the southernmost of the Maldive Islands. To get there, we had to 'cross the line' and suffered all the indignities that King Neptune could throw at us. Gan Island proved to be a perfect paradise with white coral sands, and palm trees, surrounding a lagoon of the most beautifully-coloured water that I had ever seen. Gan at that time was a Royal Air Force base with 500 men and one middle-aged W.V.S. woman. The arrival of three young wives was quite an occasion ... we could not go wrong. We were entertained royally and had a most wonderful time. Although I couldn't swim, they persuaded me to don a snorkel and flippers and took me out over the reef to view the coloured coral and tropical fish. What unbelievable colours! While there, we were invited aboard H.M.S. LOCHINCH, which was also anchored in the lagoon, for drinks and lunch in the Ward Room. We were piped aboard and met the Officers. I got talking to one young Lieutenant in my best Blundellsands' accent. He asked me where I came from. I tried to impress him by saying I came from near Southport. Eventually, he got it out of me that I came from Crosby. He put on a broad Liverpool accent and said, "We are almost neighbours then, I come from Bootle." The perfect put-down! All good things have to come to an end and we sailed for India. We suffered a hurricane in Madras and had to put to sea as it was too dangerous to remain alongside. Our final port should have been Calcutta, but due to some civil unrest we went to Rangoon instead. This was a bit of a disappointment, as I had two cousins in Calcutta that I had not seen for a long time and I was looking forward to spending some time with them.

The change of schedule had another down-side to it. The mail was in Calcutta and we were in Rangoon. The mail was forwarded to Rangoon, but missed us. It never seemed to catch up with us. I began to get very depressed, worrying if all was well at home? Was our son OK? One always imagines the worst, even though my husband assured me that mail missing the ship was not uncommon. Don't forget that this all took place long before radio telephones and mobiles.

We continued loading at various ports in the Bay of Bengal and eventually arrived at Vizagapatnam, having had no news from home for a long time. What a relief to find that all our missing mail was waiting for us! I read those letters over and over again. What a relief, we could start enjoying the trip again! While in Vizag, the tailors came aboard, copied a couple of my dresses, went away, returning about two hours later for a fitting, went back to their workshop and returned with the finished articles that evening ... amazing and the cost was minimal! While in Vizag we also attended a Hindu wedding at the invitation of the Port Doctor. It was very colourful ... a musical ceremony with lots of oriental food. I don't suppose I will ever get the chance again to attend another.

We finally sailed for home making a quick stop at Colombo to fill up with a cargo of tea and then set sail for home. We enjoyed a final top-up of the tan in the Medi, then came the excitement of the run up the channel and finally we berthed in Tibury on the 26th July, 1962. I rushed to the phone to speak to my mother. She assured me all was well and that she had thoroughly enjoyed looking after him and looked forward to seeing us both the following day.

"Thank you, mum."

For those cynics amongst you who might think our son would turn into some maladjusted young man through being abandoned by his parents, in his early years, well you were right. He went to sea as an ENGINEERING cadet with C.P. Ships and got his seconds ticket before swallowing the anchor.

Thank you, Annette and Ian. That was great.

David Gill
Master Mariner

David Gill seems to have been 'in and out' of my life for fifty years and, happily, he has recorded some memories.

THE FORMATIVE YEARS

I joined my first ship, the S.S. CABANO in Toxteth Dock, Liverpool, in August of 1958. The ship, if my memory serves me correctly, was built in Vancouver, Canada, during the war-time and was known as a Park Boat, a type of liberty/victory ship, so she had had a good innings already as many of them were lost in the North Atlantic early on.

The vessel was owned by the Elder Dempster Lines and I had been accepted as a Navigating Apprentice by them to train as an Officer. We sailed for West Africa via Madeira and Las Palmas. As I had spent a year at South Shields Marine and Technical College doing a pre-sea navigation course, I thought I was quite 'genned' up on the usual tricks played on a first tripper. These consisted of being sent down to the engine room to ask the Second Engineer for a 'long stand' or a pea for the ship's whistle or as today is Sunday to ask the Chief Engineer for steam on the organ. However, when we were in Takoradi, a boat mysteriously appeared on deck and a notice was fastened to it 'For hire. Please see the Chief Officer'. When I approached the Chief Officer, who was having a beer with the Second and Third Officers and asked to hire the boat, they all fell about laughing. The boat was, in fact, a surf boat and had been put aboard to paint around the outside of the ship whilst we were on the West Coast.

My second voyage, also from Liverpool, was on the M.V. OWERRI. Our first port of call was Milford Haven to load explosives. After the usual ports of call on the West coast such as Freetown, Takoradi and Lagos, we proceeded to the Belgian Congo and docked in Matadi. We had a lady passenger on board who was to be a missionary or work in a hospital in the Congo (I don't remember so clearly), but we often thought about her. Trouble was soon to break out in the Congo with nuns being raped and murdered and other dreadful atrocities.

The Captain on the ship was a real disciplinarian, who told the Senior Apprentice and myself to regard him as a father whilst on the ship, which was a hard thing to do. He was an excellent seaman and I remember that we were in Owendo, near Libreville, over Christmas 1958 and he had us up at 0600 hours on Christmas Day to hoist flag signals wishing the other vessels at anchor the compliments of the season. I don't suppose it did us any harm at all, but later on when I was Third Officer, I refused the honour of sailing with him again. Some years later, he was in command of the M.V. AUREOL, Elder Dempster's flag-ship and someone stuck a notice on his door which said, 'Today is Sunday. Is that alright by you? Signed God.' No one owned up to it and fortunately the person involved was not found.

After the OWERRI, I found myself sailing on the T.S.S. CALABAR from Tilbury, a wonderful old ship, built pre-war for Bullard & Kings Natal Line. She had a woodbine funnel and beautiful teak decks.

The Apprentices' cabin was situated aft of the galley and above the boiler room and was like a furnace, particularly for the thirteen days we spent alongside Apapa Wharf. I made three voyages on this ship, and on the second voyage we carried the Padre and his wife to the Mission on Apapa Wharf. A pleasant memory for me was that I had my eighteenth birthday there and the Padre's wife made me a birthday cake.

In 1960, we called in at Bathurst in The Gambia (now Banjul) for my second visit there and apart from the usual ports of call such as Freetown, Takoradi, Lagos and Port Harcourt, we also called at Winneba, Cape Coast and Keta which were all anchorage ports and the discharge was into surf boats. The surf boats were manned by a crew of eight plus a helmsman and could carry approximately one and half tons. The ship would rig a rope from forward to aft, 4 inches diameter, called a 'guest warp' for the surf boats to make fast to. Cargo was discharged by the ship's derricks into boats and then stowed aboard and covered by a tarpaulin. The boat would set off for the beach with the crew paddling and singing to keep time. On reaching the beach, the helmsman would judge the surf so as to get as far up the beach as possible. Labourers then had to physically carry the cargo across the sand to the warehouse, after which the boat would be re-launched for another journey. It is not a surprise that with such a hard life the average life expectancy of these boys was not much more than thirty-five years.

Occasionally, due to the ship rolling in the swell and the surf boats bobbing up and down, the cargo would land on the gunwhale of the boat and capsize it. The cargo would head for the bottom, if it didn't float, and the boys would all end up swimming. The boat would then be hoisted up on the ship's derrick until it could be righted. It is surprising that quite large tonnages per day could be handled by this method, especially if a ship was allotted thirty to forty surf boats.

On this voyage we also visited Sapele, one of the creek

ports in the Niger delta. I had been to Burutu and Sapele before on the CABANO. To get there, we had to cross the bar into the Escravos River, which was done at dead slow speed with soundings being taken by one of the Apprentices using the bar lead from the chains (a small platform rigged over the ship's side). Once across the river entrance, sometimes three canoes would appear with flags hoisted on a pole. These were the bush pilots hawking their services and the flags denoted their initials, thus identifying them. Favourites with Elder Dempster's were the Gula family, Emmanual and Senior, whilst Palm Line generally used the Kalaroo family.

Once it was established who was to be hired, they boarded by the pilot ladder and the canoe was lifted on deck. Usually there were three of them, the Pilot, a trainee, and a small boy who was there to learn and he generally stood on a box and steered the ship. They all wore shorts and had bare feet or flip-flops and the Pilot would generally sport a captain's cap with egg yolk which had been given to him by a Captain who had replaced it with a new one.

The ship would set off up the Escravos River and, if there was sufficient daylight, would eventually turn to port into a creek leading to the Benin River. On the way the ship had to negotiate the 'fork', an elbow bend in the creek during which the Chief Officer would stand by the anchors on the fo'c'sle. Ominously, there were quite a few 'V' marks in the mangrove swamp where ships hadn't quite made it, although all the ships I was on did.

Once in the Benin River, the vessel headed up to Sapele. The transit time was about eight hours and, if night interrupted the passage, a suitable anchorage had to be found. This was a bit of a nuisance as a careful night watch had to be maintained as sometimes the local villagers would climb up the anchor cable and try to steal the ropes and tarpaulins.

Once in Sapele, the vessel was moored to logs secured to

the bush with a bow anchor out forward and a kedge anchor out aft. Depending on the draft, a maximum of 2000 tons of logs, etc. could be loaded to allow the vessel to cross the bar out to sea.

If a vessel was bound for Warri or Burutu, the vessel had to turn to starboard in the Escravos River and transit Chanomi Creek into the Forcados River. Chanomi Creek was quite narrow and I am sure that, if a Pilot didn't like a particular village, especially at daybreak, he would go too fast when passing, resulting in the water receding from the bank and then rushing back into the huts like a mini tidal wave. This would cause the villagers to emerge from their huts, shaking their fists and hurling abuse.

We also called at Port Harcourt up the Bonny River, which was quite a regular port of call and if the port was busy, we had to anchor at Dawes Island to wait for a berth. The mosquitoes here were pretty big and very blood-thirsty. Also, in these rivers were to be found mango flies which were like a normal household fly, but ten times bigger. If they landed on you and laid an egg under your skin without you knowing, then the appropriate part could swell up and had to be lanced. Most people who knew that they had been bitten would touch the place with a lighted cigarette.

Homeward bound would consist of helping to make the ship look nice for arrival in the home port, such as painting, especially all the small items like life-buoys, side-lights, etc. Another job that seemed to be reserved for the Apprentices was recovering the handrails with sword matting, with turks heads top and bottom and securing new spats on the bottle screws on the stays and shrouds.

We had to complete sections of our correspondence courses in our free time, which were posted off to the Liverpool Nautical College (now John Moores). On my first voyage on the CABANO, £5 was deducted from my first month's wages of £9-10-0 to pay for this. Also, part of our training was to pass our lifeboat ticket after six months at sea and our E.D.H. ticket (Efficient Deck Hand) after twelve months at sea. Without these, it was not possible to sail on the OBUASI, which was manned by Apprentices and was at that time the company's training ship.

During our periods ashore in Liverpool to study for the above, we stayed at the Mersey Mission to Seamen's Merchant Navy House in Canning Street. This was managed by Miss Bridger who ran a tight ship, especially where young Apprentices were concerned. The story at the time was that Miss Bridger was the last woman to round Cape Horn under sail, although with many yacht competitions since, there have been many more. (I might add that Cathie Bridger was equally fierce with us Padres! Bob Evans.) Our nights out in Liverpool at this time were to Atlantic House for a dance, the Jacaranda Club (no alcohol), and finally the Masque for a hot chocolate. After studying for my Second Mates in 1962, Merchant Navy House was replaced by Kingston House at the Pier Head.

The OBUASI carried twenty Apprentices and no crew and although we had to have a Bosun, the Apprentices were run by the Senior Apprentice (headman) and Second Senior Apprentice (second headman) who reported to the Chief Officer. The Bosun had been on the ship for quite a while, a nice old boy, near to retirement, affectionately known as Bosun George. He took charge of the Kroo boys when we were on the West Coast. Out of the twenty Apprentices, four of them acted as Apprentices as usual and had more time for studying and the rest acted as the crew. Duties were rotated so that all Apprentices had a chance to do all jobs. When I joined, there were a couple of Apprentices I had sailed with before, but we three on joining were very much the new boys. I was given a bunk in the poop on the bottom deck with two others and very soon found my feet.

In due time by my calculations I acquired enough seatime to sit my Second Mates ... three years, three months and eighteen days, including six months remission of seatime for my year of pre-sea at South Shields Marine and Technical College. After a spot of leave I enrolled at Liverpool Nautical College, which is now based on Byrom Street, having moved from the top of Mount Pleasant.

Most candidates were quite young, me being twenty years old, and so we had to be controlled as there were far too many of us. It was like a long leave on full pay. We knew that it was essential to pass this first certificate to continue our career at sea.

On a Friday afternoon, we finished College a bit earlier and everyone had to charge up to the Labour Exchange in Leece Street to draw our dole, because although the Company paid our study leave in full, they did deduct the £4 per week which we could claim from the Labour Exchange, also I suppose our National Insurance stamp.

Life at college was pretty good as there were Apprentices I knew from Elder Dempsters and others I met who sailed with different companies, so we could compare notes.

I booked in to Merchant Navy House in Canning Street for the duration of my studying and was quite conscientious studying until 9 in the evening after a day at college, the bonus being a visit to Ye Cracke, a pub off Hope Street for a couple of pints and a chat with some of the girls from the Art College. Sometimes I would stay in Liverpool at the weekends and sometimes I would go home to Morecambe on the bus.

It was necessary to get a medical certificate while studying for Second Mates and for this we attended a practice in Rodney Street. It was a bit farcical really, because we all sat around in a circle and learnt where the pressure points were and how to strap up injuries with a triangular bandage. At our exam, the elderly doctor would move around the circle to ask you to point out a pressure point, so by counting from the first person to every fourth person, you knew which you would be asked.

After eight weeks the time came to put in my papers for the examination and face 'Fletch', a quite intimidating thought which all Second Mates dreaded as we had heard so much about him.

For the unenlightened, Captain Fletcher was the head examiner for Masters and Mates in Liverpool and certainly feared by all Second Mates and I guess by a lot of Mates and Masters. We had been schooled in College to answer many of the questions that he would be likely to ask in the oral examination, but there was no certainty that he wouldn't throw in something new. He was renowned to have a square-rigged ticket and loved to put a few sailing ship lights on the table. With you on a power driven ship on a course of North and wind from a specified direction, you had to tell him what action you would take. If you took too long, he was likely to bang the table and shout at you. Part of the problem was that he had a facial disfigurement where his right eye looked straight ahead and his left eye looked to the left, so you weren't quite sure which way he was looking.

There have been many stories about 'Fletch', one being that he asked a student from Ireland where the 'cat's head' is on a sailing ship. The guy knew that he wasn't doing well and when 'Fletch' started shouting and banging the table, he said "To be sure it's nine inches from the cat's arse!" Fletch sent him back to sea for another six months.

Another story is that he asked a Master's candidate, "You are on a ship at anchor in a strong tideway and the wind gets up, the ship starts to drag, what are you going to do?" The guy replied that he would drop another anchor to which 'Fletch' said "The wind is still increasing and you are still dragging". The guy replied "I will drop another anchor". 'Fletch' asked him where he was getting all the anchors from, to which the guy replied "The same place you are getting all the wind from!"

After a nerve wracking time doing 'writtens', orals and signals, I had passed my Second Mates.

David and Margaret tie the knot with the help of Bob Evans

MEMORIES

I sailed on one ship where the Bosun and Carpenter were always playing pranks. One such was that the Carpenter would jam a five inch nail between the finger of his left hand, wrap a white cloth or rag around it and paint it with pillar-box red paint. He would make some hammering sounds in his workshop, which was on the afterdeck, followed by a loud yell and then some groans. After this he would stagger out on the deck and confront the African crew, who didn't like to see anyone injured or the sight of blood.

However, on one occasion having played his party piece on the afterdeck, he was staggering towards the foredeck, clutching his left arm, just as the Carpenter's guests were coming aboard. One lady took a look and almost fainted on the spot.

David did not record what discussion then ensued between the Carpenter and the Bosun. Here is another memory.

One of the riggers told me a story about an old A.B. with whom he had sailed. In one port the guy had gone ashore and come back aboard totally drunk and failed to report for work the following morning.

The Chief Officer decided to parade him before the Captain for a 'logging'. The Captain said "I understand you went ashore last night, got totally drunk and failed to turn too this morning. I am going to log you two days' pay. Have you anything to say?"

"Yes, Sir", replied the Able Seaman. "How much does it cost to call you an 'Old Bastard'?"

The Captain replied. "Thirty shillings."

The A.B. responded: "Well, Sir, I would like three pounds worth."

Thank you, David Gill.

Captain John Scrivens
Master Mariner

Merchant Navy Officers often find themselves side-tracked into strange occupations. Captain John Scrivens is no exception. He has written of an event which is really part of our national history. Read on.

IF YOU HAVE NO SENSE OF HUMOUR

Two of the most rewarding features of a seafaring career are the most unexpected places and situations one finds oneself in and the diversity of people one encounters on the way. Merchant Navy Officers themselves embrace the whole social spectrum, literally from the sons of prime ministers to those of the most humble origin. It is not always those from the higher levels of society, however, who are the most interesting or competent or make the best shipmates. Occasionally, one comes across a shipmate who is both outstanding and a well known figure, a prominent person. One such person of my experience was very well known indeed and I was privileged to take him to sea for a short voyage ... a memorable happening certainly, but not an entirely happy one.

In 1961, I had served the last eight years as Chief Officer in tankers and large, for those days, ore carriers out of the St.

133

Lawrence. That year the managed part of my Company's fleet was seriously depleted and having recently made two foreign trips in temporary command, I was faced with the prospect of loss of seniority. Meanwhile, having been offered the chance of a shore appointment in about five years time, I decided to take a sabbatical from the Merchant Navy and went to work for the Queen, who graciously granted me a short service Commission. So in 1963, I found myself serving in the rank of Flight Lieutenant in the Marine Branch of the Royal Air Force at Gibraltar. It was a new and very different world for this simple sailor, but interesting and, at times, both demanding and rewarding, for both myself and my wife.

Marshall of the Royal Air Force, Sir Arthur Harris was on board a passenger liner on voyage from his home in South Africa and he suffered a heart attack as they were approaching the Straits of Gibraltar. The Captain of the liner prudently discharged his distinguished guest to the care of the Royal Naval Hospital in Gibraltar. As you might imagine, the word went rapidly round the Rock, very much a garrison town in the colonial tradition in those days, where all three services were stationed in considerable strengths, that Sir Arthur 'Bomber Harris' was in the R.N.H.

It is fashionable these days, in some quarters, to be critical of Sir Arthur Harris and I have no intention of entering into a discourse here on the merits or otherwise of his policy of strategic bombing, but the respect and regard in which he was held by his peers was firmly demonstrated to me on this occasion.

At that time, R.A.F. North Front had a Squadron of Shackleton aircraft based there. The Shackleton was a development of the Lancaster bomber of WW II fame, now used primarily in a maritime reconnaissance role by Coastal Command. Many of the Squadron's pilots and other aircrew were ex-wartime bomber command. I was in the Officers Mess as were many of the Squadron aircrew, discussing their

134

day's work over a quiet beer, when the news of Sir Arthur's hospitalisation was received. Within seconds the Mess emptied, and the sound of car engines receded into the distance as they went en masse to pay their respects to their wartime chief.

Eventually, Sir Arthur recovered sufficiently to leave hospital and he went, together with Lady Harris, to convalesce at Air House, high upon the Rock, as the Guest of the Air Officer Commanding Gibraltar, an Air Commodore at that time, and his wife.

It transpired that the A.O.C. had the privilege of being able to show his flag once a year in Tangiers, a right that had not been exercised for some years. No doubt it seemed a good idea to the Air Commodore, over pre-dinner drinks perhaps, to propose resurrecting this custom and providing his guests with an interesting diversion. In my experience Officers of Air Rank seemed rather to enjoy demonstrating from time to time that they had in the Marine Branch their own private little Navy ... particularly if they were under the very nose of the Royal Navy. Where better to do this than Gibraltar?

When news of this impending event was received at the Marine Craft Unit, the haste and enthusiasm with which my C.O. and brother Officers unanimously handed me the task, the most junior and inexperienced Officer on the strength, was most impressive. I was visited with a sense of unease and some foreboding.

I was, in R.A.F. parlance, lumbered. Never-the-less I could do no other than put a bold front on it and get on with the job. I would like to pay tribute here to the superb qualities of R.A.F. N.C.O.s and boat crews. They are the very best and never let you down. It was more a case of my having to take care not to let them down. So we set about our preparations with a will. Arrangements were made to dress the ocean-going rescue craft, HMAFV 2759, rig awnings, set out tables for a coffee reception, and prepare the craft all shipshape and Bristol fashion. That was the easy part.

The date was set, a time-table prepared, diplomatic channels set in motion, in fact the great steam roller of Service protocol and red tape took over and I was enmeshed in it. In the fullness of time, all was completed and the day dawned. I looked out of the window and was not, as they say, a 'happy bunny'. Runway windsocks streamed out rigid, indicating something approaching a gale from the west. What I could see of the sea-state beyond the harbour area was not reassuring either. I went down to breakfast in pensive mood. I was even more thoughtful after consulting the Met man. Strong westerly winds, gusting force 8 perhaps 9 at times, perhaps moderating later. How much later I asked, a shrug was his response. I began to feel a mite lonely.

Why my unease you might well ask, what manner of mariner is this that fears a bit of wind and sea in one of the strongest seagoing craft ever to be designed by a naval architect. I must explain. The ocean-going rescue launch of that time was an updated version of the wartime air-sea rescue craft. It was not in fact quite as robust as its war-time predecessor, of which it has been said "The boats never crack up, but men sometimes do," or words to that effect. It was indeed a very stout vessel, capable, in relatively moderate sea states of speeds circa forty knots. It was, however, far from sea-kindly in heavy weather, particularly from ahead. There were two main causes, firstly it was of hard chine construction and planed at high speed. Faced with a heavy head sea it simply took off from the crest of a swell or wave and dropped like an express lift into the trough where it hit with a spine-shattering thud. Strong young men have been known to weep. Slow it down you say. Here enters problem number two; you can't. The designers wanted speed and they equipped the craft with two modified Rolls Royce Merlin aircraft engines. Great examples of high rev aircraft machinery, but not designed for marine work, so they were geared down. Even running on one engine, the vessel could not operate comfortably for the purpose that I required in the conditions I suspected we might find and we would have a time schedule to serve.

My crew had as ever done a great job, the boat was spick and span and the weather in our little dock warm and sunny. The top brass and their ladies arrived and my crew hopped about brilliantly, chopping off salutes like guardsmen. Now, the A.O.C. was accompanied by his A.D.C. who of course had made all the arrangements with me. He was a very nice chap who I knew quite well, so I confided my misgivings about the weather to him and suggested he should warn his masters that we would be battening down after clearing the bay and that the ladies should be advised to expect a rough passage. I hoped this might produce some manifestation of unease amongst my passengers but if it did it was not demonstrated.

We got under way, cleared the harbour entrance and set a course westwards across Algeciras Bay. As we passed each sheltering headland conditions deteriorated and we were soon plunging about in an uncomfortable manner. The A.D.C. materialized wanting to know if conditions were likely to improve soon. I advised him that they would get progressively worse, but would probably improve out of all recognition for the return passage. He dematerialized, but shortly returned to ask if we would be able to make Tangier in time. I replied that we most certainly could, but that it would be a most uncomfortable voyage and that perhaps, in view of the conditions and the presence of the ladies, the A.O.C. might wish to consider aborting the trip.

When we cleared the point, we met the full fury of the gale head on and as everyone who has experience of the Straits of Gibraltar in a small craft knows, it can throw up a most horrible, short steep sea. Very sick-making! Surely, I thought, they will throw in the towel now, if only for the sake of the ladies. Not a bit of it, the next move was the A.D.C. to the Captain "Do you advise that we should turn back?" So that was to be the way of it. We returned because the Captain advised it. Any suggestion of failure would be laid at my door, not theirs. A nice dilemma, either I risked, perhaps, inducing a fatal heart attack in Sir Arthur and going down in Air Force history as the man responsible for the early demise of Bomber Harris, or I returned to Gibraltar with my tail between my legs. Catch twenty-two and a nice lesson in command responsibility at the same time. Well, I didn't fancy either role, but of the two I preferred the latter, so I advised our return to base. It was a case of about ship and fire off a host of signals.

The return passage was of course a very different kettle of fish, sunshine and a following sea. My passengers soon emerged on deck and beside me, on the tiny Bridge, arrived the man himself. I never knew what the Air Officer Commanding thought of my decision to return, but if Sir Arthur had any criticism, he did not show it and we chatted amiably for most of the passage. He expressed an interest in my background and it seemed he had family ship-owning interests in South Africa. He also knew my past ship owner, Mr. Fred Bowring, quite well. I was left with the impression of a quiet, erudite, well-mannered man of kindly disposition. There is no doubt from his past reputation that he was also tough, single-minded and ruthless when he had to be, but at that time he was in the midst of a terrible war, fighting for our very survival, against a ruthless and unprincipled aggressor, or so it seems to me.

Our arrival back in Gibraltar was subdued to say the least. I saw our guests off, the crew tidied up and I made my report to my Commanding Officer. Nothing was said, but I did not get the impression that I was considered to have put in a sparkling performance. Later, I sat lamenting my fate in being placed in this impossible situation to one of my brother Officers who lent a not unsympathetic ear. "Well John," he said. "You know what I always say, if you have no sense of humour, you shouldn't have joined."

Thank you Captain John Scrivens.

Captain Jim Williamson
Master Mariner

Captain Jim Williamson gives us a tale which reminds us that it is not always 'plain-sailing'. Life at sea can only be 'ups and downs' when you think about it.

It has always been a source of wonder to me how anyone can write so positively that at such a time and date certain things happened, such and such said this or that or even did this or that. This does not mean that I cannot recall events, situations, circumstances, and feelings or thousands of the images stored in my memory. I can see as plain as day the sight of my first ship alongside in Manchester Docks loading and the first huge Atlantic wave on my first trial trip as a Cadet, prior to signing my Indentures as an Apprentice Deck Officer. Most of all I recall the excitement of the initial experience of learning to steer by magnetic compass at night in a darkened wheelhouse of an old coal-burning, reciprocating-engined ship, with a very experienced Able Seaman standing behind me. And I remember the feel of his gentle hand on the wheel when he felt I was in need of assistance, and when I think back, how secretly relieved I was that he was there.

One of the years, as I remember, was 1963. I was doing

a port relief on a Company Ship in Manchester while she was being discharged. I was waiting for my promotion to Chief Officer. My Masters Foreign-going Certificate was not new, having served over three years as Second Mate since obtaining it. It was the 7th November ... Christmas was looming and on everyone's mind, but suddenly in my case all was about to change.

A summons to report to the Dock Office for what was to be the second time of the day to see the Deck Marine Superintendent, but this time it was charm beyond anything I had ever previously experienced, other than the times when I had returned with a brand new Certificate of Competency, known in the trade as a 'Ticket'. I had a great respect for the man, 'Our Boss', and would do more or less anything he asked regarding serving the Deck Department, providing it did not compromise my stricter principles. The latter was something I would put first and, incidentally, he knew it.

The bottom line was he had the MANCHESTER MERCHANT sailing in four days and due to the close proximity of Christmas and also having another ship sailing on Christmas Eve, which fortunately he had managed to man with Officers ... but this particular ship was a problem due to Officers on leave and also on sick leave.

The Master, who was senior, had agreed to cut his leave short to take the ship and a very senior Chief Officer, whose promotion to command was imminent, had also agreed to go as Chief Officer. The unbelievable climax was the fact he needed a Second and Third Mate. Apparently the first was easy; he had a volunteer, a Chief Officer, a lovely man, willing to help out and looking forward to a nice easy passage as Second Mate on his present wages, 'money for old rope', the only disadvantage being the 'graveyard watch'. So where did I fit in ... obviously Third Mate. But now the terms! Sign on as an extra-Second Mate on First Officer's wages. He knew that I had a secret passion for this particular ship and he agreed that I should remain in this ship on these particular terms until my promotion to Chief Officer in a few months time. Manning this vessel had obviously been a problem for him, resulting in a Senior Master, three Senior Officers and a promise he would get us home for Christmas.

Our passage down the Manchester Ship Canal and then seaward to the Liverpool Bar Lightship brought raised eyebrows from our Company's appropriated Pilot at such a bevy of Masters Tickets on board. The outward passage to Montreal was marvellous, the weather for the time of year was unbelievable and we made a Great Circle route from Inishtrahull to Belle Isle Strait, experiencing excellent visibility approaching Belle Isle and passing through the Iceberg limits mainly in daylight. I can remember that on approaching Belle Isle on my evening watch it was so clear that not only did I experience the 'northern lights' (Aurora Borealis), but refraction was such that when the Lighthouse on Belle Island flashed, instead of seeing one light there were five in a vertical line. This is common when the sea-water temperature is lower than the air temperature which of course is caused by the icebergs coming down in the cold Labrador Current, especially late in the year when the sea temperature falls much quicker than the air in this part of the world. I apologise for this distraction, thinking of this voyage triggered my memory.

My other memories at sea were the enjoyment of standing the 8 to 12 watch, something I had not done since my days as a Junior Officer, and in some cases having the Old Man breathing down my neck. Yes, as Third Mates we all knew what that experience could be like. During this voyage my watch-keeping was an absolute delight. As Officers, the three of us, although we knew each other well, got off to a wonderful start and I got the feeling that we all were getting an extreme amount of pleasure from this experience. There was immediate friendship and a professional trust, which gave a relaxed atmosphere, and at the same time there was a high level of efficiency, making our part of running the ship a real enjoyment. The remarkable aspect in my opinion was that two of us had in fact taken on a junior status in the Ship and under the Articles of the Agreement that we were normally used to; but this in no way seemed to be relevant, we just carried out our duties.

Our time in Montreal was also a pleasure while discharging and loading. I in particular gained a lot of experience and picked up many ideas from the two Senior Chief Officers which would help me when I got my promotion early in the New Year and in later years. I always looked forward to our 'smoko' in the Chief Officer's office, morning and afternoon. We had plenty of banter and me, being the junior, probably got the most stick. I have not mentioned the 'Old Man', he was an excellent Shipmaster, always calm, friendly, down-to-earth and a perfect gentleman and again he treated us with respect. We would see a lot of him on a daily basis.

On the 22nd of November during one of our morning 'smokos' in the Office and listening to the radio coming from the Chief Officer's day room, we were to hear something that would remain in our memories for the rest of our lives ... the assassination of President John F. Kennedy in Dallas. It was an experience where you do not ever forget the time and date or what you were doing when hearing that news. If my memory serves me right, one of my idols also died in the same month, Nat King Cole.

The S. S. MANCHESTER MERCHANT completed loading on the 2nd December, 1963, at Shed 12, Montreal and by late evening was preparing to sail. I suppose after we had all written our last letters home, we were one of the last ships departing Montreal for the winter, because the port closed down each year until the early Spring. As we were not a Lloyds Class Ice-breaking Ship, we could not afford to be too late if it were to be an early winter freeze-up. Our thoughts were now on Christmas at home and not a close call like some of us had previously experienced.

It would be about 2100 hours local time in Montreal on the 2nd December 1963, I was what is known as, 'testing the gear' on the Bridge. That is checking the Engine-room Telegraphs and Communications, plus all internal and external communications, i.e. radios and speakers to the Fo'c'sle Head and the After End Docking and Undocking Station, finally VHF and HF radios, Ships Steam Whistle and Siren, both electric and lanyard, plus many other details necessary for preparing for departure for sea. Then last, but not least, giving the Montreal Harbour Control an ETA of our departure as 2400 hours local. At this point, the St Lawrence River Pilot had not yet boarded and all that remained was to report to the Master that the 'gear had been tested and was in good order'.

The night was very cold. I cannot remember the actual temperature, but it was well below freezing as will be realized later, the visibility was excellent on a clear moonlit night and as soon as the Pilot boarded we went to sailing stations. Although our preparations for sailing were well ahead of time, we were to have problems Aft with the last two stern ropes being frozen to the bollards on the dock and subsequently requiring a Fork Lift Truck to free them. This was to delay us ten minutes, resulting in our departure from the Berth at approximately 0010 hours. This was reported to Montreal Harbour Control on VHF Radio, with the exact time we had let go. Somehow this was never recorded, except in the Ship's 'movement book' kept by the Deck Apprentice doing the Bridge duties.

The Ship's Master and our Pilot were aware of traffic movements, as Montreal Harbour Control on VHF Radio had already informed them that a Great Lakes Vessel the DONNACONA had left St. Lambert Lock in the St. Lawrence Seaway and was down-bound to the Seaway Entrance off Longueuil, then coming upstream favouring the south side of Channel and bound for the Grain Terminal to discharge her cargo. There was also a Norwegian ship, the LIONEL, that left St. Lambert Lock at 2400 hours and was bound to the Seaway Buoy, also off Longueuil, bound for Montreal Harbour and to her berth at Section 29 on the north side of the river.

After letting go, the tugs pulled us astern out of the dock, swinging the ship off Shed 12 until she was heading downstream for the south side (starboard side) of the main channel with Jacques Cartier Bridge ahead. Once heading down-stream, I took up my station on the starboard wing of the Bridge, which enabled me to operate both the telegraph for engine speeds and also the ship's steam whistle. I also kept a strict lookout and was listening for the Master's and Pilot's orders. I was monitoring the VHF, which had been on full volume since the ship had to let go, so that everyone could hear any advice or change in traffic movements from Montreal Harbour Radio or communication between ships ... it was also close to the starboard Bridge door.

I can distinctly remember that while we were still above Jacques Cartier Bridge we passed the DONNACONA, her navigation lights were so bright, particularly her starboard light, and I walked to the side of the wing bridge as she slid past. The night was so clear, with it being so cold and the river at this point was so calm, it was like glass and her lights reflected in the water. I recollect the Second Mate coming into the Wheelhouse after finishing his duties at his station aft when we let go. His main interest at this time would be the Gyro Compass which was his 'baby' and then eventually relieving me as it was after midnight and consequently his watch, once we both decided that leaving Port stations were over and we were bound down river. While passing under the Jacques Cartier Bridge and turning to starboard, I reported a ship leaving the Seaway entrance near Longueuil, approximately a mile away, on the Port Bow and turning to port near the Seaway Buoy showing a 'red sidelight'. The Pilot and Master had obviously also seen it and the Pilot ordered me to give one short blast on the steam whistle, which means I am altering my course to starboard. Immediately after this, I listened for any reply of which there was none. Being outside I was not aware whether the Pilot or anyone spoke to this ship on the VHF; the ship was obviously the Norwegian ship, LIONEL.

This ship continued to turn to port and still just slightly on the Port Bow, therefore now the Master and Pilot ordered another single blast of the Whistle. Again there was no reply and by this time the Master was becoming agitated. I got the feeling the Pilot had 'lost the plot'. The LIONEL was now end on showing both Green and Red Sidelights and, in what to me were seconds, she shut out her Red Sidelight, while dead ahead. She continued to turn to port showing her Green Sidelight only as she crossed our bows. Collision was inevitable unless as in Star Trek it could have been "Beam me up Scotty"!! They say that when asked in the exam room taking orals for a Masters Certificate, what would you do when danger is imminent, apparently, no matter whatever the situation, the answer is supposed to be "let go both anchors". Well, in this case it would have been useless I am afraid, which will be evident later, so our only alternative was what the Master did, a 'Double Emergency Ring Full Astern'. Being a Steam Turbine Ship this takes time. We were beginning to feel some of the river current with us and we were loaded quite deep, a draft of nearly 28 feet and now far too close and committed to steer our way out of trouble.

What was to follow was the most unbelievable experience of my life. The fact the nobody lost their lives can be nothing less than the hand of God, who quite often looks down favourably on seafarers. I can only tell the story of the collision as I saw it, otherwise it will become far to complicated. There will be technical details which I can only assess as I saw them in those brief moments. Then I will continue with the effect it had on the remainder of the voyage.

The Motor Ship, LIONEL, had her engines aft and the Bridge amidships. She was almost fully loaded from Great Lake Ports and was calling at Montreal to top off before sailing for Europe. She had a Gross Tonnage of approximately 4500 tons compared to the MANCHESTER MERCHANT of 7651 tons. The collision was our bow slicing into the Starboard side of the LIONEL forward of her Bridge. The noise of the impact I could say I will always remember, mainly because of its intensity. I have been on ships which have collided before, but nothing which could compare to this. I recall the first few seconds after the initial 'thud' with a tearing and crunching of steel as we split her hull shell plating apart and buried our bow deep inside her.

There was a tremendous explosion, with a huge flame climbing skywards far beyond the limits of anyone's eye-line on the Bridge of the MANCHESTER MERCHANT. It appeared to curl back over our Foredeck and come towards the Bridge. Of course in hindsight, this was an illusion. In the few seconds after the explosion, the huge flames from it made everyone on the Bridge 'duck down' momentarily.

Within a very short time we were aware of the situation we were in. The ship was on fire forward and later the stern began to swing slowly to port, down-stream in the current. Our bow was pulling out of the LIONEL, probably due to the stern way we had picked up from going astern on the engines, which the Pilot may have used, or the effect of the current. As far as I remember our engines were stopped, but the Second Mate was in the Wheelhouse attending to some orders. At the time, we were not aware that we had penetrated at least 15 feet into the hull of the LIONEL.

My immediate thoughts were how can anyone survive on the LIONEL in that conflagration amidships. I remember seeing people running aft from the midship-housing along the Main Deck with what appeared to be blankets covering their heads, evacuating the Bridge and accommodation. On the Fo'c'sle Head, ropes were going over the Port Bow and at least one or two men were climbing down towards the river. I assumed that by this time the LIONEL's bow would be aground. After that I was completely taken up with my duties on the Bridge with orders from the Master and occasionally from the Pilot with regard to the ship's position in the river, etc. I can always remember the 'Old Man', probably a nervous reaction from the awful tension he would be under, saying, "Well, bang goes your Christmas, Mr. Williamson".

As the MANCHESTER MERCHANT drifted down-stream in the current and the Pilot was able to stem the flow using the engines, the Chief Officer came from the Fo'c'sle Head to report to the Master on the situation forward. He was almost unrecognizable, as the spray from the ship's fire hoses had frozen on his clothing and head gear. The crew had been fighting the fire in the Stores forward and what was left of the Paint and Oil Store Rooms. He looked like Scott of the Antarctic after being out in a blizzard or perhaps the

Abominable Snowman. We were apparently gaining on the fire and with luck it would soon be out. The ship had a gaping hole in the bow, running well aft near the waterline and about 10 feet in depth as could be ascertained in the dark. The Fore Peak was flooded and we were down by the head, but our pumps could handle that. The Chief Officer was concerned that using the Starboard Anchor could be dangerous ... so much of the bow was missing, the Fo'c'sle Deck could be pulled downwards. He thought the Port Anchor seemed reasonable, providing not too much weight was put on it.

The Pilot eventually anchored us opposite Vickers Shipyard, Montreal, about 0240 hours, out of the current so that there was the least load on the anchor chain. We had the Engines on 'Stand-by' and a very strict anchor watch. The remainder of the crew were having a watch below and a sleep, now the fire was out and all that could be done had been. We had had tugs assisting us after the collision and the Master requested that, due to the uncertainty with our anchor, the tugs remain standing by us until at least daylight or until we got our orders for berthing. The only other item I can remember was we were constantly hounded over the radio by the local Press asking for details of the collision.

The following day, we berthed on one of Montreal's Section Berths below the Shipyard and for the first time were able to see for ourselves the enormous amount of damage to our bow, even though some was under the waterline. Apparently, the main conjecture was whether the ship was to be repaired in the Quebec Shipyard or Montreal. Due to the time of year, the concern was that if we went into the Vickers Shipyard in Montreal and the winter started early, we would be trapped in Montreal all winter when the river froze,. In Quebec we would stand a better chance as the river is tidal there and the winter freeze-up starts later.

I will never know who made the decision to put us into

the Montreal Dry Dock for our repairs and took the chance we would get out before the main freeze-up, even though it required us discharging some cargo to enable us to make the draft for the Dry Dock, but Montreal it was. My memory begins to fade a little when it comes to the length of time it took to do the repairs; all I do remember was that the temperature was hideously low. It was warm and cosy in the ship, but awfully cold when inspecting the daily repair work and going ashore to the 'loo' ... yes, that was the only thing we could not do onboard! Just think, today they have chemical toilets and Portaloos.

During the Dry Docking, news started to filter through about the collision and the other ship. She was apparently aground and would stay there until the spring when they would endeavour to re-float her, also she was burnt out for at least half her length. Montreal Harbour did not have a Fire Boat so she was just attended by Harbour Tugs with their own fire-fighting equipment. The Bridge and midship section of the LIONEL were made of aluminium and apparently at the height of the conflagration the temperature reached 2000° and the Bridge front actually started to melt.

The explosion and fire was apparently due to her deck cargo of drums of naphtha and underneath in the hold t'ween deck, drums of pure alcohol into which our bow had ploughed. No wonder there were such catastrophic results!

The 27-man crew of the LIONEL were able to lower the lifeboats which luckily were aft away from the fire. One boat landed ashore at Longueuil and others were taken off by a tug. The two tugs, HELEN McALISTER and JAMES BATTLE, who had powerful fire pumps, helped with the fire. The flames lit up the harbour for hours after the collision and, apparently, Captain Andreas Johnson, the Master of the LIONEL, returned later to his vessel to direct the fire-fighting operations. I never found out what happened to the crewmen I saw going over the side of the bow and who had been trapped in the Fo'c'sle Head by the flames. There was a story that a cabin boy who lived aft slept all through it.

During the repairs we had settled down to shipboard routine and were closely monitoring the weather forecasts daily and watching the state of the River St. Lawrence and the slow build-up of ice, hoping against hope that we would be able to make our passage out into the Gulf of St. Lawrence before the thickness of ice became too much for our ship to handle.

Anyway as luck would have it, repairs were completed and the Dry Dock flooded. We were afloat again. One late December morning, the tugs pulled us clear of the dock and swinging in Vickers Basin, we were on our way to Halifax, Nova Scotia, to load and make up for the cargo we had discharged in Montreal prior to Dry Docking.

At this time of the year, all the River navigational buoys had been taken up and replaced by timber buoys, soft-wood to starboard and hardwood to port, but one of the main navigational aids were superb 'leading lights' of very bright green, on the turns and on the varying lengths of the Channels. The winter changes to the River made it necessary that ships only move in daylight above Quebec in the Winter months.

The ship was not Lloyds-Ice-Strengthened for navigating in any heavy ice, but we were lucky. Although there was considerable ice in the River, by adjusting our speed we could deal with it satisfactorily without causing any damage. The ice between Montreal and Three Rivers is full freshwater ice and therefore much harder than sea ice which is found nearer Quebec where the river is tidal.

After two days, we were clear of the Pilot Station at Escoumains and heading for the Gulf of St. Lawrence and I think we all felt some sort of freedom after our experience locked away in Montreal. The experience has stayed with me all my life and it has surprised me how the details of the voyage, the stay in Montreal, the collision and all its trauma, even up to the Dry Docking, have remained so clear.

The finale to one of the momentous occasions in my sea-going career, and I have had a few, would be over a year later when I was Chief Officer. The Master, Chief Officer, Second Mate and myself, all off the ill-fated MANCHESTER MERCHANT, flew out to Montreal to attend the court case under Canadian law to settle the findings of the collision. It took a fortnight and, as I was almost the last to give evidence, I unfortunately was only able to sit in court towards the end of the proceedings, but even during that time I began to realise that in courts of that level where millions of dollars were at stake, the outcome was not about justice, but who had the cleverest defence lawyers and could discredit the opponent's witnesses the most.

We stayed in the same hotel as Captain Johnson, the Master of the LIONEL. What a charming man and an excellent seaman. We never once discussed the collision, but I will always remember him. We had much in common when it came to seafaring ideas. When I eventually became Master myself, I often thought of the long discussions we had together in the Hotel Lounge and sometimes the Bar, although the latter was not often because we had early nights. He had a long time in the witness box, and of course each day I never knew when I would be called.

Our Company and the MANCHESTER MERCHANT, won the court case 100% in our favour much to the delight of the Master. The whole episode had aged him considerably and he was an elderly man to start with.

Many months later the Norwegian Shipping Company and owners of the LIONEL appealed against the trial verdict and it went to the Canadian Upper House. The Appeal Judges reversed verdict in favour of the MANCHESTER MERCHANT and awarded the judgement in favour of the LIONEL, 100%.

In Canada there can be no second appeal.

I do not think there have ever have been many bigger injustices in maritime history. Instead of delight, the Master was shattered and told me he would never fully trust in anything again while on the Bridge of his ship when he had a pilot on board or in Pilotage Waters. Our pilot did everything right, irrespective of our delay, which we reported along with our departure time, when the LIONEL was still in the Seaway Channel. Once the two ships were in sight of one another, we obeyed the Harbour Rules of Traffic Movements and the International Rule of the Road.

To finish with, I have just remembered that when we shifted ship in Montreal from the berth to Dry Dock, the Montreal Pilotage Authority sent the pilot, who had been on the LIONEL in the collision. The Master immediately got rid of him in no uncertain terms. This Pilot was a Harbour Pilot and apparently a "blue eye". It was as if he was sent to spy the layout of our Bridge.

We loaded in Halifax and in a small port called Lockeport, also in Nova Scotia, taking on mainly lumber and some apples, finally arriving home in Manchester in the early part of January 1964. The Chief Officer was soon to get his promotion to Master, and within a few months I became Chief Officer myself.

Thank you, Jim. With such a galaxy of seafaring talent on board, you must have had your legs pulled. You told me that the change of verdict and its total unfairness left a real scar on some of the ship's company. The reason for that reversal was apparently never explained.

Careers are full of interest and here is a summary of Jim Williamson's 'curriculum vitae'.

Jim did his Pre-Sea training in SEACROFT Training Ship in Southshields and signed as an Apprentice with Manchester Liners in 1951. He was involved with the Great Lake ships in the old canal system from Montreal to Kingston, Ontario, prior to the building of the large Seaway into the Lakes.

Next he joined Atlantic Steam Navigation Company, owned by a man called Colonel Bustard. He owned a fleet of ex-Royal Navy L.S.T.s, trading between Preston and Larne, and Tilbury and Antwerp with a Ro/Ro Transport Service. The Colonel was to build two of the first two custom-built Ro/Ro Ships in the world, stern loaders. Jim Williamson did the maiden voyage in both of them, the BARDIC FERRY and IONIC FERRY.

Unfortunately, fate dealt him a bitter blow. When he went for his Master's Certificate, the Examiner in Liverpool told him that he was ten weeks short of Foreign-going sea time. The Company released him and told him his job was open once he had passed his Master's Foreign Going Certificate. Therefore, cap in hand, he requested Manchester Liners for the voyages he needed and they obliged him and subsequently he obtained his Master's Certificate. Incidentally, that extra sea-time was eventually proved to have been unnecessary ... thank you Captain Fletcher!

In late 1960, Colonel Bustard sold Atlantic Steam Navigation Company to the British Transport Commission. Jim was forced to remain with Manchester Liners and start to build up seniority. This entailed being Second Mate until early 1964, when he was promoted Chief Officer. During this time, there was one period of severe cut-backs when nine Senior Officers and Masters had to step back a rank and this extended the period that he had to wait for his promotion to Master, which was eventually in 1973.

Manchester Liners Ltd. was finally bought out by Furness Withy Co. Ltd. in the late 1970s who subsequently sold the company to C.Y. Tung of Hong Kong. After a short time, Jim Williamson sailed in foreign flag ships out of Cyprus and under the Panama Flag, later with Hull Shipping Company in small Bulk Carriers trading between U.K. and the Mediterranean.

In 1986, Jim joined the Marine Section of the Meteorological Office in Bracknell as the 'Sea Ice Officer'. Soon afterwards, he got the opportunity to run and modernise the World Wide Ship Routing System, 'Metroute'. Then, he relocated to Liverpool at his own request in 1993 as Port Meteorological Officer for North West England, so he could live closer to home, retiring in 1998.

Captain Roy Lomas
Master Mariner

TEETHING PAINS

On board the M.V. GARRYBANK from January 1965 to May 1966. The voyage was the Far East to South and East Africa run, calling at Mauritius and Reunion en route.

I was an 18-year-old deck Apprentice and the two guys with me were the Fourth and Sixth Engineers, both Scotsmen in their twenties. The GARRYBANK was in Port Louis, Mauritius at mooring buoys. The harbour is like a horseshoe and the line of ships was started in the mouth. The Harrison ship was number one in line and the Garrybank either number two or three.

We were ashore, having a night out, and when it was time to leave for the last boat back at about 2300 hours, people were reluctant to move from the comfort of the bar. The suggestion was made for myself and the Fourth and Sixth Engineers to go back on the ferry and return in the Chief Engineer's home-made boat ... wood and canvas with a small inboard engine, which was 'parked' alongside the gangway. Then to pick up the rest of the guys.

We did this and the three of us went back ashore for the rest of our lads. We ended up collecting up a couple of guys from a Harrison ship. Our lads said "Take them back first and come back for us." We went past our ship to reach theirs. "Come on board for a drink" was the inevitable cry … so that we did. I was getting concerned that we should be getting back for the others up, but nobody else seemed bothered and it turned out later that they all got safely back on another boat.

I should mention that I didn't drink alcohol at that stage of my life and so viewed all that went on rather differently than the two other lads with me.

On finally bidding farewell to the lads on the Harrison boat, we went down the gangway, got in the boat and cast off. There was a slow current which caused us to drift along the ship's side. This wasn't a concern at first, but the two Engineers were having great difficulty starting the engine and I became rather worried as we slowly passed by the port anchor cable. I reflected on the dark ocean which beckoned us. At that point logic kicked in and I suggested we row back the five or ten yards back to the anchor cable and make fast to it until we got the engine going.

The idea was a good one and joyfully agreed to by both my colleagues. The Fourth Engineer's attempt to get up and retrieve the oars however, caused the boat to capsize and we found ourselves swimming around in shark-infested waters in the early hours with nobody likely to know of our predicament.

My first concern though was to help Andy, the Fourth, who couldn't swim. I managed to remember enough of the school lifesaving certificate teaching to get him the short, but ever-increasing distance back to the relative safety of the anchor cable. The other Engineer managed to tow the Chief's boat back and lash it to the cable.

I then volunteered to swim back to the gangway for help. I used to pride myself on my swimming prowess, but it was a different ball game with socks, shoes, trousers, shirt and sweater on. The journey seemed painfully slow and I didn't think about how the current was delaying my progress until much later.

My thoughts took on a more frightening direction as I remembered seeing a shark around the ship during the day. I wondered what I might do if confronted by a fin approaching me. A feeble thought about Tarzan with a knife between his teeth diving underneath the shark and ripping its belly open briefly entered my head, but upon realising I didn't have a knife anyway, fear brought an amazing new speed to my strokes.

I have no idea how long the journey took, but at long last I had reached the gangway and a new problem surfaced (excuse the pun!). I was exhausted and could only just reach the gangway let alone climb onto it, so I had to shout for help and wait. My eyes were still watching the area around for signs of sharks and so I was very relieved when the Chief Engineer appeared at the top of the gangway and uttered the words "What are ye doing swimming at this time a the night, laddie?!"

After being hauled aboard and explaining what had happened I tried to get someone to launch a lifeboat. My experience seemed to have had the effect of preventing any logical thought from existing in my mind. And so, it was left to someone else to do the logical thing and throw the men a lifebuoy.

Whilst everyone made their way for'd (quite a few people had shown up with all the commotion going on), I proceeded to get out of my wet clothes and then, when down to my underpants, decided to go for'd myself and see how the rescue was going.

It was raining, quite cold and I can only assume that shock

was also setting in. I reached the guys on the fo'c'sle head and was then jumping up and down as an overwhelming need for the toilet hit me. I started to head back aft, but had to succumb to the 'sudden urges' and promptly squatted over the hawse pipe. I didn't realise till a few moments later what a close call the lads in the water had had and told them later it was pure luck I chose the starboard rather than the port one under which they were huddled.

The lads were eventually hauled along the ship's side and pulled aboard and we all had a shower and welcome hot drink. I remember the shock must have set in for the Fourth Engineer who stood in the shower for well over an hour.

On returning to my own ship I, of course, received a huge dressing down from the Chief Engineer and the Mate. I was just happy his boat hadn't sunk in the night, otherwise I probably would have had to walk the plank.

That was a terrifying experience and reminded me of the very first time that I had to break news of death at sea to a next of kin. The next of kin was the wife who was seven months pregnant. I had just been appointed as a Padre in the Mission, Kingston House, in Liverpool and was totally inexperienced. Six seamen had 'borrowed' a small boat in Rosario to return to their ship. All six were lost. Roy Lomas and his mates had a fortunate escape.

He has another tale which takes us back to September, 1968.

WHAT WAS IT !

I was Second Officer on watch mid afternoon, somewhere in the Indian Ocean on board SS. OSCILLA, a 53,000 dwt Shell Tanker. Weather was beautiful. It was flat calm, no swell to speak of, excellent visibility and not a ship in sight.

I observed about 6 points on the starboard bow what appeared at first to be a torpedo heading for our ship. My second thoughts were that it must be a porpoise or a dolphin and I, naturally, kept it under observation through the binoculars.

I can't put a figure on it exactly, but it seemed to have been heading towards us for at least a minute, and could have been a lot longer.

I kept expecting this 'porpoise' to disappear or change its track, but it just kept on coming. My thoughts ranged from calling the Captain and telling him we are being torpedoed and that World War Three was about to begin or "Sorry to disturb you, Captain, but there is a porpoise attacking the ship!"

I felt it imprudent to call him, but as the torpedo got closer and closer, I almost wished I had done, just to prove my eyes weren't playing tricks on me.

The picture was just as I had seen on many war films as various merchantmen were torpedoed.

At about five seconds to impact', at which point I was totally convinced it wasn't a porpoise, it disappeared from view. So I raced across to the starboard side half expecting it to appear there. My torpedo theory would then, therefore not have added up.

What on earth could it have been?

I saw nothing else for the rest of my watch and spent most of it looking for a rational explanation to the afternoon's diversion.

My only theory is that we were being used as target practice by a submarine with the latest radio-ontrolled torpedoes and when the torpedo I saw was about to hit its target, the cancel button would have been pressed and it would sink to the bottom and be recovered later by divers.

I have never had anyone give me a better explanation and I certainly have never since come across a gyro-controlled porpoise!

Thank you, Roy. I cannot help but observing that you might have been blown to smithereens. Happily, you are still with us!

Captain Brian McManus
Master Mariner

Memories are short and I suspect that very few of us could recall the dates of the 'Six Day War' ... 5th to 10th June, 1967. Captain Brian McManus has written an excellent account of those rather distant days, but we only have space for excerpts ... with apologies to Brian.

Egypt had 7 divisions, 100,000 men, 1,000 tanks and 500 heavy guns. The war was one of the biggest battles of tank warfare, which killed 300 Israelis and 10,000 Egyptians. Israel's success was due largely to its pre-emptive attack, destroying 400 of the enemies' aircraft while they were still parked on the ground.

Fourteen ocean-going ships became trapped in the Great Bitter Lake, which is part of the Suez Canal. These ships belonged to eight different nations and four of them flew Britain's Red Ensign. Two of these were owned by the Blue Funnel Line, a name famous in shipping, as is Rolls Royce, Marks & Spencer or Tesco ashore.

This is Captain Brian McManus's story of what was to happen to those fourteen trapped vessels.

SUEZ CASTAWAYS –
GREAT MEMORIES OF A BITTER EXPERIENCE

Besides the four British ships, there were two German, two Polish, two Swedish, one American, one Bulgarian, one Czechoslovakian and one French ship.

MELAMPUS (AGALAMPUS) dressed overall for the regatta 1st March 1969.

In mid-December 1968, I took command of the two Blue Funnel Line ships, AGAPENOR and MELAMPUS. The two ships were lying idle trapped in the Great Bitter Lake. Since mid-December 1967, the two ships lay lashed together alongside each other port side to port side so that the bow of one ship overlapped the stern of the other by 100 feet. This unit, appropriately enough, was now called AGALAMPUS, a combination of the two ship's names. Round about that time a ship's running costs were approximately £500 ($1200) a day. Economies also dictated that the original crews, totalling more than 100 men, be ruthlessly slashed to a caretaker strength of sixteen.

The ship-owners recognized Egypt's sovereignty of the Suez Canal, and accordingly, it was policy for the British ship-owners to fly everybody to and from Cairo by Egyptian Airways. They also had cash frozen in Egypt and Nasser's currency regulations prevented them from withdrawing it. Airfares were one way of using it.

162

After an eight-hour flight and two airline meals, the Boeing 707 landed at Cairo. Through the airport hustle and bustle our weird assortment of baggage was gathered and guarded with efficiency of any a platoon of Guards. Any sailor who has called at Port Said knows that the Arabs are gifted craftsmen of theft and cunning, and had no reason to suppose that Cairo Airport was different.

A new Captain and Chief Officer for another British ship, the SCOTTISH STAR, had joined the flight at Heathrow and now mingled with us. Also, two gloriously drunk Czechoslovakians waited to ride aboard our bus the next day.

Aboard the bus, Assuit Shipping's courier, a pleasant young Egyptian, told us that the Army prohibited photography all the way to the Lake, as we were travelling inside the restricted military zone. It was an exaggerated precaution, as the military activity seen comprised only a few Army vehicles.

Eventually, the coach halted at a road barrier surrounded with the paraphernalia of modern warfare. An Officer and an NCO cursorily studied our visas and inquisitively poked through the baggage. At the roadside, barefooted ragamuffins gathered and stared up at us with curiosity. I gazed equally curiously at the primitive mud-walled hutments, scraggy goats, motley sheep and bantam hens. Several veiled women, shoeless and clad in shapeless black knee length frocks, stood aside from the children, nursing their babies.

At that moment, two miles away out on the Lake aboard AGALAMPUS the departing crew revelled merrily at the lively farewell party. Despite the Great Bitter-Lake Association's short history the farewell party had become a tradition, but this time it was actually a double party, a farewell and Christmas party combined. Naturally, the invitation extended to the whole Lake society, and to put some zest into it, or so they thought, the guests brought with them all the empty beer cans saved up during the preceding fortnight. As the newcomers approached, the empty cans were dumped overboard making a sort of mock ticker–tape reception.

Although the sun was bright, a blustery breeze churned the Lake's blue water into breaking waves. At the SCOTTISH STAR, her new Captain and Chief Officer nipped agilely on to her accommodation ladder and the two Czechs, now sober, scrambled up a short rope ladder up the grey hull of their trim little vessel.

AGALAMPUS with her two great lofty hyacinth blue funnels, smartly capped with black, looked impressive. Keen binoculars spotted our progress across the Lake and as the launch neared AGAPENOR's accommodation ladder, the twin whistles of each ship started blasting forth in the long and short blasts of Morse code ... GBLA. Besides being our welcome signal, it summonsed the guests to dispose of their empty beer cans and at least a couple of thousand cans cascaded down into the water.

At that precise moment the launch wheeled about. Everyone aboard AGAPENOR stood frozen in amazement. Maybe, either the new arrivals or the Egyptians considered that they had been slighted and were leaving in a huff. But, that was not the case. The water alongside AGAPENOR's accommodation ladder was too choppy, so the launch's Coxswain was hoping to find more of a lee alongside the MELAMPUS. He did, and willing hands grabbed our baggage from the launch and led us aboard through a maze of decks and accommodation, over a solid wooden gangway between the two ships and so aboard to join the party. A gentleman called Fuad showed me to the Captain's quarters and introduced us. We had never met before, but like me, Captain Hughie Davies lived in North Wales. He was entertaining several of the other ships' Captains who politely finished their drinks, shook hands all around and left.

Fuad wandered in and out agitatedly becoming more and more fidgety. "Mr. Captain Davies, please tell your crew to come or we will be stranded," he begged. Whereupon Captain Davies went down into the bar and ended the party.

In the meantime, Fuad said to me, "Mr. Captain, how about a bottle of whisky baksheesh". "But surely you are a Moslem and debarred alcohol", I teased. "It is not for me, Mr. Captain. It is for my Austrian wife", he parried. I gave him one; after all, it was the land of baksheesh.

Captain Davies returned to say adieu and Merry Christmas. "By the way", I said, "I gave Fuad a bottle of whisky baksheesh". Captain Davies exploded with something rude and nautical, ending with "I gave him one this morning and a carton of 200 cigarettes. I remember him in Port Said before the Canal closed and he was known as Mr. Ten Percent".

Once more the two whistles of each ship, making four whistles, thundered out GBLA in Morse code as AGALAMPUS said goodbye to the departing crew. It was 16th December and they would be home in good time for Christmas.

Burt Narbarro, the cook, was the one person who could not afford the time to join the party. An experienced and skilful hand, he first went to sea in a wartime trooper. More recently, to keep abreast of today's gourmets, the company sent him to work for six months in the Dorchester Hotel. He knew that some people had skipped breakfast, and all had missed lunch, so by six o' clock everyone was ravenous.

I did not expect much, but I was wrong. Burt produced two cooked dishes, a salad and a sweet. I went into the galley and thanked him for producing such a fine meal.

Catering aboard ship is always of a high standard. It needs to be because the crew has no way of supplementing their diet. The normal shipboard breakfast is grapefruit or fruit juice, cereals, smoked fish, eggs or omelettes to order, served with bacon, baked beans, tomatoes or some such thing and finished with a griddle cake covered with syrup. Lunch will be soup, two cooked dishes, cold meat and salad, a sweet and a cheese board. Dinner is soup, fish, a roast, cold meat with salad, a sweet and a cheese board. In addition, there is early morning tea with toast, mid-morning coffee, afternoon tea with biscuits and a late night sandwich with a do-it-yourself hot drink. Life at sea at times can be monotonous and the meals help break the day up. However, I could foresee that in the Lake it was going to be difficult to even vaguely imitate the usual pattern. And, when bored, the seaman's first complaint is the food. Napoleon's adage, "An army marches on its stomach", applies equally to a ship.

Burt's day started at six in the morning. His work never ended. He baked bread, peeled potatoes, scoured the pans, washed the paintwork, wiped the working surfaces spotless, scrubbed the galley deck, kept the fridges clean and cooked three meals a day. For a special occasion, such as a birthday, he made cake. The galley became the focal point. Everyone stopping for a cup of instant coffee chatted with him. Anyone from the other ships visiting would stop off in the galley. Bob, an Old Conway, the Chief Officer from the PORT INVERCARGILL liked Burt's bread and would bisect a Vienna loaf and make a sandwich. Unperturbed, Burt would just bake another couple of loaves. Yet another of his chores was feeding the animals.

That night a film was shown and everyone relaxed. With no likelihood of any shore leave for the next four and a half months, the crew resigned themselves to their self-imposed voluntary isolation.

The next morning before breakfast, I looked through the binoculars at the other ships in the Lake. As the AGAPENOR and MELAMPUS traded to the Far East, the Blue Funnel ships were known as the 'China boats' with Liverpool dockers. The two ships had good binoculars aboard. One had a pair of Canon 7 x 50 and the other a pair of Asahi Pentax 7 x 50. AGALAMPUS was the closest of the ships to the Egyptian shore. I noted that the Polish ships and the Swedish ships had their national flags painted on their ships' sides. Later I found that the Swedish ships had also painted their national flags on the ships' hatches. Ships transiting the Canal have a searchlight hanging over the bow, whose split beam picks up the reflector buoys on both sides of the Canal. The searchlights are hired from the Suez Canal Authority, but regular users such as the AGAPENOR and MELAMPUS carried their own. Several of the ships had the Authority's searchlights hanging over their bows.

After my first breakfast aboard, I started an inspection of the accommodation on board the two ships accompanied by Alan, the Steward-in-charge. He was actually a Second Steward waiting for promotion to Chief Steward, which he would achieve after his tour aboard the AGALAMPUS. In the Officers' smoke-room, the Christmas decorations produced a festive and homely touch. "That was quick work", I said glancing at him with surprise. "The last crew did it," he laughed. "And to think that we brought Christmas decorations all the way from Liverpool," I chuckled. Alan brandished a large brass key about three feet long. "Whose twenty-first" I asked with some curiosity. 'AGAPENOR's' he replied. "I was aboard her on her maiden voyage in June 1947".

Although the MELAMPUS was the newer ship (she entered service in 1960) we lived aboard the twenty-one year old AGAPENOR. AGAPENOR's generators used heavy oil. The two ship's main engines also used heavy oil, so there was an ample reserve of it. MELAMPUS's generators used diesel oil and the stock of diesel was low. Electric cables connected MELAMPUS's switchboard with AGAPENOR's generators, so the AGAPENOR supplied electricity for the two ships.

The hordes of cockroaches infesting the galley were appalling. These vile insects coloured brown resemble a beetle and are often found aboard ships, on North Sea oilrigs and in canteens anywhere from Alaska to the tropics. They are nocturnal and one shuddered to think what it must have been like at night. Cockroachs have inhabited the earth for millions of years and never evolved. I knew that Rentokil manufactured a highly effective residual insecticide, but was there any aboard? I searched and enlisted Les Sells, the Radio Officer, to help. Several aerosols were found, but it was needed in gallons. There was no option except to use what was on hand. I started spraying and soon saw results. As I exhausted the aerosols, cockroaches rained down from the galley deck-head and overhead pipes. Exterminated and dying they carpeted the galley deck, working surfaces and shrivelled on the galley stoves. As Burt and I swept them into buckets, he remarked with awe "I have never seen so many or seen them cleaned out so swiftly either". Philip, the Chief Engineer agreed and helped sweep up the carnage. During the sweep up, I disclosed that this was my first venture into entomology.

A cable was sent to the head office in Liverpool asking for 5 gallons of the appropriate Rentokil insecticide fluid. It arrived within ten days and the cockroach problem was soon solved.

Second Officer Ian Russell had flown out and joined AGALAMPUS a week ahead of us. The idea was for him to learn the ship's routine and general way of life on the Lake. It was really unnecessary, because he had served aboard AGALAMPUS the previous year. Ian tended to talk imperiously about his previous Lake experience and was quick to explain any aspect of life on the Lake and the GBLA. Overnight he earned the nickname the Vet. He accepted it with good humour and even liked it. He possessed a nonchalant Teeside personality, which, combined with his previous experience, made him a prime asset aboard. As the caretaker crew did not have a Chief Officer the Vet was the Executive Officer.

In a ship's restricted confines, life follows a set of rules based on a mild system of discipline copied from the armed forces. I discussed the special circumstances existing on the

Lake with the Vet. "Some things are waived, for instance, everyone is called by their Christian names". He was nervous and apprehensive as he explained this. "But to retain a little respect for authority the Captains' names are prefixed Captain. "Alright" I said. "I am Captain Brian". He hesitated, "I might as well tell you the worst and get it over. The sailors work from nine till four. They don't work Wednesday afternoon because it is football. Saturday and Sunday are none-working days because it is a five-day week. Nonetheless, they are paid fourteen hours per week overtime".

I was astounded. No one had told me or hinted at this before we left Liverpool, in fact the reverse was implied, with everyone was expected to do a little extra. The Officers were expected to clean their own cabins and bathrooms and the sailors worked in the engine-room if needed.

Obviously, two sailors could accomplish little aboard the two ships, especially, if Philip, the Chief, wanted them occasionally working down the engine-room. I considered it ridiculous to pay out fourteen hours overtime when the sailors' working week was already reduced from the usual forty hours to twenty-seven.

I told the Vet this. "But Captain Smallwood (the Operations Director) recommended paying two hours overtime a day in case the sailors lowered or hoisted the boat after five o' clock" he argued. I conceded to both the shorter working week and the overtime payment. On a normal voyage, the ratings depended on overtime to increase their earnings, and at sea would expect to work eight hours on Saturdays and another eight on Sundays. So, with these hours overtime a week, they were still six hours down on what they normally earned.

In Blue Funnel, the Petty Officers, Boatswains, Carpenters, Cooks and Second Stewards were staff men on a consolidated rate of pay with no overtime and they also contributed to the Company's pension fund.

It was known that the way out to the north towards Port Said was too severely blocked with obstructions such as a demolished cantilever railway bridge and a dredger that had been filled with cement and sunk. It was a pity, because the distance from Port Said to Liverpool is 3,185 miles ... while from Suez to Liverpool, around the Cape, is 11,320 miles.

To the south, Suez was barely 29 miles away, and after passing though the Great Bitter Lake and then the Little Bitter Lake, the final section of the actual man-made Canal is only 14 miles. In these 14 miles, however, shortly before the cease-fire, the Egyptians blocked the Canal by scuttling a dredger, a tug and the Egyptian Navigation Company's tanker, NASR, 10,484 grt. NASR had been built for A.P. Møller, Copenhagen as the JANE MAERSK in 1950 and sold to United Arab Maritime in 1954. Thus our ships became permanently sealed in with no chance of escape, although it was possible that the ships could navigate past the tanker.

Credit for conceiving the Great Bitter Lake Association belongs to a Blue Funnel Captain and the Captain of the KILLARA. When ship-visiting, the men relaxed solely by drinking beer. In early October 1967, the fourteen Captains met aboard the MELAMPUS and the Great Bitter Lake Association, GBLA, was formed. By forming it, the Captains hoped to introduce more healthy activities. It was an instant success.

To enrol in the GBLA cost £1, thereupon the new member received a tie. It was in the United Nations colours monogrammed with a symbolic anchor, the number 14 and GBLA in gold, to signify the fourteen anchored ships surrounded by the desert. In addition, an enthusiastic unpaid secretary, Port Line's Captain Jim Starkey, organized a supply of GBLA tankards, car and blazer badges and issued the members with a membership card. As an exclusive extra, the Captains qualified for a GBLA pennant, but a strict rule insisted Captains only. The flag's design, blue and yellow in colour, embroidered with an anchor and the numbers 14, was based on the GBLA tie.

Anyone who visited a ship was invited to join the GBLA, and no one ever refused membership into the ranks of such a one-up association. Consequently, besides seafarers, the 1,000 members included consular officials, journalists, film and television crews of several nationalities, and quite a number of British MPs, including the volatile George Brown, Foreign Minister at the time of the Six Day War.

On joining, two dogs about the size of sheep dogs, a cat and one hibernating tortoise were inherited. Captain Hughie Davies left the cat to me as an unwanted legacy. But, I dislike cats and quickly 'emsheed' her off to Philip. Sandy, named after his colour, the male dog must have had a glorious three weeks, when Squeak, the bitch, was in season. I was astounded at such irresponsibility by the previous crews. When the pups were born, one of the Engineers disposed of them. A couple of months later, Squeak had to go the same way as she was attacking anyone coming aboard.

I judged Les, the twenty-five years old Radio Officer, to be the most versatile man aboard, capable of turning his hand to anything that cropped up. The Egyptians closed and sealed the ship's radio rooms immediately when the ships became trapped. They feared that the ships may be spying for the Israelis and could pass information on by the ships' radios.

The GPO's Portishead short-wave radio station knew the difficulties and transmitted any messages every fourth hour over a period of 24 hours. Les received them listening intently on the short-wave band of an ordinary Eddystone radio. He seldom needed a second attempt. The Eddystone was the best personal radio for short-wave reception aboard ship. But, at £66 they were expensive and few people could afford them.

Few British shipping companies employed Radio Officers direct. The radio equipment companies supplied them. Marconi was the biggest supplier, followed by International Marine Radio, (I.M.R.), part of I.T.T., with Siemens having a small share of the market. Even Cunard passenger ships relied on I.M.R. for its Radio Officers. Blue Funnel was an exception and employed its own Radio Officers. Aboard Blue Funnel ships, the Radio Officer was also the Purser. As Purser, he typed out my weekly report to the company. In the Lake, there were neither cash advances nor postage, so the only accounts needed were the bar accounts.

Normally there were strict bar hours, where the Second Steward was the barman. Cash was not used and the crew signed a chit for their drinks. This was fairly standard procedure aboard British ships at this time and even passengers were usually required to sign chits. At the end of the week, these were added up and entered in a bar book. The crew signed the book and their chits were returned. With only sixteen men, it was not possible to have bar opening hours and a barman. Consequently, the bar was open all the time and the crew helped themselves and signed the chits as they took a drink. Seafarers are honest and, at sea, cabins are never locked. The 24-hour bar worked and there were no shortages. Sometimes on a Saturday night there might be a leisurely sun-up drinking session, but there was no drunkenness.

When the original crews left the two ships in 1967, the Company paid them for personal items such as radios and tape-recorders which they had left behind. These were distributed through the ship, which enabled every man to enjoy the luxury of them in his cabin.

My day began by swimming in a wide circle around AGALAMPUS, which I estimated as approximately 400 yards. Most afternoons, I retired to a secluded section of MELAMPUS's upper decks and soon acquired an all-over suntan. Then in the late afternoon, I swam another 400 yards circuit. Later, I became more adventurous and doubled my swim by going around the dredger, KHOD, that was moored about 400 yards away.

After breakfast on the first Sunday aboard, the Vet asked in a solemn voice, "Are you coming to church this morning"? I frowned at him, dumbfounded. I had received an elaborate briefing in Liverpool about what to expect, but no one had mentioned church. "Where?", I challenged, not quite certain whether or not I was the victim of his wit. "It is aboard the German ship, NORWIND, and absolutely non-denominational," he answered, smiling. It sounded plausible. "Besides", he added "all the other captains want to meet you". He hesitated, expecting a query. "With your permission, Sunday lunch is normally a cold buffet. This gives Burt and Alan the chance of coming to church. It will also give Burt a break", he said, while studying the anchored ships. I agreed that I had no objection.

I thought it strange for two cases of beer to be passed into the boat before she cast off with the church party, but made no comment. The Vet skilfully nursed the boat alongside the LEDNICE, with shouts of "Ahoy" being exchanged. I found that 'Ahoj' is Czech for 'Hello'. She was named after a town in Czechoslovakia, whose tourist attraction was a mediaeval castle. I recognized the two Czechs who had travelled from Cairo with us. They lowered a case of beer to an elderly stout man with grey hair and moustache, who was dressed in a grey shirt and trousers. He was the ship's Captain and had only rejoined the ship a few days before us. He looked more like a farmer than a sailor. LEDNICE did not own a motorboat and depended on the AGALAMPUS for transport. Likewise, AGALAMPUS provided transport for the SCOTTISH STAR. She owned a boat, but was awaiting the arrival of a new engine from Britain. At SCOTTISH STAR her Captain, George, stepped into the boat first and next came two cases of beer. She was a fine-looking ship, so I was surprised that she was the only ship in the Lake that did not have radar.

NORDWIND's Captain, Gerhard Lomer, resplendent in uniform, greeted me and the other two Captains in fluent English. I remembered seeing him in my cabin the day I joined.

173

"Have a beer, Brian," he invited. I accepted a Tuborg. "What about church?" I asked, puzzled. "It is not really church," laughed Gerhard. George uttered a rude word. "They fooled me," he admitted, with a certain amount of gaiety. Several of the SCOTTISH STAR's ratings were on their second or even third tour of duty and knew everybody.

Gerhard had been aboard the NORWIND on a voyage from Bombay to Avonmouth, Liverpool and Glasgow in 1967 when the ships became trapped in the Lake. "Church is the main social function of the week", Gerhard told us. "It started because the Egyptians compelled us to stay aboard our ships. We demanded the basic right to go to church every Sunday".

Everyone mingled on the open deck chatting and joking. A string of international code flags added some colour to the scene. The Czech Captain, Clement, pointed out the Captains' GBLA pennant, and George and I expressed our approval. Owing to the notoriously lazy attitude of the British towards learning languages, everyone spoke English. The German chief steward took care of all the beer the congregation had contributed, and acted as barman.

Glasses, like many things, were scarce in the Lake so the congregation drank from the bottles or cans. "Are those the prayer books?" whispered George facetiously. Meanwhile, one and all greeted Klaus, the NORDWIND's Chief Engineer, with a cheery "Hello Santa". Her Bosun, a squat powerfully-built German capable of drinking huge quantities of beer, if given the right opportunity, answered to a friendly "Hello Charlie Brown". Why he adopted this misnomer no one quite knew. Maybe he cherished memories of a pub with that name in the heart of London's dockland. The pub was decorated with such nautical memorabilia as a shark's backbone, ships in bottles and model ships.

'Church' was also an opportunity for the ships' sports committees to meet and discuss forthcoming fixtures.

Naturally, the 'Church' had a 'Vicar'. At our first 'Church', the 'Vicar' was the Chief Engineer of the PORT INVERCARGILL. The 'Vicar' was elected by a free vote, which indicated his popularity. His pulpit was standing on No. 4 hatch, which elevated him above the congregation. Part of his 'sermon' was to announce the preceding week's news, and the sport and social activities for the forthcoming week. Finally, amidst bantered humour in half a dozen languages and a chorus of laughter, he called out the name of the newest water baby. A water baby was the unlucky person who accidentally fell into the Lake. So far, there were about fifty water babies and one pet dog. They claimed, jestingly, to be the most elite section of the GBLA and had designed a special, monogrammed tie for themselves. Whether or not any of the Lake's visiting guests qualified for this special tie, it was not recorded. 'Church' ended with the congregation all singing the Beatles song, "We All Live in a Yellow Submarine".

At 'Church' the Sunday before Christmas, the GBLA planned to gather around the buoy in the boats for a Christmas Eve carol concert. It was to be a repetition of the previous year's Christmas Eve, when a raft was made using empty oil drums and a 30-foot Christmas tree placed in its centre. The raft was anchored in the middle of the anchored ships and KILLARA supplied electricity for the coloured lights. All the ships boats circled it and the crews sang a carol from their country. The Czechs "Good King Wenceslas", Germany "Stille Nacht", Great Britain "O Come All Ye Faithful", and the Poles turned up complete with a piano in one of their boats. The Swedes sang one in Swedish. However, to the GBLA's indignation, fate intervened, allied with the unpredictable mysteries of the weather. A westerly gale furiously lashed and maddened the normally placid lake. It left no alternative except to hoist the boats clear from the water for safety. Instead, the GBLA listened to the BBC's broadcast from St. Martins-in-the-Field with lusty vocalists 3,000 miles away singing the

175

carols. The progress of NASA's Apollo 8 launched from Cape Canaveral on 21st December was followed until its splashdown in the Pacific in 27th December. It was the first manned spacecraft to orbit the moon. On Christmas Day the gale prevented inter-ship visits. Burt provided a dinner equally as good as the Cairo Hilton could have provided. Alan was perturbed as there were thirteen seated at the round saloon table. To break the unlucky number, he sat down for a moment before serving the meal. The MELAMPUS had originally carried twelve passengers, so she had a good selection of wines and spirits in her bond locker. Alan, showing the true professional that he was, found Liebfraumilch and Nuit St. George to wash the dinner down and served a choice of Drambuie or Benedictine with the coffee. The day ended with a film.

Once a week, all the ship's mail was put into a large envelope and sent by registered mail to the Head Office in Liverpool. All the crew needed to do was put a 2½d stamp on their letters, and our man in Liverpool, Charles Metcalfe, reposted them. He had been a Radio Officer/Purser with Blue Funnel before going ashore as a Welfare Officer. This gave an indication of how long mail took and it varied from five days to three weeks.

GBLA stamps were made for affixing to home-going mail. The first basic stamp-making equipment was a worn-out Gestetner duplicating machine aboard the SCOTTISH STAR, where Edmund Owen-Humphreys, Chief Refrigeration Engineer, designed 300 sets for distribution on 2nd and 3rd October, 1967. The Second Mate printed them and the cadets coloured them with the only colours available, blue, red and yellow felt tip pens. But, things improved with lino-cuts and etchings. Considering the limited materials available, some of the artists showed great skill and even produced very limited editions laboriously by hand. Sometimes with just a GBLA stamp, the mail had been franked by the Egyptian postal authorities to be delivered in Australia, Germany, Great Britain

and Sweden. They became collectors' items. They were in great demand by philatelists all over the world, but the greatest interest in them was in Germany. Every week, each of the two German ships received about fifty requests for them. Some collectors wanted only the GBLA stamp franked "Mailed on board" with the GBLA's own cancellation stamp. Sometimes a homeward going crewman would post letters at Cairo Airport with only a GBLA stamp on. According to the stamp dealers, Stanley Gibbons, at present they only have a curiosity value of a less than a pound.

After New Year, things became more serious as the pattern of life on the Lake was adapted. The first Tuesday in each month, the MÜNSTERLAND issued provisions. She took her name from an agricultural area in North West Germany. The ships handed in their orders at 'Church'. With typical German thoroughness, sharp at nine the next Tuesday each indivual ship's stores, eggs, lamb, mutton, liver, kidneys and jam were stacked neatly ready for transferring into the boats. Although nearly two years old, the eggs still whipped up into a good omelette. The frozen stores issued were, in fact, cargo for Aden. On her way home to Bremen from Australia, striking Aden dock workers caused the ship to sail right past and into the Canal. Besides fridge cargo, she carried wool, skins and rutile sand. Also, a Herr Kirsten, the son of the Kirstern Shipping Line family in Hamburg, was shipping his furniture home from Australia for his new house in Hamburg. For Sunday lunch aboard the MÜNSTERLAND, the Germans barbecued a whole lamb on an improvised spit over a wood fire, and imbibed a seemingly endless supply of beer. They had once reared a pig for a barbecue. On arrival in the lake, the ship had had Australian grapes aboard and had given the last twenty cases to the LEDNICE to make wine.

By trading between one another, the ships remained almost self-supporting. Everything was signed for to be settled one day between the various owners.

Stocks of some commodities were abundant. For instance, tinned goods from Australia included fruit, jam, steak and Irish stew. From Japan, tinned apple and fish. From Tsinkiang in Communist China, tinned asparagus, chicken and white peaches. From Malaya, pineapple in chunks, slices, or crushed in juice. From Pakistan came potted shrimps.

Tea was no problem, as MELAMPUS had loaded one thousand tons in Ceylon. She had also loaded desiccated coconut, which after two summers in the lake would be no use to Cadburys. At the end of the Six Day War, Brooke Bond wanted to land bridge the tea to Alexandria, but the Israelis forbade it. Chinese sugar was plentiful.

The Agents boarded the ships Wednesdays and Saturdays. They accepted any cables for dispatch and after a journey to Cairo, it could take eight days before the cable reached its destination.

All the crews received a bonus while serving in the lake. The British bonus of £60 a month was the lowest. An AB was paid £50 a month with an overtime rate of 6s (30 p) an hour. The £60 a month bonus did not provoke any serious complaint, but paying income tax on bonus money earned 3,000 miles away from Britain did.

From 19th January, Egypt's winter started with an overcast sky and little sunshine for the next 23 days and in mid-February the swimming in water temperatures of 65° was cold. After that, it was good weather, and most seafarers enjoy the sun. The PORT INVERCARGILL's Chief Engineer was a suntan addict. Every time I went aboard her, he was sitting in a deckchair in a brief pair of swimming trunks, soaking up the sun. Periodically, he would walk around with his fingers spread open to catch the sun and get tanned between his fingers. Jock, our Third Officer, thought the secret of a good tan was to use raw linseed oil, which he said would stain the skin so that it looked like oiled teak. But, he abandoned it after a couple of weeks as he found it was too difficult to wash off.

During February, Captain Jürgens of the MÜNSTERLAND with unprecedented boldness began dumping 400 tons of Australian apples and pears with the candid explanation that after almost two years continuous running the fridge machinery was tired.

The MÜNSTERLAND was our closest neighbour. She had a dog aboard and got rid of it by putting it aboard MELAMPUS's. Gerhard was disgusted with such behaviour by his countrymen and said, "Waste no time and return it". But, not wanting to create a tit-for-tat situation it was easier to give the Agent a case of pineapple and send the animal ashore.

The dumping met with Eric's approval and he set to on a massive dumping operation. A quantity of frozen trout and 800 tons of Australian fruit were dumped discreetly, only at night. Apples floated everywhere. They spoilt the swimming. When I told Eric that his apples were drifting towards the Egyptian shore he delayed further disposal until the wind blew westerly towards the Israeli-held shore.

I joined in the dumping spree and spent one afternoon throwing 3 tons of garlic overboard. It was packed in wooden crates and two summers in the Lake had dried and wizened it, so that it no longer reeked. It was thought that the Egyptians would salvage the crates. A couple of weeks later, garlic ensnared between the two ships continued bobbing up and down in the water.

179

On 21st August, 1968, Russian, Bulgarian, East German, Hungarian and Polish troops invaded Czechoslovakia. In protest the LEDNICE hoisted her ensign upside down, and flew it at half-mast. Philip asked Clement if he had ordered this. Clement's English deteriorated until Philip changed the subject. Captain Vladimir was in command at that time. The next day the Captains of the two Polish ships and the Bulgarian ship went aboard the LEDNICE and declared that despite the political situation it would not affect their comradeship. The one thing they held in common was that their Shipping Companies were state-owned.

On 19th February, 1969, the London and Liverpool Steamship Owners Assurance declared the PORT INVERCARGILL a Constructive Total Loss with an insurance valuation of £1,141,100. The insurers set up the Invercargill Shipping Company as her new owners.

At the end of 1969, seeing no possibility of the ships being released, the underwriters paid up and Ocean Fleets withdrew their crew from AGALAMPUS.

In May 1974, a joint operation by the Royal Navy and United States Navy began clearing the Canal of military ordinance and hardware. In the Canal, it found personnel carriers, some with the personnel still in them, 2,000 kg unexploded bombs, anti-tank rockets, unexploded shells, small arms etcetera. An Egyptian Air Force Mig fighter was found in the Great Bitter Lake.

The minesweeper HMS MAXTON transitted the Canal from north to south on 15th July, 1974. She was the first ship to make a complete Canal transit since it closed in June 1967. It was declared to be 99% clear on 20th December, 1974.

On 5th June, 1975, the eight anniversary of the Canal's closure, President Anwar Sadat reopened officially the Canal. Surprisingly, none of the ships' owners were invited. Shipping had made immense changes since the closure in 1967. The Far East and Australian trades had been containerised, the supertanker evolved, too big to transit the Canal evolved and the size of a ship's crew halved.

Captain Brian McManus' script has been greatly edited and for that I apologise. Here are his concluding thoughts.

After leaving the lake, I never saw any of AGALAMPUS's crew again. One reason was that I was declared redundant by Ocean in August 1972, and joined Denholm Ship Management Ltd., Glasgow.

Today, the once great names in British shipping are no more and the fleets have declined to not much more than the big oil companies' tankers, container ships, a few cruise ships and short sea ferries.

All these years later, most people might remember England winning the World Cup in a football match against Germany in 1966. Even fewer will remember the Six Day War of 1967, and recall that the Suez Canal was closed for eight years. Memories are short and possibly people working today in shipping may not know about the ships trapped in the Great Bitter Lake some forty years ago.

Thank you, Brian, for your memories. I asked for some career details.

While growing up in the 1930s it was my ambition to go away to sea and one day become Captain of the QUEEN MARY. After leaving the CONWAY, I seemed to be on an early road to success and boarded the QUEEN ELIZABETH bound for New York on Easter Monday, 1944. In New York, I joined the Cunard White Star managed Liberty ship SAMHOLT.

After obtaining my Temporary Second Mate's Certificate in January, 1947, I was appointed Third Mate of the BANTRIA. She was not a Cunard White Star owned ship, but owned by the Cunard Line. In Cunard White Star, a Third Mate was paid £33 a month, in the Cunard Line only £30-10s-0d a month. After the luxury of a Libertyship, the no-frills BANTRIA with her fresh- water pump and no hot water was not for me and one voyage was enough.

One of my friends, an Old Worcester, persuaded me to join the War Department fleet in Portsmouth. The pay was £28-10s-0d a month. I stayed six weeks and then joined the Bibby Line. Every Master in Bibby was a b .... d. They were 'anti' because before the War one needed a Master's Certificate to join. I was promoted Second Mate with my First Mate's Certificate, but after one voyage, as their fleet was decreasing, they were going to put me back to Third Mate. I left and joined Elder Dempster. In 1967, the E.D. personnel were integrated with Blue Funnel into Ocean Fleets. E.D. was a good employer, but Ocean Fleets the best.

However, Julian Holt disliked me and put me on the redundancy list. In 1972, I joined Denholm Ship Management, but was made redundant in 1982. They were good employers, but not as good as Ocean Fleets.

I did one six-months voyage for Unishipping. One voyage was enough. They were the worst employer I ever had, but luckily I got back into the Denholm Group with Denholm (Bermuda).

I left my last ship at Jeddah on 30th July, 1987. I was sixty and a half to the day.

Captain Brian McManus could have written so much more and, along with his many friends, I am entertained by his endless production of twinkle-making e-mails

Captain Dave Ramwell
Master Mariner

Captain Dave Ramwell ran out of Manchester from 1968 to 1987. The laws of chance delivered the occasional heart-stopper in the restricted waters of the Ship Canal. Regularly throughout the year, the sludge vessels of the Manchester and Salford Corporations made the passage down the Canal to the deposit grounds in Liverpool Bay, beyond the North West Light Float. Life certainly became easier when the operational base shifted to Sandon Dock in Liverpool in 1987, until finally all dumping at sea ended in 1998.

Dave's memories are recorded in the well-loved publication, Sea Breezes, and we are much indebted to the publishers. Let Dave unfold his memories.

PASSAGE TO THE NORTH WEST

One long ... one short. The blasts shatter the silence of early morning. After a while, a uniformed figure emerges from the small brick office and waves a white handkerchief about his head. A "Thank you" blast on the whistle sends him scurrying back to the warmth and, on board, the securing ropes and wires all except one are slipped with a speed which speaks of much practice.

Slowly, under the power of her twin Mirrlees engines, the vessel slides along, the jetty. "Give her a check!" and the strain is taken on the starboard head-rope, canting the bow to starboard. Now the starboard engine is put astern, the port ahead and soon, a barely perceptible upsurge of the bow indicates the nose has taken the soft mud on the bank. The engine revolutions are slowly increased and a musty odour of stagnation rises from the propeller boil, tainting the freshness of the dewy mist. The swing is well under way and, looking aft, its rate can be judged by the movement of the ensign staff against the background of Barton Airport. Just a little too fast perhaps ... ease the port engine ... bump ... the thick protective belting makes contact on the port side with the wooden bullnose that extends from the Barton Lock island ... full astern on the starboard engine ... not coming off the mud quite quickly enough ... touch astern on the port ... "Heave away for'rd" ... stop the port ... ahead the port ... not much room aft now ... not much ahead either! "Let go the headrope." She's swinging well and the stern is finding deep water in the big lock entrance. She can even be brought astern again; the nearer the point of contact to the ships' fulcrum the better the swing.

At last she's round. The apparent disinterest of a lock gateman indicates that all the timbers have remained in place on the extension, but the wheelman already has her under control as both engines now throb slowly ahead.

"As she goes." Not that, without the words, he'd steer her straight into the bank ... but the true seaman is a neat creature who works to a pattern whenever possible and this simple dialogue indicates a set stage in a pattern, the end of a manoeuvre, the full stop at the end of a sentence.

"As she goes", and the Wheelman, Officer of the Watch, and the ship settle down like a broody hen on its eggs for the short run to Irlam.

On the Irlam Lock Island, a white light flashes at the side of the big lock. Good ... much easier making the big lock, especially first thing Monday morning! Just stop the engines in good time, steer her in, keeping well clear of the gates, and pull her up. She'll take a run to port as she's going in, but she always does and the corrective helm and engine movements maintain the pattern.

There must be some shallow water on the starboard side; whenever it's shallow the stern is attracted to the least water. This attraction varies directly as the speed of the vessel, the depth of the water and the shallows. Was there a formula in 'Danton's Seamanship?'

Enough day-dreaming! Full astern both ... line out fore and aft. "Heave her alongside." Behind us chains pull the giant gates slowly together and the railings on their walking platforms judder as the gate is closed. Paddles are lifted and the island hut moves slowly upward until it is finally obscured by the oily black wall.

Ahead the gates of the bottom reach crack open as the pressure equalizes on both sides. Chains move on massive sheaves and slowly, reluctantly, the two leviathans edge back to their recesses in the lock walls. A megaphone is poked through an open window ashore ... "One coaster and a light tug this side ... there's a liner just leaving Latchford now." Quite busy. We can meet the tug anywhere, not so the others.

"How long's the coaster been left?"

"Forty minutes."

Not bad; we might not even be delayed.

"Let go fore and aft." Lines snake inboard and "All clear" is shouted from aft, a signal for the vessel to glide out of the lock ... the noise of her engines fading suddenly as she clears the exit. It's hardly worth giving her much headway ... once under Irlam viaduct, speed will have to be reduced to a crawl. There's an ore boat working on the Irlam steel wharf.

Through the viaduct ... she can be seen now, rust-red grabs dropping hungrily into her holds, lifting cargo and dropping it ashore to be digested somewhere in the depths of the sprawling conglomeration of smoke and dust in the hinterland.

The Mate stands on the fo'c'sle head, chewing an unlit

Mancunium

pipe, arms folded on the upper rail, one leg resting on the lower rail, in the universal stance of all Mates on the fo'c'sle heads when nought else occupies their attention. He has one eye on us, one eye on his own moorings. Our speed ... or lack of it ... satisfies him and before we are past, he pockets his pipe and picks up his cup of tea.

One long and one short ... the outward signal; the coaster should be showing up at any time. The red light at Partington South bank is flashing, so there will be at least one ship working with low flash cargo. Again the telegraphs are eased back and the engines quieten in direct response. Here's the coaster ... couldn't have timed it better. One blast and go to starboard. The tug is right behind him. As soon as we're out of the way, he will be blowing to overtake. The Pilot returns a wave as the vessels pass port to port in the widest part of the canal between Irlam and Latchford.

Cadishead viaduct catches the engine roar for a few seconds, then Partington lies astern. Full Canal speed ... ease up for Bob's Ferry ... then away again. Now the ninety-foot cutting from Mill Bank to the Warburton high-level bridge. Not much can be met here, nothing upwards of a barge or light tug.

How deep did Irlam say the liner was? They didn't.

"Latchford, Latchford.This is MANCUNIUM, MANCUNIUM."

"Good morning, MANCUNIUM ... over to channel twenty and go ahead."

A short conversation reveals the liner to be 26ft. draft. Deep ... he'll be wanting the middle.

Rounding Rixton now, where the Mersey flows out of the canal. Ahead, on the Latchford straight, the liner is squatting in the middle of the fairway. Speed is adjusted. The Pilots like to meet ships this side of the M6 viaduct.

No golfers out this morning ... too early. Single columns of smoke spiral lazily upwards from the roof tops of Lymm, still sleeping in its cosy niche on the hillside. There's no wind, so even if the ship has to hang back, she should behave. But she doesn't have to.

Long and a short ... let the liner know we're coming ahead, and from the liner ... a long-short-long tells the stern tug "There's a vessel about to pass me from the opposite direction. Ease the engines ... mustn't go too fast or she'll run to port, and the first thing to stop her will be the liner. Not too slow or we'll lose steerage way.

"Stand by fenders".

Tied bundles of cane drop over the side to absorb the initial shock of impact should she touch ... a token gesture.

"Steady at that, Wheelman ... we're just clear."

"Just ... !" A wholly descriptive adjective in this case ... he's not giving much.

187

"O.K. your side, Wheelman?"

"Just."

Hell, not much room, hope she behaves ... have to watch the starboard propeller on the bank. The way the propellers stick out each side ... sore thumbs pale into insignificance.

Now a wall of steel is pouring horizontally past the bridge window. It's clearing.

"Hard a starboard."

Stop the starboard engine, full ahead on the port. The stern is being dragged to the bank, the bow is trying to fill the 'hole' in the water astern of the liner and his tugs. Helm and engine work against and finally overpower the fierce couple. The stern moves slowly clear of the starboard bank.

"Wheel amidships."

"Wheel amidships."

"As she goes."

"As she goes."

Hope we get a clear run down. That Pilot didn't give much room. Still at that draft, he probably couldn't. He's probably echoing the same sentiments on the Bridge of the liner. They earn their money those Pilots ... wonder how they get that CARCHESTER through the ninety foot when she's deep laden. Grease the sides and slide her through with a shoe horn! Yes, they certainly earn their money.

The white light is flashing by the small lock at Latchford. There's no wind to speak of and no sluicing, so there should be no complications. The small lock is forty-five feet wide. Now the twin screws come into their own, shoving and pulling to position two thousand tons for a straight run into the confines of the small lock. She brings up well, the gates close and on the other side of the lower gates the water begins to boil as the vessel drops to the next and last reach before the open sea.

The vessel slides ahead as the lower gates snuggle into their recesses. A satisfying "Nothing to meet" is shouted from the other side of the lock. The water though by no means clean, is much fresher now ... more brown than oily black. Stop the engines under Latchford viaduct ... ahead again as the vertical members on the Knutsford Road Swing Bridge move out of transit and a green light begins to flash. Hurry along ... don't keep the road traffic waiting.

Here the Canal sides are steep, the banks sheer and this somehow heightens the impression of sailing along a giant ditch.

On Latchford High Level Bridge, two children out with their mother wave frantically to the ship.

Through 'The Wide' now. Whoever called it that had either never met a 'tug job' in it or had a rather cynical turn of mind. It's not bad outward when the vessel can pull well over to starboard, but inward, when meeting one of the big ones, it's a different situation. His length won't let him pull over to starboard too far before his tug has to heave the bow to port to middle in the fairway again. No, inward bound, bilge keels and starboard props are ripe fare for the South bank, 'wide' or no.

Through the 'Wide', and Northwich Road Swing Bridge lies safely along the bank and even as we pass this, Chester Road Swing Bridge starts to move clear.

The Canal will remain narrow now until we reach the Moore Lane Dolphins on the other side of the Moore Lane Swing Bridge.

The head yaws from side to side as the vessel gathers way, the ship won't steady despite immediate wheel against the swing. The single plate rudder makes evident its inefficiency in this stretch more than any other. It seems unfair that all the effort expended by the Wheelman should be translated into such lethargic movements of the ship's head.

Acton Grange viaduct, Acton. Grange Wharf ... now Moore Lane Bridge swings open ... past the Bridge and finally the Dolphins draw abeam. She will steer more easily now ... one course will take us almost to the Wiggs Wharf and there's a comfortable distance between the ship's sides and the bank all the way. Time enough to light a pipe and relax, discuss the fortunes of United before having to ease back the engines once more to negotiate Old Quay Swing Bridge.

The Quarry Hole ... difficult to believe that people actually swim here when the weather is warm ... must have brick-lined stomachs.

Long and short! The outward signal warns Old Quay of the vessel's approach, but even as we take the bend, the bridge is swinging off. They always give a good swing, but they haven't the same traffic to contend with; only cars and lorries having business with the small I.C.I. factories on the North bank.

The Bridgeman waves his signal trumpet. He's got orders for us. "Hang back at Old Quay for a tug job just passing the lay-by now."

The engines are stopped, the vessel loses way and, off the first of the Dolphins lining the estuary, a touch astern on both, brings her gently to a halt.

Not long to wait. Even now the head tug appears in the Runcorn Bridge hole. Its charge lumbers slowly after it, a clanking steaming hulk, a water-borne, pre-historic monster.

Under a 'flag of convenience', now hardly recognizable as a vessel that's seen better days under the 'red duster'. The engines of the stern tug scream astern, struggling to over-ride the sheer awkwardness of the mass it's fastened to.

Both engines slow ahead ... the stern tug has cleared the bridge hole. "Stand by fenders." There's plenty of deep water here. Any vessel that can proceed above Ince can tie up at these Dolphins. Kill the run with the engines, square her up for the bridge hole beneath the viaduct.

For a while now the engines must run slowly ahead so as not to part the moorings of the little grey tanker barges always alongside the Runcorn Dock wall, nor those of the coasters within the dock itself. Nothing on the lay-by, but a coaster on the Salt Works. A long and short well before the bend, though it should be all clear.

But it isn't! Stop ... full astern both ... she's paying off rapidly to starboard ... stop the starboard engine ... three blasts on the whistle. "My engines are going full speed astern." The head's steadying ... full astern both again. Like a clearing flash of smoke reveals the theatrical magician, the Captain appears on the bridge, his worried look asking the obvious question.

"Not a word of warning, Captain. We're just rounding the bend and there's this coaster backing out of the Weston Docks."

He looks around. The engines are stopped. She's holding nicely with plenty of room ahead. He tuts his annoyance, then satisfied that danger is past, descends in steps more measured than those of his ascent.

The coaster's completed her swing and heading outward rapidly, unravelling the disturbed water of the wake from her stern.

"Eastham, Eastham. This is MANCUNIUM, MANCUNIUM". Eastham soon know about the maverick from Weston.

Weston Mersey Lock. The lock master and his further gesticulations convey clearly his opinion of the mental state of the navigator in the vessel ahead. He's right, but, unfortunately, the Manchester Ship Canal does not constitute a compulsory pilotage area. Pilots should be taken, for apart from their knowledge of basic Ship Canal procedure, only experience can teach the hazards of this deceptively tricky stretch of waterway.

There's a dredger working at the Weaver bend. The vessel ahead blows the outward signal (at least he knows that) and the dredger trudges wearily to the estuary bank, hauling on its shore-wires and sending up a large ball on a halyard to indicate the clear side. Ease the engines right back and stop to go over his wires. Buckets continue their slow journey round, tipping over at their highest ascent and emptying their contents, thick, grey, sticky mud, into a chute that channels it into the barge alongside to splash like spoonfuls of duff in a thick gravy.

Must be a monotonous job that. Still if they want a change, they can always send the buckets round the other way!

Frodsham Score now, the Weaver's well astern. Always a pleasant run along the Score in good weather. Sheep graze on the sea-washed turf ... rabbits scud in and out of burrows in the hard ground of the bank; a skylark fluttering, like a piece of paper caught in a telegraph wire, sings its happiness across the estuary.

The warmth of the sun has consumed the faint mistiness hanging over the water, and the blueness of the sky is reflected on the surface of the water camouflaging and belying its true colour and pollution.

Ease down again. On the port side Frodsham Pumps sucks Canal dredgings from a barge and take it ashore and out of sight. We pass; the barges creak as they range alongside the wooden jetty, their ropes stretching and relaxing as we draw abeam and finally clear. Ahead again.

Now, the 'magazines' draw abeam to starboard. A red-brick building, its floor raised on brick stilts to a level above high water mark, it was used for storing the explosives that blasted the cutting out of the rock at Ince. Now the cows and sheep use it for shelter during inclement weather. Its prominence as a landmark makes it useful too, for judging the relative positions of vessels inward bound when the observing vessel is outward bound between Weston and the Weaver.

The 'bottleneck' now, where the Canal narrows considerablty. No cynicism in the naming of this point. Wonder why it wasn't blasted to a uniform width when the canal was built. The 'bottleneck' drops astern and the sheer rock wall of Ince rises out of the Canal.

The signal light on the estuary bank isn't on so there's nothing berthed or unberthing at Stanlow ... safe to proceed beyond Ince. Have to go slow in any case as from here to Eastham it's virtually one big dock and cargoes being worked include low-flash petroleum products, lead-based compounds and liquid ammonia.

The change from the flat lush green of the Score to the sprawling mass of tanks and tangled hissing pipes that is the Stanlow complex is startling in its abruptness.

Ince oil berth ... Ince coaster berth ... Stanlow Ferry, then Stanlow Hailing Station. "Nothing to meet MANCUNIUM" booms through fixed megaphones above the industrial din.

Past the Stanlow Oil Dock entrance ... the barge berth ... and then Associated Octel. At this berth a complicated vessel, under the Norwegian flag, lies alongside secured with over twenty parts of rope, each one carefully adjusted to the tautness of its neighbour. Should she break away, it's a safe bet that a goodly portion of the quay will remain alongside her! On the quay, drums are stacked high and binoculars show each to be emblazoned with a skull and crossbones. Figures wearing gas masks and rubberized suits lean on the rails and watch us pass.

Stuart's Wharf ... a good berth to be alongside whilst waiting for the tide or for more favourable weather reports from Mersey Radio. Ships passing have to go easy for Octel astern and Ellesmere Port ahead, so moorings are rarely overstrained. It was a pity the developers had to demolish the Canal Tavern for, truth be known, that haven of cheer, enhanced the attraction of the berth more than anything for many on board.

Ellesmere Port is full ... couple of Russians in ... there seems to be one in all the time lately ... another dredger, but he's tucked in the corner out of the way; must be waiting for a barge. Clan boat ... but he must be going up along, as his masts are struck and his radar platform lies on the 'monkey island' above the Bridge.

Now the cutting, and the sweet odour of pine gets stronger as we near Bowaters. A pyramid of timber spars avalanches now and again as an elevated conveyor tips more on to the peak. Funny, it must be a sign of the times, but the mind now associates the smell with after-shave lotion instead of tall, green pines marching shoulder to shoulder down to the edge of a mountain lake!

Bowaters falls astern, Jack's Castle draws onto the port beam, the vessel rounds the bend and is in the"home straight".

"Eastham, Eastham ... this is MANCUNIUM, MANCUNIUM ... we're just passing Jack's Castle now. Over."

"Thank you, MANCUNIUM, keep your eye on the small lock signal."

"Thanks Eastham will do."

Passing the crane berth, where vessels are 'cropped' to a suitable height for the journey to Manchester, the ship enters the Eastham Basin. The small lock signal is 'on', the engines are stopped and the vessel drifts easily into the 50-foot gap and brings up easily on her engines as the stern line tightens aft.

It doesn't take long to run down ... high water is only just over, so there won't be much difference between the Canal and sea levels. The gates behind are closed and almost immediately the gates ahead crack open.

"Let go for'd. Let go aft" and with engines going ahead faster than they ever did in the Canal, the vessel leaves the lock.

"Favour the starboard side, Wheelman." The ebb runs strongly from our starboard quarter to the port bow.

E 6, the first of the buoys when outward bound, and the engines are put full ahead for the first time since last the vessel was in the Mersey. Full ahead and as the clutches begin to bite, the 'scream' of their slip diminishes and the needles on the tachometers edge toward maximum revolutions.

The red buoys move quickly past us to starboard as we gain the speed of the ebb. Bromborough draws abeam. The WINSTON CHURCHILL lies in the dock, a synthetic replica of a bygone age of grace, but graceful no less.

Slow down for the Dingle mid-river tanker moorings.

Full away again, bring her to starboard at the red and white chequered Pluckington Bank buoy and bring the Duke's buoy and the Liverpool Landing Stage onto the starboard bow. Plenty of masts and funnels sticking above the sheds of the Liverpool dock system. A Palm boat ... brings back memories ... Cammell Laird's over at Birkenhead seem busy ... must have a full order book.

The Langton wreck buoy slips by to starboard. "Port wheel." She steers well in the river and the bow comes round to put the first of the sea channel floats onto the starboard bow ... C 22 and the start of the Crosby Channel.

Seaforth Container Terminal with two or three ships in. The hull itself seems but a large modification of the boxes it carries. Still their names have a good ring ATLANTIC SAGA, ATLANTIC SONG, ATLANTIC CHAMPAGNE.

Two low clangs on a deep-toned bell ... Crosby Light Float draws abeam to port and falls rapidly into the wake. Now the narrowest part of the channel ... 'Alpha across to C 1. Wouldn't like to meet one of the supertankers here ... over 200,000 tons feeling its way to Tranmere Oil Stage; ten years ago 80,000 tons was a behemoth!

Into the Queen's Channel ... "Bring her off the reds a bit." A strong ebb setting her to starboard.

Formby clangs its single stroke, the fairway buoy is brought ahead, pass fine to port and a course can at last be set on the magnetic compass.

"Steer 280."

"Steady on 280."

The Bar Light float is passed to starboard and for the next half-hour there's nothing but open sea and anchored ships between us and the North West Light Float.

It can be seen now on the port bow. Ring the engine room: "Ten minutes more."

Green lights glow on the converter panel ... the valve motors are operational ... ease the engines back. The North West is over five minutes astern now. "Hard a starboard ... bring her round to 100."

Sailors appear on deck .. buttons are pressed on the Bridge and valves lift in the tanks. The ship rises bodily and in less than ten minutes over 1,400 tons of sewage sludge has poured into the Irish Sea.

Thank you, Dave, that was a great contribution to our stories. However, as with all raconteurs, the stories keep coming.

STEADY ... STEADY AS SHE GOES

"This is going to be dodgy" said the man at the wheel
as the ship hurtled headlong into the lock.

Almost parallel and in a line with the outer bullnose of the now-disused most eastward lock, there is a row of wooden Dolphins. Just behind these Dolphins, and clear of the lock approaches, a bank dries out at low water, its dry height increasing towards the locks. This bank, while it remains uncovered, affords vessels making the lock into the Canal protection from the tide.

When the bank covers, the flood sets in a south-easterly direction, diagonal to the line of the locks, so that a vessel, approaching from the river, has it running from her starboard quarter to her port bow. Just off the locks though, and especially a couple of hours before high water, the run is more across the entrance, and the mariner must be wary of the sudden set to port.

There's nothing gradual about the set; the banks are dry and there's no run ... the banks cover and there's a strong run, growing rapidly stronger towards half flood.

Thus, once the bank covers I will not take the 50ft lock and, on the bigger tides, even the 80ft lock is too small, the run being too powerful to counter safely by hugging the land to westward.

Approaching from the river one day, I was keeping the vessel close to the starboard buoy line. It was about two-and-a-half hours to high water of a tide that was more spring than neap ... a good flood was running.

Although once in the lock, the vessel was to go alongside a barge, the barge was far enough from the entrance to offer the whole width of the lock for the initial and most critical phase of the operation. I could see no problem, and experience had taught me what to expect, but I had that degree of tenseness I always felt when holding the concentration necessary to monitor the effects of the helm, engine and tide on the ship. I had to bear in mind that the ship's course was now the resultant of all three and that I only had command of the first two. I was glad she was such a positive, responsive vessel, but the flood called the tune and I had to harmonise.

Suddenly Lock Control came over the radio: "You'll have to take the small lock. The barge has got big tyre fenders down her sides and you won't fit in."

Could I go astern? No chance ... lose all control ... flood tide too strong. Round up? Too near the dolphins. Nose in the 80ft? Stern would pay off before the ropes went out. Nose in the "putty"?

The options presented themselves as a blurred kaleidoscope of ideas simply because there was no time for any analytical consideration of the individual alternatives. I was out of step with the dance and the flood was up my stern.

Lock Control were right, however, I would have to take the small lock.

"This is going to be dodgy," remarked the Wheelman, more to himself than to enlighten me. Both of us were about to have our professional abilities stretched to the limit.

The dolphins rushed by the Bridge window at an alarming rate. My trepidation mounted, goaded to new heights by the next utterance from the Wheelman, rigid as a statue in the intensity of his concen

"Ain't never, ever been in this fast before!"

I had no choice; my speed had to overcome the lateral influence of the flood. I had to keep my nerve and fight the instinctive impulse to slow down.

The bow entered the lock and immediately dived to the outer west gate as it fell into slack water while the stern was pushed eastward by the flood. The Wheelman already had the helm hard to port as I crossed the engines, checking her just before she took a bite out of the timber.

She flattened nicely alongside the wall and I put both engines full astern. Had they fired? Yes! So why wasn't she slowing down? A line snaked ashore aft, another for'rd, assisting the engines in countering the headlong hurl.

The ship was alongside, the after gates closed. It was like a dream. I was drained. I was one of those half-lemon shells that live in ship's gash cans. My stomach was playing its own version of the 1812 Overture.

But I was ecstatic with relief that washed over me in waves.

The Wheelman's voice penetrated my trance. "Skipper, can you hear me Skipper? I said I'm going to make us a bucket of tea. How many packets of sugar would you like?"

Yet another Dave Ramwell extravaganza. But, let's try again. Swinging at Runcorn on the Manchester Ship Canal can be an everyday event, an exercise in expert ship handling or, just occasionally, a near disaster. Read on.

SWINGING SHIP AT RUNCORN

Some 14½ miles up the Manchester Ship Canal and about two miles up-Canal from the Old Quay Swing Bridge, Runcorn Sewage Works berth is let neatly into the straightness of the south bank. A vessel loading there would have come from sea in ballast, swung at the Quarry Hole about half a mile away, and be berthed head out.

The swinging area, although known to the Ship Canal fraternity as the Quarry Hole, will not be found on any Admiralty chart under this name; on such it is designated Stonedelph. I remember this because I once held the rapt attention of my Chief Officer all the way from Weaver Bend to Wiggs Wharf with the completely fabricated tale of how the place got its name. I told of the tiny man who brewed his own moonshine and was permanently drunk. I contrived to stack as much padding as I could coax from my imagination until the final "Hence, 'stoned elf' ".

The ungenerous response to this entertainment was a suggestion involving a rather unconventional use for the parallel rules.

Runcorn Sewage Works berth is a relatively new addition to the Canal and I was Master of the SALFORD CITY before it fell to me to load there. Having not done the swing at the Quarry Hole, nor even seen it done, I was glad on this first occasion that my Second Mate had executed the manoeuvre on the MANCUNIUM and was now on hand with sound advice.

We arrived in daylight, there was no sluicing current and little wind. Ian, the Second Mate, pointed out the marks on the small sandstone cliff and, keeping as close as possible to the north bank commensurate with good port propeller bank clearance, I endeavoured to complete as much of the swing as possible before gently "taking the putty".

Ian's quiet assurance that we would touch sand with the forefoot before sandstone with the bow was a more effective tranquiliser than a pipeful of thick twist. Nonetheless, I was somewhat nervous; mariners have an instinctive aversion to sailing towards solidity, even slowly, and when the ship finally touched the unseen sand we seemed very close to the cliff.

Immediately contact was made, the swing slowed as its centre moved from around amidships to right forward. An iron railing on the estuary side provided a good measure of swing rate as the ensign staff moved to transit with each rail in turn. Coming astern at first opportunity, the SALFORD CITY took the centre of the fairway and proceeded down to Runcorn.

Although the manoeuvre had been straightforward, I could well imagine the difficulties injected by adverse weather or sluicing ... a strong southerly would halt the later stages of the swing and a strong northerly could blow the ship ashore.

It was extremely difficult to make out the natural features used as markers during the hours of darkness, that is until one of our mates (one Black Angus) shinned down the cliff one weekend and highlighted as appropriate with white gloss. Although the paint eventually weathered away, by the time it had disappeared the Canal Company had positioned a couple of buoys to mark the approach. By time the buoys had been plucked by some errant ship, the manoeuvre been inculcated suuficiently to make it automatic ... in fine weather, that is.

The winter gales would send the Runcorn loader up to Warrington for the lee of high banks and buildings and safety of a bullnose to swing on. Sluicing after heavy rain or, below Latchford a level tide, also rendered a Quarry Hole swing difficult and sometimes impossible. Often, if sluicing wasn't too fierce, the Canal authority would close the sluice gates until the ship was round. But heavy sluicing, particularly if it involved the gates beside the Latchford Lock, just two miles up-Canal, gave a Warrington swing its own problems.

The MANCUNIUM, at 263ft, was the longest of the three smaller vessels in the five-ship fleet and was given a dispensation to swing at Warrington, being several feet over the recommended length for ships turning there.

Imagine a ship swinging in the open end of a letter V; as long as she is pivoting centrally on the bullnose there is adequate distance between the extremities of the vessel and the two tips of the 'V'. The vessel's chances of wedging between a rickety wharf on one side of the 'V' and an iron piling and concrete bank on the other are directly proportional to her beam distance from the bullnose, when across the line of the fairway. This should convey the dangers of a sluicing current, though, of course, in reality the base of the 'V' is not closed.

One night, I took the wheel at Chester Road bridge to allow the AB to assist on deck, and to see for myself the effects of the sluicing. Jim, the Officer-of-the-Watch, approached the bullnose, his positive use of engines against the current a testimony to his many year's experience.

I expected the swing to be quick because from her bullnose

fulcrum to forward the ship was in the main fairway where the sluicing current ran. The quick movement to starboard of this part should help press her up to her point of contact. If it didn't, then at least, with the stern in still water, she shouldn't soak downstream. But ...

Maybe the moving body of water met the forward part of the hull and having little other rapid means of escape, ran along the whole portside of the hull as the ship went broadside on to the Canal's course. Whatever the perverse hydrostatic law that was guarding its own integrity that night, I am cognizant of its effect, if not its principle.

The soak downstream happened so suddenly as to render consideration an impossibility; there was only time to pluck a decision from instinct. Jim beat me to the draw. I was just about to tell him to reverse everything to bring the bow back to port ... we would at least be narrowing our aspect ... when he increased the starboard engine to full astern, eased more balancing ahead revs into the port engine and built up the bow thrust revs at 'three o'clock'. Jim had played the card I'd have thrown away and there was no going back now ... it was win or bust with 'I'll stick', a prediction and not a statement of intent.

How much of the bow's dizzy movement against the backdrop of Warrington houses was owed to Jim's action? How much was rooted in unwanted lateral soak? My heart synchronised with the throbbing starboard Mirlees ... I was chewing blotting paper. Down aft, darkness and rapidity had turned the timbers of Naylor's Wharf into giant misshapen teeth, hungry for a bite of rudder and prop.

'We're going to wedge fast', I thought ... and 'fast' in its every sense! The AB forward signals to go astern, his face in the floodlight giving alarming indication of the bow/bank distance or lack of. The port engine is eased, but not stopped ... every force that translates to starboard swing is now crucial.

She's moving astern ... we're going to hit Naylor's ... we're still not clear forward ...

Suddenly the bow is pointing at Chester Road bridge, and the stern, in quieter water, moves rapidly away from the timbers it had been threatening to rearrange just seconds earlier. A sluice gate opens somewhere in the top of my head and relief floods through.

Maybe if we had reversed the swing with that first frightening soak ... maybe we would have succeeded; there would have been a healthy contribution from a "Full ahead" starboard engine assisting the bow thrust to move across the flood. Yes, we would still have soaked down the Canal, but it would have been with a decreasing aspect, bow and stern clear of obstruction. Maybe we could have middled her again, then proceeded up to our Davyhulme base ...

But never mind the "maybe"! Jim had made a brave, instant decision at a critical moment and he had been right ... the MANCUNIUM was alongside Naylor's and safe.

"Jim, that was dodgy," I exclaimed.

"Oh ye of little faith," he replied, but his smile did not eclipse the relief that coloured his features too starkly to stay hidden.

Luxuriating in the freedom of now being able to pick our own mood, we engaged philosophical gear and, between us, we decided that if we were to put the alleged truism, "A miss is as good as a mile" on trial for fraud, "Exhibit A" would be a partly used packet of washing powder.

When she was swinging at the Quarry Hole, the MANCUNIUM would only use her bow thrust for the initial and final stages of the manoeuvre; otherwise there was great danger of the intake grill clogging. Once she touched forward the movement of the ensign staff against the rails aft was painfully slow. The single plate rudder did not contribute much to proceedings; I'm sure it would have made no difference if the wheel had been put back amidships from its hard a'starboard lock. The position of the wheel fulfilled a psychological need rather than the ship's.

Only the turning moment of propellers opposed was, I'm sure, providing such movement as could be teased out of the old ship. It was heart-breaking when, after gaining hard-fought ground against wind or sluicing, it became obvious the battle was uneven and we had to retreat to Warrington. With both ends of the ship free and continuous bow thrust, the turn there was so quick that I would sometimes go to Warrington when fairly certain she could have managed at the Quarry Hole. Grumblings suggest displeasure at my judgement occasionally, but timing comparisons more often than not had us passing the ghost of others' intention still struggling at the Quarry Hole as the MANCUNIUM berthed at Runcorn, post-Warrington swing.

The PERCY DAWSON, built 22 years after the MANCUNIUM in 1968, had twin rudders to direct a more powerful flow along their axis. She could complete the Quarry Hole swing in a fraction of the time.

I remember a MANCUNIUM Officer swinging the PERCY DAWSON there the first time. Even in the imparted knowledge that the newer ship was much faster, he was startled by speed. The MANCUNIUM's lethargic efforts had so conditioned his approach to the operation that he looked quite shocked when the rails blurred down aft. However, he soon settled himself and relished in the novelty of a ship which was doing what he wanted when he wanted … and fast at that!

On warm summer days families would picnic on the flat grassland behind the sandstone cliff. The sight of a ship so near to their hamper must have added interest to their day but it was easy to identify a family observing our swing at the Quarry Hole for the first time. I'm sure I can script the words unheard to go with their actions seen.

"Look children! Here's a ship. Get ready to wave."
"Children stop eating. Gaze down Canal".
"Oh! The Captain's bringing her a bit closer for us."
Previously seated children now kneeling.
"He's turning, he's coming right at us! What does he think he's up to?"
Children and parents now standing.
"The daft beggar! He's going to hit the rock!"
Children and parents adopt flight posture. Retreat called off as she comes gently to a halt just a few feet from the rock face.

When the picnickers had gone home and the sun had gone down, the courting couples would arrive. They parked their cars so as to be obscured from the road, but this left them visible from the Canal. Not that the ship's crew would be interested in their goings-on, but angular deflection of the Aldis to transfer the beam from rock face to car window was so slight that trespass was to be forgiven now and again.

What sudden light from an unexpected source does for the composure of young lovers, sudden smoke from an unexpected place does for the composure of the ship's Officer.

One of the MANCUNIUM's clutches had been screaming all day. We had all, Master and Mates, nursed it, coaxing out the revs with gentle cumulative movements of the telegraph. It would expedite our programme if we could keep running until Friday's maintenance day. An ability to proceed on one engine, and the bow thrust facility, placed the decision well within the prudent safety threshold.

By the time the vessel came to swing at the Quarry Hole that night, our nursing had seemingly resulted in an improvement in the health of the patient; the clutch appeared to have bedded in, its screaming had become less frequent.

I pressed "Thrust Stop" and a short time later the bow lifted almost perceptibly as the forefoot touched the sand.

Now the extra strain came on the engines and clutches as cavitating increased and the forward turning moment lay trapped under the bow. Slowly now did the ensign staff tally each rail; more frequently now did the clutch scream its complaint.

Suddenly the intervals between screams joined up and grew louder and as if that diabolical din wasn't enough to unnerve me, smoke poured out of the engine-room skylight. I stopped both engines and rushed to the phone.

"You beat me to the draw," said the laconic voice at the other end. "I'm in the Wendy House, it's all smoke, there's no fire, but there will be if you try again."

The tone of a man long-resigned to the eccentricities of others was soothing this time, its familiarity dragging normality back from the wings toward centre stage.

The same smoke had billowed out of an open engine-room door on the main deck, where it had been seen by Bosun Stan and Seaman Harry. Their reactions had been unbelievably fast. I caught sight of them just as I put the phone down, grabbed the megaphone and bawled "Don't go down, everything's OK." Stan, already rhythmically foot-pumping the bellows, gave three tugs on the line attached to the harness (a nice touch when a tap on the shoulder would have done) and Harry withdrew his foot from the other side of the engine-room door.

I knew there was no fire … Stan and Harry didn't; I knew the Second Engineer was safe … Stan and Harry didn't. Had there been anyone prostrate on the plates, he would have been lifted to safety in the shortest possible time.

Later, while the clutch was being renewed, I wrote a letter commending the action of the two men. I never did receive a reply and they did not hear any more about it.

There are many forms of discipline in ships … some subtle, some blunt, some formal, some not so. But it's what happens in an emergency that really puts the team to the test.

The most important discipline of all can only dwell on a plane that is completely horizontal. That was the message finally signalled by the acrid smoke from the screaming clutch the night we swung for Runcorn at the Quarry Hole.

Thank you, Captain Dave Ramwell. In all honesty, I cannot claim to have understood all that cavorting on the Manchester Ship Canal. Having been trained, in the rather distant past, to fly an aeroplane in wartime ... it seemed easier, as all that was required of us was to go up and down and basically forward. Dave obviously was into gyrations and backward flips ... we could cope with gyrating but, as far as I recall, I never ever went backwards.

We cannot let Dave depart without a peep at his colourful career ... his own words, of course.

I joined Palm Line in January 1961, my desire to go to sea cemented by an anonymous arsonist who burnt the Scout hut down, which resulted in my joining the Sea Cadet Corps.

My time in Sea Cadets made up to some extent for my lack of pre-sea training of the formal variety, and gave me the opportunity to boast to my grandchildren that I once spent a week aboard Britain's last Battleship, VANGUARD. (Cost me a whole eight bob.)

I joined my first ship, NIGER PALM, in Rotterdam. She was fitted with a triple expansion reciprocating steam engine ... i.e. an "up and downer". (I remember the amazed Chief Engineer of an American ship in Genoa chasing his Apprentices across to have a look at the "Goddamned floating museum" parked over the way...)

My next ship, the renamed ex-TEMA PALM, was MAKURDI PALM, an ex-German vessel and another up and downer. She often confused Pilots who didn't know how to categorise her type on their official paper; she was half dry cargo ... with three holds and the rest was tank space. The tanks carried palm or groundnut oil.

I was delighted to be sent as Senior Apprentice to the LAGOS PALM. She was on the mail run and trips could be as short as six weeks ... a brevity especially appreciated in view of my having just become engaged to be married.

Well, I made it to the Church, got married to my wife, Julie, and we soon started a family. Much as I enjoyed sea life, I wanted to see more of my family and, having by this time obtained my First Mate's 'Foreign Going' Certificate, I applied ... unsuccessfully ... for a Helmsman's position on the Manchester Ship Canal.

At the interview, the Pilot Manager told me there was a long waiting list, but, he asked, had I heard there could be a job going on the Sewage Sludge vessel belonging to Manchester Corporation Rivers' Department? My adverse preconceived notions as to what that ship looked like were dispelled by a visit to where she lay berthed just below Barton Locks. She was named MANCUNIUM, was exceptionally clean, with pleasant accommodation ... though there was a tell-tale whiff about her.

February 26th, 1968, my First Mate's Certificate stamped to show I'd passed Master HT, I joined MANCUNIUM as Second Mate. I was 24.

Occasionally I'd be seconded to Salford Corporation's SALFORD CITY in the reciprocal training programme Manchester had with Salford. Two years after first sailing as Relief Master, I was appointed permanent Master on the SALFORD CITY in 1972. Two years later the ships all fell under the management of the newly established North West Water Authority.

We had many adventures in the different ships over the years. I was on MANCUNIUM when the Canal just astern ignited and killed several men. After striking the gates in Eastham small lock, I was told in the subsequent enquiry that I nearly succeeded in doing in thirty seconds what the Luftwaffe had failed to do in six years. Collisions, groundings (gentle!), rudders falling off ... sounds bad, but the close quarters and time scale gives it less alarming perspective.

At the end of 1998 under a European edict all dumping at sea ended and the two crews were made redundant. We had a farewell party in a pub on the Dock Road which prompted the landlord to remark ... his eyes brimming with nostalgia ... "It's just like the old days."

The crews still keep in touch, most of us meeting up once a year in a large Liverpool pub sometime in November. We tell and retell all the old tales and thoroughly enjoy our nostalgic wallows.

That was the Dave Ramwell story ... and many thanks again to Sea Breezes for allowing publication.

John Tebay
Liverpool Pilot

Anyone who has any knowledge of Liverpool and the maritime world will remember John Tebay with love and affection. Certainly he was a Mersey Pilot, but his career made him a source of all knowledge and, if you had a problem ... "Ask John Tebay!" In retirement, he became involved with the Merseyside Maritime Museum and with the Liverpool Nautical Research Society ... he was a superb 'Bag Carrying' pilot, known and respected nationally and internationally. His Pilot son, Tom, happily affords us a tale or two about his father.

ALL GREEK TO ME

About 30 years ago, in the late 70s, he was on the Pilot launch at Point Lynas on the way to board a rather old and dilapidated Greek tanker bound for Eastham Locks and Stanlow. The weather was not good, and, unfortunately, the ship was already running late for the tide. As the launch approached the ship's side, it was quite apparent the Captain had failed to make a proper lee, and the ladder, which was damaged and lopsided, appeared to be too high to step onto safely. Despite several requests from the Coxswain of the Pilot launch for the Captain to bring his ship onto a proper heading and for the crew to lower the ladder nothing was happening and valuable time was being lost.

My father decided that to waste any more time would probably mean the ship missing the tide, and instructed the Coxswain to move in close to the ship's side so he could make a carefully timed 'leap' onto the rickety old ladder.

The launch was crashing up and down in the swell and by now the ship was rolling heavily. As he reached for the ladder, the launch slipped into a short sea and he lost his footing, managing only to get one knee on the bottom rung, but thanks to a good grip with both his hands, soon had both his feet on the ladder, which, to his horror, was covered in oil.

When he finally got to the Bridge, the Captain greeted him somewhat indifferently and apparently oblivious to everything, including the layer of crude oil that was covering his clothing. Looking straight at the Captain, he said "If you ever come to Point Lynas again for your Pilot without making a proper lee and with a ladder in that dreadful condition then so far as I'm concerned you can go to The Crack of Doom".

The Captain looked slightly perplexed and disappeared behind the curtain into the Chartroom. Over the next ten or fifteen minutes there was a lot of mumbling and shouting in Greek and the sound of chart drawers being opened and shut.

Presently, the Captain re-appeared, and addressed my Father directly.

"Please Mr. Pilot, I have looked at all my charts, but I cannot find this place. Where is this place you call 'The Crack of Doom"?

Tom has another one. The second story is in the days before radar was commonplace, obviously pre-war. A predecessor of Tom's found himself on the Bridge of a large ship inward bound to Liverpool from Point Lynas.

BY GUESS AND BY GOD

Soon after boarding the ship the visibility had quickly reduced, and now in thick fog, the Pilot had only a dead reckoning position with allowance for tide to find the Bar light ship.

Some time later, the visibility improved enough to allow the Pilot to catch a glimpse of the North West light float ship pass the ship on the port side. The Pilot also noticed that no one else on the Bridge had seen this.

Knowing the exact course and distance now to the Bar light ship, he was able to quickly calculate when the ship would arrive.

The Pilot, a well known personality of the time, instructed the Midshipman to fetch a strong bucket, attach it to a lanyard and collect a sample of sea water from the ship side. The 'Middy' was to bring the bucket to the Bridge together with an empty glass and a tumbler of fresh drinking water.

As the Pilot, and a respected man of local knowledge, no one questioned this request. There was, however, considerable interest on the Bridge, particularly from the Captain when the bucket of sea water arrived and the Pilot took samples of it to taste, rolling it around in his mouth, spitting it out and alternating it with drinking water, apparently to clear his palate and even smelling it like a wine taster. Finally, holding it up to the light and dipping his fingers into it, the Pilot announced that by his reckoning, the ship would pass very close to the Bar Light ship in exactly thirty minutes time. Extra lookouts were posted ahead and aloft, and then before long, the fog signal could be heard, and then later at exactly the time predicted, right ahead, out of the swirling fog, so close that the Pilot instructed a hard a starboard to the astounded Helmsman, there it was … the Bar Lightship.

As the saying goes "A Pilot is a Man of Local Knowledge".

Thank you, Tom ... I enjoyed that. And here is one which John Tebay wrote for the Liverpool Nautical Research Society.

HOUND OF THE SEA

On the 13th February, 1980 a Boeing jetfoil, to be named CU NA MARA ... (HOUND OF THE SEA) ... arrived in Gladstone Dock on the deck of the ANTONIA JOHNSON. Built in Seattle, and intended for the B. & I. Line, she was to carry 250 passengers on a three and a quarter hour passage between Liverpool and Dublin at approximately 45 knots.

Foreknowledge of the B. & I.'s plans had resulted in prior meetings between representatives of the Port and Pilotage Authorities and senior B. & I. staff, when safety and practical operational aspects were discussed. Prior to the CU NA MARA coming into service, there were to be at least six weeks of working-up trials and crew training. Initially, an American Bridge team of Captain and Engineer would instruct a small number of selected B. & I. Masters and Mates until they were officially qualified to operate the craft. Amongst the Port of Liverpool's requirements would be the employment of a Liverpool Pilot when navigating the River and Mersey channels. The Pilots to be used would have to be current members of the Pilotage and Examination Committees and would report back on any potential problems whilst in the Pilotage area.

B. & I. also suggested that, before the jetfoil arrived, a small team should travel to Brighton to have a look at a similar craft then running a service to Dieppe. This team consisted of Captain G. Barry (B. & I. Line Commodore), Captain J. Devaney (Superintendent, Dublin), Captain A. Jones (B. & I. , Liverpool), and Pilots Tebay and Webber. Arriving at the Brighton Marina, I think it is fair to say that, considering the craft was intended to carry 250 passengers across the Irish Sea, she looked a mite small ... actually 99 feet long with the foils up, and 30 feet beam ... and she was moving gently in the sheltered waters. Whilst manoeuvering when sailing or berthing, the jetfoil did so in displacement mode (i.e. floating on the hull), and with a vectored jet aft and a small bow thrust forward she could turn in her own length. Displacement speed was about 10 knots. In this trim and once out in a slight swell, she tended to roll uncomfortably, probably due to her flattish hull and light draft. However as she swiftly accelerated past 30 knots with the foils down, she rose up and became pleasantly steady, the twin 4,500 hp gas turbines drawing in water at the leading edge of the engine pod and ejecting it with great force through the rear jets. Despite the speed of 43 knots with her hull clear of the water, she did not appear to make a broad or high wash, and from a passenger seat on the upper of two decks it was like being in a low-flying aircraft as we skimmed the waves. This sensation was encouraged by the seating layout being similar to a wide-bodied jet, plus the use of aviation terminology such as 'take off' or 'landing'. On the Bridge ('cockpit'?) the instruments were grouped in a semicircle around the two command seats.

On arriving at Dieppe, the Captain kept the power on as we entered the harbour, and if it was intended to impress, it certainly induced some palpitation in this observer! However, once he 'lifted the handles' the power fell off and, dropping back into displacement mode, she lost way immediately. From a navigational point of view, we noted how quickly the crossing situations built up with the traffic in the Channel, and how it involved some re-interpretation as to the visual assessments on radar.

In the third week of February 1980, the Mersey trials and training began. If the CU NA MARA was in Liverpool, she would be berthed in the Waterloo system. Joining time for those required was around 0730 and we would be in the river by 0830. With Langton abeam, she would be up on the foils and passing the Rock at 43 knots through the water. Initially at this speed it took some time to adjust as to how quickly we closed with other vessels. The same applied for the other port users! The CU NA MARA could come off the foils and thereby bring up very quickly (actually five seconds from full speed), she would then need a clear straight stretch to take off again.

Apart from the River and Bar Lightfloat shake-down trips, the runs to Dublin also started in February 1980. As it was neither practical nor desirable to discharge (or pick up) a Pilot at Liverpool Bar, I would carry on for the passage to Dublin, and then make the return trip. In good weather it would be quite a novelty to be passing Lynas Pilot station in little over seventy minutes after leaving the stage! With reasonable weather the trip was a pleasure, but if the sea and swell started to increase beyond four to five feet, it became less comfortable. Whilst not rolling or pitching, there would be an element of slamming or jerkiness, and as the tops of the seas hit the bottom of the exposed hull, it made an unsettling noise. An operating limit ten feet (three metres) wave height had been imposed. On the trip from Dublin something went wrong and we started to 'porpoise' ... that was not at all pleasant and we had to 'land' whilst the fault was rectified. Fortunately the passengers had seatbelts. On the humorous side was the astonishment registered by the seagulls as they made their customary 'laid-back' take off from near the bows and suddenly realized that they were not going to make it!

Full passenger services commenced on 25th April 1980, but inevitably the Irish Sea had plenty of weather tricks to play. As a result, trips were cancelled to an unacceptable degree, and unreliability of service is a quick commercial killer. After the summer season of 1981, the jetfoil service was wound up. I understand that the CU NA MARA was sold to the Japanese and renamed GINGA, which sounds not an unreasonable name for a hound!

Let there be another item from John Tebay.

M.T. MYRINA

On the evening of the 2nd January, 1976, I was on turn as an inward Pilot on the Bar Pilot Boat, sheltering in the River during a westerly gale.

At approximately 2045 hours, I was informed that I was to be boarded immediately on M.T. MYRINA, 208,000 tons deadweight, the vessel having broken away from Tranmere Oil Stage. Pilot launch, PUFFIN, took me from the Pilot cutter towards the MYRINA, which was then S.E. of Pluckinton Bank Buoy and heading about N.N.W. River conditions were extremely bad with an exceptionally high wind and a confused sea being aggravated by a strong flood tide.

Conditions aboard MYRINA were also difficult, so that it took about twenty minutes before the Pilot hoist was rigged and the PUFFIN was able to get alongside. Contact had been established by V.H.F. from PUFFIN to MYRINA, but communications were difficult. However, the Master of the MYRINA was advised and was endeavouring to get his vessel towards the west side of the River and away from shoal water.

Three tugs in the vicinity were requested to help by pushing on the starboard side of the vessel, but they were experiencing difficulties in the bad conditions. At approximately 2110 hours the MYRINA appeared to have taken the ground aft and swung to a heading of about N.E., presumably with the bow ashore as well. At this point I was able to board the vessel.

From then on, both anchors and available tugs were used in an attempt to get MYRINA head to tide and wind, but despite combined efforts this did not stop the vessel slowly setting towards the S.E. until she brought up across Garston Bar heading at about 030.

At about 2140, Pilot Westwood had joined and it was later decided to attempt to bring the ship off at near High Water (2358 hours) using the available tugs on the starboard side and with the most powerful boat made fast aft. Despite these efforts being reinforced with full main engine power from between half an hour before until one hour after High Water, the MYRINA remained fast aground. Both anchors had been lifted and stowed during this time. At 0130, the attempt was abandoned and soundings taken around the vessel with thought as to the ship's safety over Low Water and the next attempt at flotation on the day tide.

Plans were made for the subsequent attempt and these were put into operation during the morning of the 3rd January. At approximately 1130 hours, MYRINA started to lift clear and, although main engines were not then available, the tugs were deployed to the most advantageous use and the vessel brought away from the bank at about 1200 hours and towed stern first to a position of comparative safety off Tranmere Jetty. At about 1330 hours, main engine power became available and MYRINA was swung and taken to sea.

During the course of all these operations, MYRINA came into contact with both G.1 and G.2 and with Pluckinton Bank whilst swinging to proceed to sea.

This script is John Tebay's report to the Pilotage Committee. Wind speeds were in excess of 70 knots and MYRINA had been discharging a full cargo of crude oil when she had broken free of her moorings. A total of fourteen tugs were deployed in the successful operation to refloat the MYRINA, which was drydocked in Rotterdam and after repair carried on trading for another five years before being scrapped.

There is no doubt that his courage and the endeavours of himself and fellow Pilot, 'Jock' Westwood, contributed to avoiding a major environmental disaster on the Mersey and there is obviously no need to add anything to this account.

Thank you, Tom Tebay. Great memories of your father!

Captain Peter Daniel
Master Mariner

Captain Peter Daniel has excelled himself in producing a photograph of himself with his mother and father enjoying a Christmas lunch aboard LANDFALL in 1948. His Father was a member of the Master Mariners Club.

That young lad was to become a Master Mariner and here are some memories.

SHIP'S SURGEON

I was the Master on a vessel en route from Panama to New Zealand and I was having a pre-dinner drink in the Officers' Bar. It was the Electrician's birthday and we were pushing the boat out.

The Chief Officer appeared at the smoke-room door with the West Indian Bosun, and a towel covering the Bosun's left hand. The Mate said to me, "How are you at the sight of blood, Captain?" "Why?" I replied. He took the towel off the Bosun's hand ... the Bosun was carrying the second finger of his left hand in a towel. He had severed his finger whilst working on deck.

The Mate and I took him down to the ship's hospital. I gave him morphine, but it took three of us to hold him down whilst the morphine took effect. I prepared sutures and a steriliser and set about right away to sew the finger back on. There was no air-conditioning in the hospital and it was like an oven.

The operation took about half an hour. I dressed the finger, and by this time the morphine had taken effect and the Bosun had passed out.

I had an Officer keeping a watch on the Bosun through the night. That night I did not sleep. I kept thinking if I had sewn the finger with the nail facing the right way and not back-to-front. We were still two weeks from New Zealand. The Bosun came to in the morning. I gave him aspirin, but I could not examine the finger as the blood had congealed to the dressing. In fact I could not change the dressing throughout the voyage.

On arrival at Wellington, the Bosun was sent to hospital and he returned to the vessel four hours later with a letter. Much to my surprise, the finger had healed perfectly and the hospital could not have done better! And to prove it the Bosun was waving his finger, much to his delight.

I sailed with the same Bosun at a later date and he was always grateful to me for saving his finger.
I was always tickled to find a copy of The Ship's Captain's Medical Guide in the Master's bookcase and we always smiled at the details on the final page of that useful volume ... Burial at Sea. It was the ultimate long-stop. Of course, all Merchant Navy Officers acquired a First Aid Certificate through the Red Cross. I am told that when first appointed as Master, the poor

victim was sent for a couple of days to the A & E Department. There he would observe all the gory activity and at some point was given a chunk of severed pork to practise his suturing art. In the fairly recent olden days there was always the radio telephone, but today with satellite and T.V. and cameras there is much more guidance available. But, however clever that might be, the Captain is still at the sharp end!

Peter has other anecdotes

HOLY ORDERS

Whilst sailing in the same Company en route from Honduras to New York, I was informed by the Agent that I would be taking two passengers ... two Catholic nuns would be joining the vessel around 11 p.m., We were due to sail in the early hours of the morning.

We had an Owners' Suite on that vessel, in which we could carry two passengers. I turned in sharply that night ready for sailing in the early hours. I got up at midnight and thought that I would look at the Owners' Suite, the door being on the hook, to see if the passengers had everything. I was greeted by a rather attractive nun dressed in jeans and sweater. "I am Sister Mary and this is Sister Angelina." Sister Mary was an American from New York and Sister Angelina was from Belize. "I hope you don't mind carrying a couple of off-beat nuns with you, Captain, and if we leave our habits off." "Not at all," I replied.

We sailed around 0200 hours. At about 0830 the Nuns arrived in the dining saloon for breakfast, dressed in jeans and sweaters. They were, of course, the talk of the ship.

That evening at dinner, the Refrigeration Engineer Officer, who always missed meals, apart from liquid ones, decided to join us at table. Coffee was served in the lounge, and at the end of dinner, the Refrigeration Engineer, who was, shall we say, rather on the stout side, decided to put his arms around the two nuns and lead them into the lounge for coffee and drinks. The three of them got stuck in the doorway leading from the saloon. I said to the Chief Engineer, have a word with the Refrigeration Engineer, he has already had too much to drink.

At coffee and liqueurs, the nuns decided to leave early. I thought that the least that I could do was to go and apologise to them for the behaviour of one of my Officers. They were taking a stroll around the boat deck. "Don't worry," said Sister Mary, "Sister Angelina here has a black belt in judo. We both teach at a convent in La Ceba, Honduras and when we have a roll-call in the mornings, if any of the girls are missing, we telephone their parents. More often than not, we are told they should have arrived at school by now. Sister Angelina knows exactly where they will be. She has been in every brothel in La Ceba and pulled them out with a sharp clip around their ears and drags them back to the convent. So, Captain, you have nothing to worry about, because Sister Angelina can look after herself."

And there was more from Peter Daniels.

PERESTROIKA

Another time I was on a vessel around Central America, carrying bananas. We called at Turbo, a small banana port in Columbia. There was no berth, but you loaded bananas direct from barges in mid-stream.

One of the engineers injured his back working in the engine room. There was a Russian vessel anchored close by, and as every Russian vessel carries a doctor, I called up on VHF and spoke to the Captain. I asked if his doctor would examine our engineer. As this was in the 1970s, at the height of the cold war, the Russian Captain agreed, but explained that it would not be possible for a Russian doctor to visit a British ship. We therefore lowered one of our lifeboats, and sent the Engineer across to the other vessel on a stretcher, accompanied by the Chief Officer.

After about two hours, the lifeboat returned with the patient. The patient had been given lotion and pills. All the directions were written in Russian. I naturally thanked the Captain on the VHF, but thought a nice gesture would be to present him with a bottle of whisky.

The following morning I visited the Russian ship by lifeboat with the bottle of whisky. After long negotiations at the gangway with the Commissar, the Communist Party Leader, I was shown to the Captain's cabin. He was having breakfast with his Agent. I was welcomed with open arms and offered coffee and vodka. As it was too early for vodka, I joined him for coffee.

We got into deep conversation about world affairs in general. The Commissar was present. The Russian Captain then said to me: "If all the world's heads of state were seafarers, Captain, then there would be no more trouble in the world." How right he was! Since then I have sailed on foreign flag vessels, being the only European on board, having in one vessel seven nationalities, Muslims, Philippinos, Indians, Chinese, Burmese, Thai and Tamil Tigers. Everyone got on well together, there was no friction. It was one of the happiest ships that I sailed in. They all took their turn in the galley, cooking their own speciality dishes.

Shortly after that voyage, I was on charter to the M.O.D. in the South Atlantic towards the end of the Falkland's conflict. The company I was in traded to South America, including Argentina. A number of the Officers were married to Argentine women and lived in Argentina and had taken up Argentine citizenship. Our Chief Engineer was one and unfortunately his son was doing National Service in the Argentine Navy. He was serving in the BELGRANO when she was sunk. Luckily he survived.

I often think now what the Russian Captain said to me ... If all the heads of state in the world were seafarers, there would be no trouble.

Perhaps I too should not have been surprised that, after working in the Mission for some thirty years with seafarers from all over the world, my outlook on life had changed. I had met all colours and creeds, I had shared the lives of committed men of all faiths, had acquired deep insight into the joys and pains of mankind and had slowly reached a conclusion which might be challenged by my Church ... we are all brothers and sisters and there truly can be only one God. If I had been born in Bombay (is it really called Mumbai these days?), I would probably have been a Hindu! But, Captain Peter Daniels has not quite exhausted his repertoire.

DOLLARS

When I was working for a foreign flag company, based in Hong Kong, I had to fly out to a ship in Mexico, via Miami. The crew were paid in U.S. dollars and the owners had given me $50,000 U.S. dollars to take out to the ship. When I arrived at Miami, the coloured lady Customs Officer shouted, "Hey, guys, there's a Limey here with $50,000 ... let's have a party." Thanks very much I thought, as everyone in the queue now knew that I was loaded with cash. If I went to the toilet on the plane, I made sure I had the cash on me and not in my brief case. Was I glad when I arrived safely on board without getting mugged!

Thank you Captain Peter Daniels.

Captain David Allen
Master Mariner

Captain David Allen, an ex-Master of the Club, has other claims to fame. In the 70s he was Staff Officer in H.M.S. EAGLET and retired from the Royal Navy in 1975. Next, he was in charge of a dumb barge (no means of motivation!) burying pipelines in the North Sea. Back at sea with Mobil, even though he had his Master's Certificate of Service from the Navy, he completed his Master's Certificate of Competency in Liverpool in 1980. Seven years later he became Deputy Naval Regional Officer, West Midlands and North West. David is the perfect example of a Naval Officer who became a Merchant Navy Master and a R.N.R. List One Officer.

LAMBARENE

In October 1961, while I was serving in H.M.S. DIANA in West Africa, we visited the Gabon port of Libreville and during that port call some of us from the ship had the opportunity of visiting Doctor Albert Schweitzer's mission hospital at Lambarene ... those of you who are of my generation will of course know of whom I am speaking but may I for a few moments remind you of some of his achievements. He was born in France in 1875 and studied theology and philosophy at the Universities of Paris, Strasbourg and Berlin. He also became a world renowned authority on music and was an accomplished organist. At the age of thirty, however, he commenced new studies in medicine and on qualifying went out to Gabon, then a French African colony, to establish the hospital and effectively spent the rest of his life there. He was awarded the Nobel Peace prize in 1952 and was made an honorary member of our Order of Merit.

The party was flown from Libreville to Lambarene by the Gabon Air Force in a transport aircraft with, I might add, few modern day passenger comforts; Lambarene is situated about thirty miles south of the Equator on the banks of the river Ogowe. On arrival at the town's airport, we transferred briefly to lorries, which took us to the river where we then embarked in boats for the final stage of our journey to the famous hospital. Doctor Schweitzer, who was by then 85, personally met us at the jetty and conducted the tour of the hospital himself. He still stood very upright, remained active and looked remarkably fit despite the obvious strains of working for so much of his life in equatorial climes, where disease was inevitably rife. During our visit he spoke only French but his commentary was translated very ably for us by a charming Dutch nurse, who naturally impressed the young unmarried Lieutenant of the day! Out of doors Doctor Schweitzer wore his characteristic white pith helmet but indoors he removed it and then appeared to match the impression we had of him in those days with long flowing hair and a bushy moustache.

Most of the medical staff were either French or Swiss, but there were also Belgians, Dutch, Germans, Norwegians and one American and one Japanese. The staff had their own separate accommodation and mess room. Several of Doctor Schweitzer's own family had worked in the hospital and some were still there at the time.

The hospital was built primarily to treat those still suffering from leprosy. Most of the patients brought along with them members of their families, many of their personal belongings and even their domestic animals. The village was, therefore, swarming with dogs, goats, ducks and hens that sheltered under the raised floors of the huts. Even a young monkey had been adopted by a mongrel bitch that escorted us throughout the tour of the hospital; whenever the youngster was tired it jumped on to its adopted Mum's back for a few moments and took a ride. We also saw several parrots, but these were generally kept chained or caged.

The wards were all crowded and not especially clean ... MRSA seemed not, however, to be a problem there! The patients we saw appeared happy and seemed pleased to have European visitors. The cleanest ward was the maternity ward where the babies slept peacefully in small wooden cots, covered with mosquito nets ... remarkably we heard little crying. The drugs and medical equipment, which seemed old but adequate and perfectly hygienic, were kept in separate rooms. One resident in the village had arrived five years earlier and had since refused to leave ... she was of pygmy origin and spoke no known dialect. She continued to live primitively and occasionally stole food and firewood from others in the village and became violent if any attempt was made to take it back from her.

We learnt that Doctor Schweitzer was loath to institute any major changes to the way of life there because he preferred the natives to retain the lifestyle they knew best. They clearly had great faith in him as a doctor and healer and travelled huge distances to be treated by him. For me that was a particularly memorable day and I feel privileged to have had the opportunity of meeting him.

When David Allen first left the Royal Navy in 1975 he found a job with a firm of maritime civil engineers, which fortuitously was based just a few miles from his home in the Wirral; the company doctor was also his own GP and a good friend! Land and Marine Engineering were specialists in burying oil and gas pipelines and these skills were much in demand at that time. The company's engineers designed their own trenching equipment, which was fitted to their own dumb barges. His first non-naval command was as the Master of one of these, on the strength of his Master's Certificate of Service.

POST-R.N. REINCARNATION

The barge was towed when underway by tugs but positioned for trenching operations using several anchors; the vessel was fitted with eight. Once in position the trenching machine was lowered to the seabed and water-jetting commenced. When the trench had been dug the pipeline would sink into it and be covered in due course by the regular action of the sea.

Inevitably such operations were often very slow. During one operation in July 1975, when the barge was working off Peterhead, it took fourteen hours to move the barge just over a mile - truly snail's pace!

Although accommodation was available in some of the barges operated by the company the staff and crew members were frequently billeted ashore. On one occasion the staff were living in a hotel at Hillswick in the remote north western part of the largest island in the Shetland group, simply known as Mainland, and the proprietors had recently employed two young Filipino waitresses, whose English was by no means perfect. One evening when being served fruit salad as the dessert several of our group asked for cream to add to it. The girls kindly brought salad cream but had to have explained that this was not what was required. Despite their acute embarrassment they retained their beautiful smiles throughout the rest of our stay and were very good friends thereafter. At the time they must have been some of the earliest Filipinos to be employed anywhere in the UK.

BOAT PEOPLE

Some twenty years later in 1981, in the South China Sea, I was Second Officer in a product carrier and I had been in the employ of Mobil for about four years. Around midday we encountered a group of Vietnamese boat people, crammed together in a small boat. The boat was about thirty five feet in length and relatively crudely built; we estimated that there were approximately eighty people onboard. The boat was equipped with both an inboard engine, probably diesel, and an outboard one, which drove a very deep propeller ... this latter engine was not running, probably, we believed, because there was no fuel for it. In the wheelhouse we were able to see a crudely fitted magnetic compass and a well worn and probably out of date chart; the boat flew a simple white flag on a bamboo pole. As the boat approached our ship we had to request that the crew extinguish a small fire they had on the deckhouse, presumably for cooking ... this they readily understood and complied immediately.

The boat people comprised women and small children and mainly young men ... there seemed to be very few older men. Three youths who stood on the deckhouse appeared to be in charge of the group, although there may have been someone with greater sea experience in the wheelhouse. The main spokesman for the party, however, was a girl of barely twenty, who had an excellent working knowledge of the English language.

When their boat first came alongside, the group inevitably asked to board but, because of' company rules of the day, we were not permitted to let them do that. If their boat had been unseaworthy, we would, of course, have been able to embark them and land them at our next port, which was to be Singapore. We did, however, transfer certain stores to them ... fresh water, fuel, milk, rice, bread, butter, some simple medical stores, an up to date chart and some cigarettes, all of which they appeared to be very grateful for. They hoped to reach Malaysia and we, therefore, pointed them in. the right direction ... at the time they were some two hundred miles off the Mekong delta and about four hundred and fifty miles north east of Singapore. We had a duty to report their position to the United Nations refugee agency in Geneva and it was expected that they would be intercepted and probably picked up by an American warship, which was kept in the area specifically for that task. The great concern of the boat people, however, was that their position should not be made known to the Russians, who were staunch allies of the North Vietnamese at that time. Clearly they hated the Communist regime and were prepared to take the greatest risks to escape from it. We had, therefore, to have the greatest admiration for them. Sadly we never heard anything more of then, but obviously we would like to think that they were successful in their undertaking.

EARLY COMMAND EXPERIENCE

David Allen first took command of a powered merchant vessel on 8 October 1981 and quickly gained experience of a Panama Canal transit ... and all its perils! He joined a Mobil lightering tanker at Balboa, took passage south to Puerto Bayovar in Peru with his predecessor still in charge but once the ship sailed from that port he finally enjoyed the full responsibility of command and one of the first major tasks was to complete the return transit of the Panama Canal.

The ship entered the canal before daylight and perhaps the most daunting part was, on the advice of the pilots, driving the ship towards the inner lock gates at a considerable speed and waiting for the water cushion to stop the ship before it struck them. The cushion was effective but for a new master, who had only been in command a few days, there were a few nervous moments - and a few concerns that his command would not last long!

STOP ENGINES!

In May 1982, when I was on only my second trip as Master, I had the horrifying experience of having my ship, a Mobil lightering tanker, drift with a total power failure towards a bridge straddling the Delaware River.

We had discharged our cargo of crude oil at Paulsboro oil terminal and had just sailed from the berth. The tugs had slipped, but were fortunately still not too far away. We suffered a complete electrical and propulsion failure and started drifting towards a pillar of the bridge.

I had visions of the ship severing the bridge span and watching cars and other vehicles tumbling into the river. I remembered seeing a film which featured that very theme!

In order to prevent us causing a major disaster, I ordered the starboard anchor to be let go. Although the cable ran out to its full extent and the brake band burnt, the anchor successfully dredged on the river bed and thus slowed our progress. That gave us sufficient time to secure four tugs, which were then able to hold our position on the side of the channel while effecting repairs.

It was indeed an anxious time for a relatively new Master!

VOYAGE UP THE AMAZON

During my time with Mobil I sailed twice in a product carrier up to Manaus, which is almost one thousand miles from the open sea. The sheer size of the River Amazon is perhaps the feature that impresses one the most. Its entrance is over two hundred miles wide and the distance travelled to Manaus is greater than the length of the British Isles. Even at this inland city it is still over a mile wide and what is more amazing is that smaller ships can continue upriver another thirteen hundred miles.

When I completed this transit, in October and November 1984, the river level was comparatively low. In the middle of the rainy season (January) that level can rise by up to fifty feet and hence the shape of banks and islands may alter radically. Native huts near the river have to be built on stilts to prevent them being swept away. The downriver passage is made much more rapidly and ships may achieve speeds of up to twenty knots.

Thank you, Captain David Allen. I suspect that your career is the widest of all the Master Mariners in the Club.

Gerry Davies
Master Mariner

Many seafarers progressed to obtaining their Master's Certificate, but never sailed as Master and Captain of a ship. Gerry Davies is such a person. He sailed with Shell, Esso and Elder Dempster before coming ashore and later becoming a Chief Port Health Inspector ... a post he held for many years.

What is the task of Port Health Inspector? The dangers were evident in the 14th century when the Black Death swept Europe, killing millions of people. The Venetians in the next century introduced a quarantine system ... ships were detained for forty days (hence the word 'quarantine'). In this country, we tried with difficulty to deal with the problems and the first Quarantine Act was introduced in 1710. Many decades were  to pass before Public Health became a matter of concern. The first Act to control shipping was in 1866, and in 1872 Port Sanitary Authorities came into being, under the control of local government. In the early days of the last century, the Authority accepted the responsibility for the importation of disease. Times now have changed and, in reality, air travel poses a far greater threat. Today the main function is the inspection of imported food, pest control and the issue of de-ratting certificates, although containers have almost eliminated that problem. Port Health Authorities have no direct responsibilities in relation to crew accommodation, but, by use of Section 'Bluff', the most used section of the Act, there have been many cases where improvements have been secured, long before the introduction of Port State Control.

Gerry Davies obtained his Masters (Foreign-going) Certificate in 1955 and came ashore the following year to qualify as a Public Health Inspector. In 1966 he was transferred to become a Port Health Inspector and, in 1972, was the Chief Inspector.

Here is one of his tales.

THE SKUNK!

When one becomes involved in pest control, two things are very quickly learned. The first is that all rats are at least as big as a fully-grown domestic cat ... it would seem that they are that size from birth! The second is the rather strange fact that no two people have ever seen the same rat. If there are six sightings, there must be at least six rats ... the possibility of two people seeing the same rat does not exist. Scepticism becomes instinctive in my trade.

One Saturday lunchtime, my wife and I had just sat down for a well-earned G and T after the weekly trip to the supermarket, when I received a telephone call from the Royal Seaforth Dock. The message was that a docker had seen a skunk on board a South Korean ship discharging packaged timber.

I had no idea what a skunk looked like and I thought it highly unlikely that the docker knew either. I vaguely thought that he must have seen some small creature such as a guinea pig. I looked up a description of a skunk confident that I would then quickly scotch the idea of such a creature being on board. I duly set out for Seaforth, not in the best of tempers at having my weekend spoilt.

The ship was equipped with a stern ramp and the cargo was being discharged using forklift trucks. I interviewed the Master who stated categorically that there was indeed a skunk on board. Efforts had been made to trap the animal without success and one of the men had been squirted at by it.

This was serious. Skunks are frequently affected by rabies and the possibility of it getting ashore by means of the stern ramp could not be ignored.

The Master should, of course, have notified the Port Health Authority of its presence before arrival. I duly 'read the riot act' and advised what precautions should be taken to deter the skunk from getting ashore.

I managed to contact a colleague, and together we searched the ship from stem to stern, truck to keel, to no avail. We found no evidence whatsoever of its presence, not even a single dropping. The next day another thorough search was made, again to no avail.

The crunch came on Monday morning; the skunk had been seen ashore!

We set up some cat traps, but what should we use for bait? We decided to use a mixture of cat food and dog food. Goodness knows what the City Treasurer thought of these items on the petty cash sheet!

An inspection of the traps the next day revealed that the one set up in a disused freight container had been sprung, and it was clear that some well-meaning idiot (or animal lover, depending upon your point of view,) had released the creature.

The trap was reset and Wednesday proved to be our lucky day. The skunk was caught and caged in the back of my car.

One of my colleagues followed in his car to take over in the (hopefully) unlikely event of an accident. It showed no sign of rabies.

Chester Zoo said that they would be delighted to add the skunk to their collection, but unfortunately the Ministry of Agriculture, Fisheries and Food thought otherwise. It was sent to one of their laboratories so that a proper scientific evaluation could be made. The poor skunk was killed and its brain examined, but no sign of rabies was found.

Much to the dismay of some of my less charitable colleagues, my car did not stink after carrying its most unusual passenger.

Thank you Gerry Davies ... I asked for more tales and was not disappointed.

RACOON

Sometime in the late seventies or so, the Master of a tanker bound for Tranmere Oil Terminal sent a message to Liverpool Port Health Authority advising that on board was a racoon, which had sneaked aboard the vessel at a port in Canada. Great efforts had apparently been made to catch the animal without success. It had been seen many times in the centre castle, but how it had managed to survive without food or water was, officially at least, a mystery. Knowing the average seaman's fascination with animals, I have no doubt that it was well fed and watered.

The Master of a ship entering a British port from a foreign port is required to inform the Port Health Authority of any animals on board. The reason for this requirement is to prevent the importation of rabies into the U.K. All animals are capable of becoming infected with rabies, but some are more likely to carry the disease than others. This disease is carried in the saliva and humans are usually infected by being bitten, but it can be transmitted by an infected animal licking the skin if the skin is broken, however slightly. In most animals, rabies causes changes in the animals' behaviour. Animals which are normally shy and wary lose their fear of humans and become aggressive.

Rabies in humans is usually fatal. Treatment is very painful and seldom effective, even when begun immediately after the infection occurs.

Regulations require that animals must be securely confined at all times when the vessel is in port and must be prevented from having any contact with persons other than members of the crew. Obviously the regulations were formed to deal with animals as pets or cargo.

It would be wrong to consider taking action against the Master in a case such as this, but nevertheless it was vitally important that the racoon be prevented from getting ashore. The question was … how? One of my colleagues suggested that we enlist the help of Chester Zoo.

The Curator of Mammals seemed delighted at the prospect of securing a racoon for the Zoo's collection. He suggested that the best plan would be to tranquilise the animal. This would be achieved by using a dart-gun. I quickly pointed out that the ship was carrying a highly inflammable cargo, berthed at a jetty surrounded by oil storage tanks. However, I was assured that there was no risk as the dart was propelled by compressed air. This seemed the ideal solution.

The Zoo had its own approved quarantine station and it would be acquiring a racoon for very little expenditure. The team from the Zoo duly arrived and in a short time the racoon was resting peacefully in a secure cage, ready to be taken to the quarantine station.

There were congratulations all round, until in the course of casual conversation it emerged, to my horror, that although the dart was indeed propelled by compressed air, this was released by means of a percussion cap!

The thought of a large section of Birkenhead going up in flames gave me nightmares for quite some time.

Well done, Gerry, you could have made the headlines!

Captain Michael McClory
Master Mariner

Extracting these tales from seafarers is akin to extracting teeth ... until they start and the proverbial floodgates are opened. However, Captain Michael McClory responded happily to my requests. We start with snippets.

LISBON

Maria was the laundry lady and she looked after our problems through the Company's agency. Back in the 1960s, detachable paper white collars had just arrived and so Maria had been given a batch for her laundry system. Incidentally and of no interest to this little tale, Maria had a wooden leg as a result of an accident with a tram when she had been a child. We spotted her coming down the quay weeping copious tears carrying in her hand a mass of soggy paper. Need we add that she was not amused when we explained the truth to her.

HAIFA

We noticed that a little kitten was being tormented and ill-treated by the dockers, so we rescued the animal and it was placed in my room. So it remained on board for several weeks, well fed and thoroughly spoilt. We came to Liverpool, Glasgow and sailed around Europe before we were outward bound again for Haifa. We tied up alongside and placed the gangway in position. The cat emerged from my cabin, along the deck, down the gangway and strolled off with tail erect back home!!

Like a measured drum beat in these seafaring tales, you should be able to discern the meaning of the phrase 'Brotherhood of the Sea'. The sea is dangerous and unforgiving and lives are at risk, regardless of modern technology and scientific know-how. A rather ancient Cape Horner describing the 'cruel sea' told me that when you are up aloft 'you have one hand for the ship, one hand for your mates and the other hand for yourself.' And that actually made sense! Captain Mike McClory, Master of CITY OF NAPLES, has such a story which I have culled from newspapers and reports.

STORM

Extracted from Lloyd's List 13th October 1976. VLIELAND (Cyprus).

Land's End Radio, Oct 11 … Following received from Brest-Le Conquet Radio

At 1506 GMT, on 2,182 kHz: Mayday (distress) relay, following received from motor vessel VLIELAND, C4QI.

Antwerp for LATTAKIA at 1500 GMT Mayday, approximate position lat. 46N, long 08W, ship listing, require immediate assistance.

At 1520 GMT, on 500 kHz: following received from motor container vessel; CITY OF NAPLES ETA about 30 minutes.

At 1550, GMT: VLEILAND: At 1544 GMT, crew abandoning ship in position lat. 46 12N, long 07 21W.

Following received from CITY OF NAPLES: Now one mile off VLEILAND position and standing by.

Following intercepted from PHJU (motor vessel SCHOONEBEEK): At 1755, GMT, on 2,182 kHz: crew in liferafts, now CITY OF NAPLES trying to pick them up.

At 1817, GMT ... All crew members of VLEILAND picked up by CITY OF NAPLES. VLEILAND now drifting without crew.

Following received from Brest-Le Conquet Radio at 1822, GMT, on 500 kHz VLEILAND still floating adrift, dangerous for navigation, position lat. 46 12N, long. 07 21W. No assistance required. Normal working may be resumed.

Following received from the CITY OF NAPLES at 2002 GMT Picked up 11 survivors from VLEILAND, abandoned without lights in position lat. 46 12 30N, long 07 17W, drifting in direction 100 deg. from that position. Proceeding Leixos and Lisbon.

London, Oct 12 ... CITY OF NAPLES ETA Leixos, 0300, Oct. 13, with survivors from VLEILAND.

Brest Oct 13 ... All crew taken on board CITY OF NAPLES which proceeded to Leixos. VLEILAND, drifting with 10 deg. list, was taken in tow by salvage tug PACIFIC.

Oporto, Oct 14 ... Eleven survivors from VLEILAND were landed at Leixos yesterday morning by CITY OF NAPLES.

Land's End Radio, Oct 14 ... Following received from St. Nazaire Radio at 0421 GMT: Following Mayday received from PACIFIC at 0417 GMT: "We have lost four crew members. All ships in vicinity lat 47 38N, long 05 31W, please keep sharp look out." Following intercepted from PACIFIC at 0416 GMT: "Crew members abandoned towed vessel."

Following intercepted from PACIFIC at 0447 GMT: "At 0444 GMT, all four crew members picked up and saved. Please cancel Mayday."

London, Oct 14 ... VLEILAND sank at approximately

0400, local time, today in position lat 47 38N, long 05 31W.

Ellermans, Liverpool sent the following report to the Journal of Commerce: This report was dictated by Captain M.A. McClory by telephone from Portugal, approximately 1300 hours 15th October, 1976.

REPORT ON ASSISTANCE GIVEN
TO M.V. VLEILAND, ABOUT 1,500 TONS

On passage from Rotterdam to Lisbon, via Leixos. A Mayday was received at 1515 GMT from the Cypriot vessel VLEILAND that cargo had shifted and she required immediate assistance. VLEILAND's given position was 46 degree 30 North and 7 degrees 20 West and she was in our close vicinity.

I turned on a reciprocal course and shortly afterwards sighted the VLEILAND listing heavily to port. Weather conditions at this time were wind WNW Force 8 to 9, heavy sea and high confused swell with rain squalls and conditions deteriorating. I was in Radio contact with Brest-le-Conquet, keeping the radio station informed of positions and my intentions. VHF contact was made with VLEILAND and I informed the Master that I would take up station on his port quarter and stand by.

At about 1700 hours Master of the VLEILAND decided to abandon ship. I told him I would close as safely as possible and attempt to drift a liferaft to him. This attempt was made, but conditions were now such that this was found to be impossible, our liferaft being lost and drifting away.

VLEILAND then launched her own raft and the crew abandoned ship and after some considerable difficulty succeeded in getting clear of their own vessel. I then manoeuvred between the ship and the raft giving the raft as good a lee as possible.

We began to rescue the survivors at about 1800 hours and at 1920 hours all the crew were safely on board the CITY OF NAPLES.

I continued on passage at a reduced speed, my intention being to land the survivors at Leixos and this was done at 0730 on the 13th October.

OCL container ship ENCOUNTER BAY stood by during the operation and relayed my messages to Brest-le-Conquet, my own transmitter being faulty due to excessive rain.

Many messages were sent. 'The success of this operation without loss of life under very severe weather conditions must have required great skill and expert seamanship. Congratulations to you, your Officers and Crew.' 'It was a most gallant action and one which has enhanced the name of Ellerman's.' Messages were received from the Cyprus High Commission in London ... 'Without help the loss of the VLEILAND could have resulted in tragedy.'

Thank you, Michael.

Captain Peter Corrin
Master Mariner

Captain Peter Corrin was born in 1949 in Port St. Mary, Isle of Man and did all his training around the waters of the Irish Sea. In 1978, he was given his first Steam Packet command, the CONISTER, was promoted to Marine Superintendent in 1987 and ended his career as Marine Operations Manager. He oversaw the introduction of the 'fast craft' in the Isle of Man Service. Apart from our long standing friendship, Peter serves as Trustee in the Mersey Mission to Seafarers.

ANCIENT AND MODERN

I was commanding the MANXMAN in 1982, which was the last operational steam-powered traditional cross-channel passenger ship operating under the Red Ensign and in her final year of service. I remember I was standing on the gantry platform, which provided access to the vessel at the landing stage, when an elderly lady approached me laden with two heavy-looking suitcases. After informing her that the 1530 hrs vessel was actually the car ferry lying farther up the stage in the North berth, I took hold of her luggage and began to escort her along the stage. In conversation she told me she had just crossed from Birkenhead on the HIGHLAND SEABIRD, which at the time was a fast craft on a trial on the Mersey to possibly replace the conventional ferries. It was an experience she obviously had not liked explaining that the older type of ferry was much more comfortable. I replied that few things stayed the same to which she retorted, "These old Isle of Man boats don't change much!"

WHERE ARE WE ?

Excursions to and from Llandudno were a very popular part of Steam Packet schedules from both Douglas and Liverpool for many years. We left Douglas in dense fog one day bound for Llandudno ... happy in the knowledge it was a rare feature on the North Wales coast. We were confident it would clear before our arrival at the Welsh resort. Sadly though, after establishing contact with the Pier Master via VHF radio, we were informed that visibility at the pier was about fifty yards. As the ebb tide was setting towards the land, this added to the pressure. With extreme caution, we edged our way slowly towards the pier. Some half a mile seaward from it, we had to pass less than quarter of a mile from a sheer and daunting headland. We could not see it! Continuing to conform to the statutory whistle signals as well as monitoring our position by radar, we edged ever closer to the sound of the Pier Master's whistle. We could now hear the voices of the people talking on the pier, but still could not see them! Suddenly like a bullet from a gun, the dome on the pier loomed out of the fog and gradually we saw the people, who seconds earlier were just a choir of voices. As the mood on the bridge changed from despondency to delight, the Chief Officer shouted to the crowd, "Is this Llandudno?", to which they replied in unison, "Yes". I shudder to think what our reaction would have been had they replied, "No, it's Prestatyn!"

That sums up the way of life on the ships which was a mixture of dedication and professionalism, coupled with a sharp sense of humour. Berthing and un-berthing operations at Llandudno were always vastly different to those at Douglas or Liverpool, for example, which had well established port controls. In those ports you would be given accurate wind speeds and directions. In Llandudno, the Pier Master was actually the Carpenter who looked after the pier in the winter time and was not from a nautical background at all. He would tell you that the wind was on or off the pier and the tide was flowing in or out. The approach to the pier was usually undertaken using visual marks, such as the end of the pier in line with the pink hotel. This was fine until you went back the next year and they had decided to paint it blue!

STARDOM

During the MANXMAN's last year she was in great demand with film companies and on one occasion was chartered by Barbra Streisand for part of her film, YENTL. The MANXMAN was transformed to that of a tramp steamer called the MOSKVA. The proud Steam Packet red funnel became a dreary grey. Filming lasted about a week, encompassing most of Liverpool Bay, sailing from the stage in the morning and returning each evening. The days were long and tiring, dispelling the myth that the film world is one of glamour and grandeur. Any fantasy of Hollywood was also very quickly dashed by the reality of the British climate and the onset of autumnal gales. The extras, of which there were as many as four hundred at times, and who were depicting pale under-nourished pilgrims, certainly didn't require any make up. The rigours of the Irish Sea did a much more authentic job.

JACK OF ALL TRADES

All the passenger vessels carried a sailing carpenter and he had a seaman assigned to him who was known as the

Carpenter's Mate. During the winter, several of the vessels were laid up in Birkenhead. On one occasion the carpenter on the MANX MAID, one of the car ferries, told his 'mate' that after arrival at the landing stage at 1300 hrs he would need to deliver some equipment to one of the ships laid up across the river. He further informed him that the mode of transport for this task would be a handcart. They duly loaded it up with various pieces of equipment and sent him on his way with strict instructions for him to remain in the 'slow' lane in the tunnel. He was already heading for Chapel Street, when he had to be called back and told he was a victim of the carpenter's sense of humour.

Speaking of carpenters, the Company at one time had a large workshop task force comprising of welders and carpenter/joiners. During one particular slack period, one of the joiners was complaining to the foreman that he had little to do. The foreman thought about this for a while and came up with the idea that the joiner could make him a coffin. This he started to do, but shortly afterwards work picked up and they became busy again. The joiner approached the Foreman and said "Sorry, I'll have to leave the coffin for now and could you hang on a few days for it!"

Thank you, Peter.

My contact with the Isle of Man Steam Packet Company lasted for thirty years. It was always good to visit the vessels at the landing stage about forty-five minutes before sailing. There was a good reason for this. The Master always had a pot of tea and hot fingers of toast before going up to the Bridge ... at least three times I failed to disembark in time and inadvertently had to spend twenty-fours hours in the Isle of Man. The welcome was stupendous!

At the outbreak of World War Two the Company owned a fleet of sixteen ships. Three were converted into armed boarding vessels, and eight became personnel carriers conveying part of the British Expeditionary Force to France. Operation Dynamo, the Dunkirk evacuation, saw the eight ships bringing home 24,669 troops ... three vessels were lost in twenty hours. A further 9,800 were evacuated from France, including 1,800 children from Guernsey to Weymouth. Naturally, there was great involvement in the D Day landings.

There are so many names in my memories of visits to the Isle of Man ... Captain Lyndhurst Callow, Captain Frank Griffin ... one of the founders of the Mariners' Choir, and how many Captain Kinleys are there, and especially Captain Westby Kissack. Then there was Captain 'Ernie Mac' McMeiken ... the Quaules, the Quines and the Quirks ... the list could go on.

Again, thank you Peter Corrin. We all love the Isle of Man.

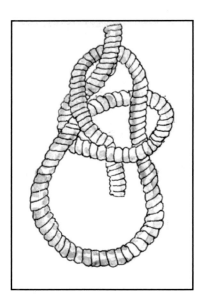

Captain Ian Drummond
Master Mariner

Perhaps I should have counted the number of veterinary tales in this book, or maybe collated them by species. What I do know is that each one is a gem! Now it is the turn of Captain Ian Drummond to swing the lamp.

ALL IN A DAY'S WORK

"That mare is waxing" was the shout from the stockman on the wharf as we lifted the last horse aboard. We had just completed loading livestock for our voyage north to Singapore.

General cargo had been completed the previous morning and the fodder for the voyage completed by noon. As the  'Wharfies' took no part in the loading of livestock in those days, the crew rigged up the races and gates and got the ship ready to receive the sheep. By the evening, we had loaded 5,500 wethers, a full complement, and all that remained to load was 14 milking cows, 20 bulls and 18 horses, which would arrive the next morning. The

251

bulls and cows would be run across races through the side doors, the same as the sheep, but the horses had to be lifted aboard.

When the government vet came aboard with the paperwork, I asked him when he thought the mare would foal. "About

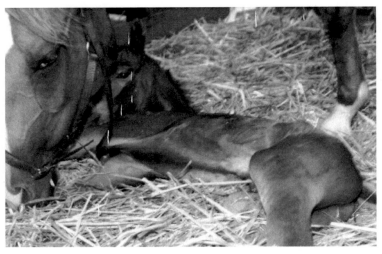

another week" was the answer. As it was only five and a half days to Singapore, there was a chance that she wouldn't foal onboard.

I was the Mate of the CENTAUR, a multi-purpose ship, carrying 190 passengers, general and freezer/cooler cargo, and with deep tanks for oils and livestock. The livestock were carried in the wings of the 'tween and orlop decks in pens. The pens had moveable decks which could be lifted up and made fast to the deckhead so as to be able to carry cattle or let down to carry two tiers of sheep, or a mixture of both. There were also dairy and portable milking machines to milk the cows. There were stalls on deck for the horses.

As soon as we departed Fremantle, I had a look at the Mate's bible on that ship, namely 'Hungerfords Stock Diseases', and read up on pregnant mares and what to expect if she foaled en route. Everything was going fine with less than a day to go. During the early morning inspection of the livestock, the mare looked good with no signs of distress. At about 0900 hours, a sailor came up to say the mare was foaling. As a lad I had lived next to a dairy farm and was quite used to seeing cows give birth. I had experienced having a few lambs born onboard when we carried crossbred ewes and usually found that the mothers coped quite well when giving birth.

I walked down to the foredeck expecting it to be all over by the time I got there. I arrived to find the Malay Bosun looking a bit concerned and no sign of the foal. The Bosun was very experienced with livestock, having worked with them since pre-war days. He told me he thought the foal was stuck, so we climbed into the stall and had a look. Luckily the foal was coming out the right way, but seemed to be stuck. The mare was getting quite distressed. The front legs were showing and we could just see its nose. So we decided to give it a helping hand, tied a piece of rope round the front legs and commenced to pull in unison with the contractions. Just as well I had lived next to a dairy farm and watched the cowman do the same thing. The crew had meanwhile moved the horse in the next stall to a spare stall, which gave us room to work, and filled it with plenty of bedding. Eventually, the foal came out. By this time the mare was down, absolutely knackered. We cleaned the colt up ... it was a male. We then got the mare up and gave her a bran mash, after which she recovered very quickly. The colt then began to suckle and, as it was lunch time, we knocked off leaving a sailor to keep an eye on them. I cleaned up and then had a large gin for medicinal purposes as well as to wet the colt's head.

A cable was sent to our agents in Singapore informing them of an additional horse, and mother and son were doing well, and to inform the consignee who happened to be H.R.H. The Sultan of Johore.

The ship arrived at Jurong the next day. The government vet came aboard and cleared the livestock for discharge. Sheep and bulls and cows through the side doors and the horses over the side.

The Sultan's Captain of Horse arrived with the Royal Horse Box, and his Australian Polo Agent came aboard. I asked him if he would like to buy a young polo pony as we had a spare one. We came to an agreement. The ship would sell it to the Sultan for a dollar in cheque form and he would recompense the sailors for their endeavours.

I never got the cheque, but I did get the satisfaction of helping a colt into this world.

Thank you, Ian. I find the mixture of some two hundred passengers, five thousand sheep and assorted cattle and horses rather peculiar. Ian added another piece of wisdom that is worthy of note. "The secret of success was that never let them mix!"

Jim Cowden
Chief Purser

Jim Cowden is an author in his own right, having written an excellent 'History of the Elder Dempster Fleet, 1852 – 1985' and also 'The Price of Peace (Elder Dempster 1939 – 1945)'. After his retirement the Company afforded him a round voyage to West Africa in order to bid farewell to friends made over many years. He has written a fully comprehensive account of his time aboard MARON. I am forced to be exceedingly selective of what I am able to print ... with apologies to Jim. The year was 1983.

MARON

MARON was one of three 'M' Class vessels, built by Scotts's Shipbuilding & Engineering Company Greenock, entering service in May 1980, followed shortly by MYRMIDON and MENTOR.

After a break of some fifteen years, I was again to face the elements of travel by sea. MARON had moved from her berth in the Huskisson Dock to a container loading berth in Canada Dock. The intention was to sail direct from Canada Dock to West Africa via Tilbury. Unfortunately however, a labour dispute arose at Tilbury which resulted in MARON moving back to Huskisson to load additional cargo to replace what tonnage would have been loaded in London.

As I stepped out of my car, MARON simply dwarfed the adjacent sheds and other shipping in the vicinity. With all her accommodation aft, she looked like a leviathan of the sea. Ten large Samson posts evenly spaced out on the fore-deck reached into the sky above. These Samson posts housed a total of nine derricks with safe working loads ranging from 10 tonnes to 35 tonnes. Looking at these derricks one would most certainly not envisage any difficulties in loading 'sinker' logs down in Gabon ports.

Standing on the quayside, one had to keep 'monkey eye' and not miss a trick. Nowadays the essence is on speed, quick turn-round, both in loading and discharging. Thinking back when one joined a 'monkey boat' loading in South-West Brunswick or the Centre-West Harrington, the sheds would be crammed full of bagged salt, galvanised sheets, baled cotton goods (with the code number on the side), hurricane lamps and not forgetting the three-legged mission pots. All of these were man-handled from delivery lorries, stacked in the shed and later man-handled again to the shed door and aboard ship … salt in large blocks stowed into Number One lower hold (Berewa … Lion Elephant brands). One would hear from the hatch foreman, "Righto there, 'arry, gis us a little galvy to block this effing lot off."

Standing on the quayside at Canada Dock, there were no stacks of cargo or comments from the hatch foreman to be heard. In the old days, one could quite easily nip to one side as the small hand-trucks made their way to the ship's side. I was now confronted by many large Lancing Straddle Carriers, each and every one with a twenty-foot container tucked safely between its legs, making their way toward the heavy tackle which was slung out-board of MARON.

The age of break-bulk cargos has almost disappeared from the West African scene. The age of containerisation, unitisation and palletisation had arrived. The once thousands of tons of salt coming from I.C.I. Cheshire salt mines, carried in the familiar 'salt flats' had now completely gone. Salt is nowadays loaded at site into Lo-lift bags, each capable of holding ten tons. After being carted from the mines by road the complete unit is then loaded aboard the ship. Everything is geared to 'quick turn-round'. Time is money. Remember that old West African saying 'Time and tide stands still for Man'.

By this time, MARON had 'singled up'. The Rea Tugs, BRACKENGARTH, HAZELGARTH and WILLOWGARTH were in attendance. Orders from the Bridge are all given by 'walkie-talkie' to those on station fore and aft. MARON had now let go her moorings and moved dead slow ahead. With a cargo of some 24,000 tonnes and a draught of 31 feet 6 inches MARON was a very heavy lump to be moving about. One hour later, MARON was safely moored in the Canada Dock Basin. After the gates had been closed, the water level was duly reduced in readiness for MARON to steam into the Mersey.

Shortly, MARON cast off and sailed into the river. Hard-a-starboard and half ahead, she headed for Liverpool Bay to adjust compasses, as necessary; after which MARON nosed toward Point Lynas to disembark Pilot Lacey and the Compass Adjuster. As they scrambled down the ladder, both clutching their small bags which, of course, contained their bottle and two hundred cigs (one of the old customs that appears not to have changed), the Pilot launch gathered them aboard.

One thing has continued from the old days was Boat and Fire Drill. As soon as was convenient, the whistle was sounded and all hands went to stations. Both lifeboats were duly swung and various appliances tested in accordance with Board of Trade requirements.

Much aboard MARON then settled down to a routine.

I, therefore, took time off to look around this modern ship's storerooms. Long gone was the time when cases of eggs, beer, etc., were manhandled from the deck, through the accommodation to practically inaccessible storerooms below. On entering the well where fridges and storerooms were situated in one complete block, it could not go unnoticed that some considerable thought had gone into planning such an arrangement. First, the alleyways were completely empty of any stores. Remember in the past, when barrels of beer were stored outside the main storerooms, together with bags of potatoes. MARON had been provisioned for approximately four months. Nowadays, so much pre-packed stores are carried. In looking over the storerooms, one could see hundreds of pints of fresh milk, sliced bread, gateaux, pork pies, sliced bacon. No carcasses of meat are carried to be cut on board. The Second Cook turned out feather-light rolls that went down so well with half-a-pound of best butter, or, perhaps, dipping into your 'potage soubise'.

Even before we had actually cleared Liverpool, the various U.K. shipping journals had advertised to the trade that MARON would arrive at Freetown on the 9th July. Travelling at well below her normal full speed, we approached the entrance to Freetown Harbour in the early hours of the 9th of July. Our ETA. was 6.30 a.m. abeam of Cape Sierra Lighthouse.

Some hours prior to our arrival, numerous lights could be seen ahead. Drawing a little closer, MARON came upon a large Russian fish fleet, consisting of a mother ship, two supply ships and some thirty catchers in all. It appears that both the Russians and the Japanese operate large fishing fleets between the Canary Islands and Sierra Leone. The factory ship was about 30,000 tonnes. The various catches are placed on board the factory ship, gutted, cleaned and then deep frozen for export from Freetown. Large supplies of tuna fish are caught and despatched to the United States.

After rounding the fishing fleet, MARON slowly came abeam of Cape Sierra Lighthouse. Now situated high up on the Cape itself stands a beautiful new hotel ... The Cape Sierra Hotel, which has magnificent views out over the Atlantic Ocean.

Alas, the harbour was devoid of shipping. No ships waiting to sail round to Sherbro for a cargo of kernels and piassava. No handy-size bulk carriers waiting to steam up to Pepel for a cargo of iron ore. At least, the bunkering station at Kissy was being used. A fairly large Italian-flag tanker was discharging petroleum products which apparently are in short supply throughout Sierra Leone. The Queen Elizabeth the Second Quay has been lengthened to accommodate an additional three vessels with a container park at one end. As MARON approached the quayside, there was very little activity at all. No hustle or bustle.

Sierra Leonne, like a lot of countries, is presently going through a very bad economic spell. However, in spite of this, one comes across newly-completed or part-completed buildings. With Chinese aid a huge sports complex is being completed in addition to other projects ... many of them running out of funds. How times have changed for this once very busy port.

The Pilot came aboard ... he turned out to be a Nigerian who had served his time in the Palm Line of London.

The Agent stated "I must see a complete manifest covering all cargo aboard MARON." With the usual pleasantries of saying that it is not available, more shaking of heads and waving of hands and "I will accept a carton of cigarettes instead." Some things never change!

So we departed from Cotonou at 0700 hours, 13th July, destination Lagos.

Thank you, Jim Cowden.

Phil Hockey, M.B.E.
Liverpool Pilot

For the past few years I have become a member of the Seagulls ... a happy group. This odd 'society' comprises retired Mersey River Pilots and their spouses. All that they achieve is to 'fly away like seagulls to a warm seaside hotel, eat good food, drink an amplitude of wine and talk a lot'. As an 'Honorary Pilot of the First Class', it is a privilege to be allowed to join in their foreign journeys. Their waves certainly get bigger in the telling, but their yarns are all the better for that!

Lying alongside the pool at Nerja, (Spain somewhere) a good friend, Phil Hockey, began to chat and out came a tale which will gladden every seafarer's heart. Let Phil take up the story.

THE SECOND MATE WHO FELL OVER THE SIDE

I was boarded on a 'Harrison Boat' some years ago, and it's no good asking me the name or date of the event. I didn't keep a diary, but it seems to be about the mid 1980s, as I retired in 1988.

I remember quite clearly that it was daylight and the ship was waiting to dock in Brunswick, when the Captain nudged me and said "That's him," and pointed to the Second Mate who was standing on the port wing of the Bridge. He repeated this a couple of times and, eventually, said "You don't know what I am talking about", and gave me a Readers Digest, saying, "Read this". I read the account.

'The Second Mate, who came off watch at 4 a.m., went down to the poop (stern of the ship) to check the log. This was an instrument hanging from a bracket affixed to the stern rail, and operated by a rotor attached to the end of a long rope. This rotor turned the log instrument and a dial showed the distance run. It was quite possible for this to become entangled and the whole length of the rope sometimes had to be hauled inboard, a two-man job at the best of times. The Second Mate, not wanting to get assistance, had climbed outboard, slipped and fell overboard into the Indian Ocean.

'With great presence of mind, he realised that the weather was kind, the water temperature was warm, and that he would not be missed until the Steward brought him a cup of coffee at 10.30 a.m. He worked out that by the time the crew had searched for him and found the log rotor entangled, they would know that he had fallen overboard and the ship would return for him. His estimate was that the ship would take about seven or eight hours before it returned, so he settled himself to waste no energy and float. An hour or two later, he realised that he was being investigated by at least two sharks.

'His horror was alleviated, when he realised the he was being circled by a number of dolphins, who kept the sharks at bay until, wonder of wonders, his ship appeared, lowered a boat, picked him up, still circled by the dolphins who followed the ship for the rest of the day.'

The ship I was on, in Brunswick Dock, was not the ship this event took place aboard, nor was the Captain involved, but he did tell me that the Second Mate did not return to sea, except for short round-the-land voyages.

So, Bob, that's the story, make of it what you will.

I have discussed this happening with many seafarers and not one of them has expressed any doubt about its veracity. Strange and miraculous things have occurred too often at sea and the improbable is ever possible.

Captain Michael Jones
Master Mariner

Captain Mike Jones is a well known character on Merseyside. He is a Trustee and the Deputy Chairman of the Mersey Mission to Seafarers. In 1989 ... the year that I retired from the Mission ... Michael was appointed Marine Superintendent of T & J Harrison. Here are some of his memories.

HIGH NOON

By the time of the Millennium, the management of any business or organisation had a great wealth of electronic and other aids which permitted them to operate their enterprises efficiently with vast numbers of people and over great distances.

But the now-gone, great Liverpool Shipping Empires had their own particular management styles, which enabled them to run their large organisations without the advantages of modem technology. Once their vessel had left the Mersey, the only real contact with their Owners was by telegram or later by telex through their

Agents' offices in ports overseas. Direct radio contact with ships at sea was for a long time of very short range, just a few hundreds of miles.

It follows that it was extremely important that the Masters of their ships had full confidence in those supporting them ashore and that the same confidence was held by the Owner in the Masters of their ships.

One particular Liverpool shipping company operating services to South and East Africa, India and to the Caribbean area held a management or 'Board' meeting at precisely noon on each and every day, Monday to Friday. Their wood-panelled Boardroom on the second floor looked out onto the church-yard of the Sailors' Church of St. Nicolas and on over to the River Mersey.

The noon daily meeting was always chaired by a Director, if not the Company Chairman himself. Seated at the long table were other Directors and all the Departmental Managers and it was here that a Master attended both prior to his sailing for overseas and on his return home.

It all started a few minutes before noon when the Masters of the ships for that day assembled in a small waiting room adjacent to the Boardroom and connected to it by a simple bell arrangement. The Masters had already circulated the Head Office to confer with departmental managers. Each would sign the attendance book before taking his seat in the waiting room. After a short period, once the routine business had been completed, the bell in the waiting room would sound inviting the first Master to join the Directors and Managers. There was always a uniformed member of the Corps of Commissionaires in attendance, known as 'Sergeant', who on hearing the bell, would open the door into the Boardroom and the Chairman would then ask him to invite a particular Master to join their meeting. The order in which the Masters were interviewed was strictly dictated by seniority, but all rather unspoken, as everyone knew who was senior to whom.

The Master was faced with a long table with probably a dozen people sitting around it and he took his place at the end, sitting next to the Marine Superintendent.

There would be an outline of the coming voyage, ports of call, the cargo loaded for each port, special items of difficult and special cargo etc. and the probable homeward loading programme. The Chairman would ask whether the Master was familiar with the ports and conditions, and then turn to questions about the vessel. Had the Master been to his vessel, was the cargo loaded to his satisfaction, were the lifeboats and other safety equipment in good order and had all tests been completed? The Master was asked whether the main engines had been tested and was the ship in a good condition to proceed on the coming voyage. Did the Master know his Officers, was another of the many questions. There was a legal aspect to all these questions and all facts were written into the minutes, but the most important question came as the Chairman asked, "Is there anything, Captain, you would like to ask us or anything you would like to tell us?" It was at that moment that the Master had direct and public access to the person who was ultimately responsible for running the Company. Nobody could stop the Master making any statement or raising any subject and therefore there was no Department, Official or Superintendent who could conceal or suppress any subject which might concern the Master. Finally, the Chairman would wish the Captain a successful voyage.

The Master would attend a similar meeting on the conclusion of the voyage, slightly more stressful as the Captain might now have to explain the things which went wrong during the voyage. Similar subjects were questioned and discussed as in the outward meeting, but now the Chairmen wished to hear of the current situation in the lands and ports overseas, how the ship and her complement performed, the condition of the ship and her equipment and details of the cargo. He asked how the port Agents had taken care of the ship and its business, which always ensured good treatment in overseas ports!

Finally, the Chairman would ask the Master whether he had anything to tell him or anything he wished to say about the voyage, which once again was the moment when the Master was free to speak to the principal persons of the Company and freely express any concerns he might have.

At last the Chairman would thank the Master for the conduct of the voyage and wish him a happy and well-earned leave at home.

The most significant moment of these meetings was when the Chairman asked the Master whether he had anything to ask or say to the Board. Here the confidence and trust, so important to the venture, were established and the Master could speak directly and freely to his ship owner without hindrance from anybody. The practice went back over a hundred years when the original owner briefed his Captains of his small sailing ships before they set out on their ventures.

Thank you, Michael, I suspect other companies must have held such sessions, but possibly Harrison's 'High Noon' was unique.

This book has been an anthology of past adventures, battles won and battles lost, of wide-open seas and narrow inlets, of memories strong and memories fading.

I have pondered long as to how this book must end as it comprises such a mixed bag of memories and reflections. In the end that choice was simple. Let Captain Michael Jones have the last 'wake' of memory and speak for 'all that go down to the sea in ships and see his wonders in the deep.'

VOYAGES OF YESTERYEAR

We remember the days when the letter arrived with instructions to rejoin your ship. There was even time to reply by letter.

We remember the warm comfortable feeling when walking through the dock shed full of cargo with the realisation that sailing day was not quite yet.

Then the day came when the dock shed was almost empty and the dockers were sweeping up ready for the next ship's cargo. Our time at home and all the fun was almost over.

We remember when we walked into the docks for the last time on the way to our ship about to sail, seeing a last bus of the night which would go close to our home and thinking we could just get on that bus and never go away.

When the moment of departure came, usually at night and in the rain, we remember we all went about the business of leaving the dock in silence and with little recognition of others and once out into the river we retreated into a private world of work and solitude as we coped with the misery of leaving our homes.

The weather did not help with its rolling and pitching world, and the damp blankets and the fiddles to hold the crockery on to the saloon tables did not bring any cheer. There was only the yet-unpacked suitcase in the middle of the cabin deck to give any feeling of home.

But then, we remember the day when suddenly we could feel the warmth of the sun on the back of the neck and life then did not seem quite as hard.

When the ocean became calmer, leaving the ship with a gentle roll, and the sun shone and warmed the air and the whole ship, then came almost the best moments in a seafarer's life. With all the outer doors and ports open and the warm air circulating throughout the ship, all the cabin doors were open with the door curtains gently swaying in the minimum rolling. We were being paid, well fed and cared for, had left our problems behind us at home. We knew where we fitted into the social structure of our ship, a world governed by the discipline of convention, respect knowing the Captain of the ship was the Master. With the promise of the ports to come, life had a good feeling of wellbeing and contentment. There was nothing to hassle us, we slept well, our watches were a pleasure, we read and had good company. Life was good.

We remember the long balmy rolling days in the Indian Ocean, but also the misery of the southwest monsoon, the long Cape rollers and the loneliness of the passages between Australia and Africa in the big Southern Ocean where the rest of the world was at the top of the chart ... with only an occasional whale and the ever-present albatross for company. We remember the welcome sight of a ship of another Liverpool line going in the opposite direction.

We remember the long night watches on the Bridge in the southern oceans with just the sound of the ship pushing through the waters and that silent Helmsman at the wheel. Looking up at the majesty of the great dome of the clear night sky, unpolluted by any light source other than the navigation lights of the ship, with millions and millions of stars from horizon to horizon ... who could question the spiritual strength and reason of nature?

We could recognize all the principal stars and find the planets. We can still feel the hair on the back of the neck stand up when, after a long ocean passage with only a sextant and chronometer to find the way, there low on the horizon was the first sight of land for many days. Who needed Global Positioning systems?

We remember the noise and excitement of moving through Port Said and the Canal. We remember the magnificence of Table Mountain with the sun rising behind it and the greenness and peace as we anchored off the West Indian islands.

At the first port, the dock labour came aboard almost as trespassers to discharge the cargo. They took over the decks and the holds of the ship completely as if it was all their very own. They made noise, disruption, untidiness, dirt and smells and those parts of the ship were no longer ours.

Strangely, while we made lifelong friends of the Dock Superintendents and often the foremen, we never spoke to the dockers themselves or they to us, no matter which part of the world. We looked upon the Companies' Port Agents as aristocracy and their wives, if we met them, as duchesses.

The only real nightlife was in the major ports, but as Junior Officers mostly worked nights in such ports, there was little experience. So we remember mostly going ashore into the towns of these ports during the days, and what fun that was with everything strange, but in some ways so like home. As young seafarers we remember the warm and secure feeling of the Seamen's Missions, which felt even more like home as they were places of safety and welcome.

We remember finishing the night's work on the ship and before going to bed drinking the last mug cup of tea at the ship's rail, looking out at the harbour in the bright fresh light of the early tropical morning and seeing one or two of our shipmates slinking along the wharf back to the ship after a night ashore. Nobody spoke, nobody asked and nobody told.

Almost always, the poorer and under-developed countries and their ports came a long way down the 'run' and by then most of the cargo had been discharged and the ship's holds were just one big rubbish dump of dunnage, dust, broken cargo and filth.

All this had to be brought up on deck by the crew and thrown into the sea on the passage to the loading area. A great wake of rubbish was left behind the ship for miles and miles on an otherwise clean ocean; and one wonders what the present officials with their regulations would say in these environmentalist days.

Loading was almost always a great joy for it was often in some new and prosperous country. We remember the southern United States where they had everything twice as good, and twice as big, and five times faster than anywhere else in the world. But they also had segregated buses and that sort of thing, which we did not really understand.

We can still recall the lovely smells of some of the homeward cargoes. The sweet smell of sugar, coffee and tea obviously, but also other pleasant odours from many cargoes which told us we would soon be homeward bound.

As the holds filled we worried about uncompleted correspondence course papers, company forms and journals to be completed, and too much money spent during the voyage as slowly our carefree dream-world began to evaporate.

In the late forties, we bought groceries in these lands of plenty to take home to provide a little joy in the remaining years of food rationing. Tins of ham, tins of fruit, jam and even sugar. We called them 'our stores'

The homeward passage was a time of rising excitement until almost everybody had the 'channels'. It was also a time to get things done, the ship painted from stem to stem until she looked like a new ship ... did anybody ashore really notice? ... letters to write, washing to be done, suits to be ironed and excuses to be prepared.

The bad weather during the homeward passage had little effect on us, in fact we found it almost exhilarating.

When the Company Pilot boarded at Point Lynas, he was greeted like a long-lost ancestor, a person from the real world with all the Company gossip. The Superintendent meeting the ship at the lock nodded to us without a word as if we had met only the previous day. We mumbled to others that we should now put our brains in the lockside boxes where the shore gang kept their fenders because the ship was no longer ours and we had no say in anything.

We were paid off with a pittance, but had the feelings of millionaires and set off home. We did not go round saying goodbye, for we had become a brotherhood of 'shipmates' and were sure to sail together again.

In less than three weeks the recall letter would arrive on the doormat and the whole thing would start again.

What a wonderful life for a young man!

Sunset

EPILOGUE

THE HISTORY OF THE MASTER MARINERS' CLUB

This Epilogue was written by Captain Graeme Cubbin, a long serving member of the Master Mariners' Club, and was published in 'Sea Breezes' in October 1998 when the Club in its present form celebrated its 50th anniversary. Captain Cubbin acknowledges the research of Mr. George Evans whose book, 'The Landfall Story', was published in 1972.

The Master Mariners' Club of Liverpool was formed in 1938. It was a late arrival in the story of the port for very obvious reasons. Seafarers are away at sea and none more so than Master Mariners. There was never a pool of such men by the nature of their trade, but the events of the First World War were to alter all that. Perhaps it was the simple fact of survival and the need for companionship that proved to be the catalyst leading to the creation of the Club. Whatever the reason, after the armistice of November 11th, 1918 and the end to the trauma, a group of shipmasters came together on the 20th January 1919 and met in the office of the Principal Officer of the Board of Trade, Captain Lyle Leitch. This was just a beginning, but it led to the founding of the Master Mariners' Club as we know it today.

That first 'get-together' produced the need to form a loose Association of Master Mariners with the purpose of meeting informally to discuss 'matters maritime' in a friendly and well-informed atmosphere throughout the year and to organise an annual dinner. The Association worked well for the next twenty years. They met in the Constitutional Club. The Annual Dinners attracted many famous people. Apart from the succession of Lord Mayors of Liverpool and of the surrounding boroughs, there were Sir Sydney Jones, the Duke of Montrose, the Marquis of Graham, Signor Guglielmo Marconi, several Admirals and, of course, a number of notable ship-owners.

It is fair to say that the Club will be ever grateful to the late Captain Sam Jones, who became Secretary in 1929. It was due to his enthusiasm that the idea of a social club was born. Thus in 1938, the Association became the Merseyside Master Mariners' Club. For the first time, meetings were convened every quarter, characterised by a talk, a discussion, and a hot-pot supper, with the annual dinner taking place in November. Commodore Sir Bertram Hayes became the first President of the M.M.M.C. and Captain E. A. Woods was elected its first Chairman. Membership recorded at the time of the annual dinner in November 1939 was 110.

Meanwhile war clouds had been gathering for some time, and at last the storm had broken. Britain had been in a state of war – or "phoney war", as it was billed in the press – with Germany since September 3rd. However, while the opposing armies glared at each other across the Maginot Line, and Royal Air Force bombers sallied forth to shower leaflets on enemy towns, there was nothing remotely "phoney" about the war at sea. From Day 1 when the ATHENIA was sunk by a U-boat with dreadful loss of innocent lives, naval and merchant ships sustained heavy losses, while their crews suffered and died.

By the time the Master Mariners had sat down to their annual dinner that year, two Royal Navy capital ships, and over

315,000 tons of British merchant shipping had been destroyed. (Figures compiled from British Vessels Lost at Sea 1914 – 18 and 1939 – 45, published by Patrick Stephens Ltd from HMSO Publications, 1988.).

Inevitably, World War Two severely curtailed the Club's activities, for it did not meet again until the war was over. This, naturally, was an infinitesimal misfortune of war compared with the devastation and havoc wrought on two Continents, but it was a misfortune, nevertheless.

Could the Club ever be revived again?

In late 1945 a rump of the old Club met with the object of trying to resuscitate the apparently moribund organisation and restore it to its pre-war glory. Out went the word, and a dinner was arranged to take place at the Constitutional Club on February 11th, 1946. Presided over by Captain A.E. Webster, Marine Superintendent of Elder Dempster Lines, it was attended by no less than 100 members and guests. Clearly there was life in the old dog yet!

The success of this event prompted a desire to recruit more members, and to acquire permanent premises where members and their wives could meet for lunch, or simply a drink, on a daily basis.

It was at this point that Captain T. Atkinson, OBE, Harbourmaster for the Mersey Docks & Harbour Board, and the club Chairman, made an astute move. He invited Commander the Honourable F. H. Cripps, DSO, RN – yes, brother to Sir Stafford of that ilk, who had just become Chancellor of the Exchequer in the recently elected Labour Government – to become President. In all walks of life, that what you know is very important, but arguably of even greater importance is WHOM you know! Commander Cripps, at that time a director of Elder Dempsters, brought a gravitas to the club's hierarchy, and he invited many influential people to become patrons. They included a succession of local Mayors and Lord Mayors, two

Earls, a Viscount, two Admirals and at least two ship-owners.

At a dinner held at the Tudor Restaurant, Liverpool, on February 12th, 1947, Commander Cripps revealed a scheme which had long been in a process of gestation; to wit, the procurement of a surplus tank landing craft, and converting her into a clubhouse permanently moored in Canning Dock, near the City centre! Such a vessel was even now in the Club's possession, and had been provided gratis by the benevolent Admiralty! This news was greeted with loud acclaim, and in the weeks that followed, Landing Craft (Tanks) 7074 was brought round to the Mersey to be converted at an estimated cost of £9,000. This sum was defrayed largely due to the goodwill of local businessmen who cheerfully purchased debenture shares in the venture. The work of converting the craft into a first class club was placed in the hands of Messrs. Bell & Burnie, Ltd. of Bootle and J.A. Mulhern.

7074, commanded by Sub Lieutenant John C. Baggot, RNVR, took part in the historic D-Day landings as part of "Operation Overlord", and is the only LCT involved in the invasion of France to survive today.

Towards the end of 1947, the work was well in hand. The vessel was formally registered as a club and named LANDFALL, a name destined to become a byword at ports throughout the world wherever, in those days, the Red Ensign was seen to fly.

Eventually, on September 21st, 1948 the club-ship LANDFALL was duly declared open by Vice-Admiral C.S. Holland, CB, RN. Staff were promptly appointed: a resident steward, who with his wife, made their home in the accommodation provided; also on the 'Crew List' were a chef, a kitchen maid, two cleaners, a barmaid, six African waiters and a ship keeper to tend the moorings. For at this time the LANDFALL was berthed in the north-east corner of Canning Dock, very convenient for the City and James Street Station, and consequently well attended.

Early in 1949, Commander Cripps, the man who had done so much to launch the LANDFALL project, retired from Elder Dempsters and went to live in the south of England. Consequently, he felt obliged to resign as President of the Club, albeit with great reluctance. Sir Robert Burton-Chadwick, a founder member of the Honourable Company of Master Mariners, was invited to succeed him. He was subsequently installed at the Annual Dinner (the first to be held on board LANDFALL) on May 7th, 1949. Commander Cripps was appointed the first Master of the Club, a gesture to mark the members' appreciation of his work, though it was but seldom that he could make the long journey north to attend the Club's functions.

Landfall

Another highly respected name was added to the distinguished list of club Presidents in April 1951 – that of Captain W. H. Coombs, CBE, RNR, the President of the Merchant Navy Officers Federation. At this time, in a move to supplement the Club's income, the premises were hired out on occasion to outside agencies for functions and conferences. Thus by 1955, the Club's finances had improved so much that the subscription rate was reduced from £10 to £7.10s.!

The 1960s, however, proved to be a difficult decade. That was when another notable personality came to the fore. He was Captain F. W. (Bill) Skutil, CBE, RNN (Rtd), who worked tirelessly on behalf of the Club. He was elected Master in 1963, President in 1964, and eventually shouldered the demanding job of Hon. Secretary in 1967. It was his casting vote at an extraordinary general meeting that kept the club alive.

Incidentally, Clubship LANDFALL was the last vessel to make use of the Canning Graving Dock. On May 11th, 1965, she was warped out of her berth and across the basin to the Graving Dock to undergo a Lloyd's survey while having her hull scaled and coated with a new bituminous epoxy paint under the watchful eye of Captain Skutil. After two weeks she was escorted back to her berth, and the Canning Graving Dock was closed for good after almost 200 years of continuous use.

Early in 1968, rising costs and difficulties in administration prompted the management committee to seek professional help. Consequently, on February 1st, 1968, the catering element of the Club's activities was transferred to Compass Catering Ltd. In return for the profits from the bar and restaurant, the company would accept responsibility for administration, insurance, and maintenance. The Master Mariners would retain exclusive use of the facilities as a luncheon club, while Compass Catering reserved the right to open the club to other reputable organisations for evening functions. That year, the club's legendary reputation was further enhanced by the engagement of a London Ritz-trained chef. That the move north had not adversely affected his talents was amply confirmed by the handsome compliments paid to him on the occasion of the 20th Annual Dinner by the Lord Mayor of Liverpool, Dame Ethel Wormald.

Later that year, the launching of the LANDFALL as a night-club, licensed to remain open until 2.00 am, doubtless provoked murmurs of disapproval from the more conservative members, but complaints were soon muted by the obvious success of the initiative, which helped finance the introduction of such simple benefits as improvements to lighting, plumbing and décor. However, the status quo was not destined to remain static for long.

A decision by the Mersey Docks & Harbour Board to close Canning Dock meant that LANDFALL would have to move, and on April 16th, 1971, she occupied a berth in the adjacent Salthouse Dock – adjacent certainly, but not nearly so convenient. And, of course, a big question mark was even then hanging over the future of the whole of the South Docks system. This uncertainty provoked, in July 1971, the sale of the LANDFALL to Compass Catering Ltd., though the Club still retained its luncheon club facility. The sale was effected none too soon, for the M.D.& H.B. made its decision to close the docks south of Pier Head in the following year. Lock gates would be left open to the river, so that the docks became tidal, and filled with silt.

The LANDFALL was once more obliged to get under way – with the aid of a tug, of course – and seek refuge in Collingwood Dock, a safe enough berth, but a long way from the City centre. This move away from the hub of things almost brought about the demise of the Club, as attendances declined and membership diminished.

Matters had reached such a pass by the end of 1975 that an extraordinary meeting was called on December 18th. Conditions on board were deteriorating, and it was decided to withdraw the Club from the LANDFALL to seek more adaptable quarters in the City. Thus on January 6th, 1976, a final LANDFALL lunch was served to just eight members (out of 146 on the register) and the last link was severed.

Before pursuing the Club's later history, let us pause for a moment to consider what lay in store for LANDFALL. Her status as restaurant and night-club continued to decline, until she was virtually derelict, her comfortable fittings and furnishings stolen or vandalised. Then in 1994, a maritime species of fairy godmother, Sir Philip Goodhart, of the Warship Preservation Trust, became interested in this careworn Cinderella of a Landing Craft, and was moved to save and transform her. For the vessel was in a sorry condition by this time, badly damaged on two occasions by fire, and sinking at her moorings. Urgent temporary repairs were carried out, and the leaks stopped. But salvation was to prove a long and drawn-out process. Funds had to be raised, only to melt away, then to be raised again – and again. However, in 1995, an opportunity arose to transport the old ship across the river to a slipway in Cammell Laird's Shipyard, and work began on a complete restoration to her original 1944 condition. Eventually, on April 27th, 1998, the veteran warship was towed to a berth in the East Float, there to join her younger consorts, PLYMOUTH and ONYX, and allow the work of restoration to continue. Thus in due course, LCT 7074 would be established as yet another fascinating unit in the Royal Navy's Museum Fleet at Birkenhead.

Meanwhile, a tireless Club Secretary, Eric P. Moss, had found a haven for the Master Mariners in Kingston House, headquarters of the Mersey Mission to Seamen, situated within a cable's length of James Street Station. With the kind permission of Padre Bob Evans, the Club moved thankfully to this more central site. As anticipated the change breathed new life into the Club, and membership was further improved by extending the privilege to executives within the shipping and related industries. Nevertheless, the aura of a Master Mariner's Club was scrupulously maintained.

However, the Port of Liverpool was, at this juncture, itself falling upon hard times. Within the next ten years, the British Merchant Fleet would be decimated, and the port would lose much of its trade to burgeoning east coast ports such as Sheerness and Felixstowe. The reasons for Liverpool's decline were many and complex, and could be attributed in more or less equal measure to the growth of jet travel, the intransigent attitude of dockers' unions, containerisation of cargoes, and the proximity of the east coast to a prosperous European Common Market. All this, of course, had a knock-on effect on all local services and enterprises, and Kingston House was no exception. A sudden dearth of seafarers, particularly of the British/Christian tendency (though it should be noted that the Mission was quick to cater for the spiritual and material needs of a growing number of foreign, non-Christian seamen) left the Mission with no choice but to close down its residential and dining facilities, including the Club's dining room, and find new premises near the still-active docks to the north of the city, at Crosby. On October 1st, 1982, the Club held its last luncheon at Kingston House attended by 27 members. However, the devoted endeavours of Eric Moss prevailed once again, and were instrumental in forging an amicable agreement with the Liverpool Commodity Trades Association, whereby members were welcomed at their premises in the Atlantic Newsroom in the Corn Exchange Building, Fenwick Street. Rather disappointingly, the first luncheon to be held there on October 4th 1982 was attended by only ten members.

Nevertheless, for a brief season, matters seemed to have settled on an even keel, but six months later the LCTA announced regretfully that they had entered into voluntary liquidation, and would cease trading on April 5th, 1983 – yet another baleful circumstance in the port's apparently rapid recession. Once again the Club, which seemed to have taken on the mantle of some oriental, nomadic tribe, was left out in the cold with no home to go to. Once again, Eric Moss found himself wandering the streets of Liverpool on this perennial quest to find a permanent berth for the Club. And once again he was successful, persuading the management of the old Lyceum Club to accept the Master Mariners as associate members of the Lyceum, but preserving their distinctive identity. The first Lyceum luncheon, attended by seventeen members, was held on May 3rd, 1983.

Thereafter for eight happy years the Club continued to meet at the Lyceum. In 1989, Eric Moss retired from his labours as Hon. Secretary after fifteen years of resolute support to the Club, which owes its present state of well-being to his spirited efforts whilst in office.

Then, in the fullness of time, the seemingly inevitable happened, and the old Lyceum closed down. However, during this period, some encouraging developments had been taking place in the abandoned docks south of Pier Head. The retreat of commercial shipping seemed to have triggered a boom in leisure pursuits. Where salt-stained freighters, jostling barges, and busy tugs had once held sway, pleasure yachts and launches now dominated the scene. Their presence had prompted the establishment of a marina in the Coburg Dock, and the Liverpool Yacht Club had established its headquarters there in brand new premises, purpose-built, on the adjacent wharf.

Application for a form of associate membership was made to the proprietors of the marina, and accepted. Thus, on July 1st, 1991, the Master Mariners moved into yet another new berth within sight and sound of the docks and the Mersey, with every prospect of a long and happy tenure among the yachting fraternity.

But once again, the bane of economics intervened. The proprietors, South Quays Marinas PLC, were suddenly beset with financial problems which resulted in the closure of the bar and restaurant areas during the last quarter of 1993. Once again that indefatigable Secretary, Captain Ron Baldwin, went in search of alternative accommodation, and found it. Not for the first time in maritime history, the Royal Navy came to the rescue of their merchant brethren, in the person of Commander F.J.C. Bradshaw, LVO, RN, the Commanding Officer, who kindly offered the superb dining facilities 'aboard' H.M.S. EAGLET, a naval shore-establishment, headquarters of the R.N.R. in Liverpool, situated near the northern end of Princes Dock.

Thereafter, for nigh on eighteen months, the Master Mariners availed themselves of the hospitality so generously dispensed by their sister service. However, it was accepted from the beginning that moorings at EAGLET could only be a temporary measure. Consequently, when it became apparent that the marina bar and restaurant were to be re-opened under new management, the Club committee lost no time in re-applying for the restoration of their former privileges.

And so it transpired that the mariners bade farewell to their naval hosts, with many expressions of regret and respect, appreciation and goodwill, and moved south once more towards the welcoming embrace of the Harbourside Club, as it is now called.

Meanwhile life goes on and, as always on the last Wednesday of every month, as many as seventy members sit down to a savoury lunch.

An Old Friend . . . Joe McKendrick

285